Dude I Think Your Mom Healed Me

❧❦

*How to Believe For and Receive
God's Promises of Health and Prosperity So
You Can Fulfill Your Dreams
...and Change the World*

❧❦

Betsy Beers

©2013 Betsy Beers Ministries
All rights reserved
BetsyB.tv
me@betsyb.tv

≈Dedication∽

To my grandfather, Herman Zeissler
who showed me to the water and to the fire,

If I impact this world,
it will be because of you.

Special Thanks to Maureen Freitas, Intercessor and BFF,

*To my great rewards and sources of material
My children, Courtney, Joey, Sammy and Lucy*

*And to my husband Patrick,
who no longer has to ask,
"Aren't you done with that thing yet?"*

Preface

This book will empower you to pursue and accomplish your wildest dreams. I pray you will carry these secrets for protection, healing and success to everyone you encounter along the way.

And I impart these truths to you, not because I have degrees and doctorates, which I do not (okay one in film production). It is not because I am uniquely favored with divine wisdom. My expertise comes not from a gushing intellect or moral transcendence, but by trial, error, stubbornness, perseverance and death-grip persistence. I have found the keys to getting the healing principles of God's word off the pages of the Bible and into my real life experience. Healing and miracles are working for me and my children, and they can work for you too. Every time.

"What we hope to do with ease we must first learn to do with diligence." -Samuel Jackson

By doing nothing, we naturally default to eventual poverty, disease and often, early death. Here is your chance to be proactive and find your way out of every curse! Struggle with it till you get it. The process is an adventure. Would you rather climb a tough mountain or languish on a couch, a spectator of others' greatness?

You will never be the same again --and the view is breathtaking.

-Betsy

Table of Contents

Introduction

Part 1 You Should Never Be Sick

1 Why is Healing Such a Big Deal?	17
2 Church Snobs Church Snubs	23
3 Saved: Spirit Soul *and* Body?	27
4 Faith Healers Faith Stealers	29
5 More Faith? Me?! How Offensive!	35
6 Q. Healing? A. Yes!	41
7 Satan's Top 10 Lies That Bind	53
8 God Bless It!!! *&%#*^%*$@!!!	73
9 Saved *and* Healed in The Atonement	87
10 Two Damned Doctrines	107
11 Stop Saying Sorry!	127
12 False Humility & Self-Sacrifice	141

Part 2 When Suffering is Wrong

13 I'd Rather Be Healed Than a Hero	147
14 Christian Suffering Isn't Being Sick	153
15 No Trouble With Trouble	157
16 Glorifying God in Suffering? Hmm...	163
17 So You Think You're a Martyr	169
18 My Kidnapping Testimony	187

Part 3 Thorny Lies That Make You Sick

19 No More Child Organ Donors	203
20 Emo-Faith & Child Sacrifice	211
21 Do-It-Yourself Healing	225
22 Will He Do Wonders Without You? Hail No	229
23 Be Aggressive & Possessive	233
24 "Feed My Baby to a Crocodile"	237

ᴇ Table of Contents ᴈ

25 Mega Pastor Mega Death	245
26 No Matter How Grim	251
27 Sitting In An Open Prison Cell	257
28 Surrender Your Wheelchairs!	261
29 Satan Pain in the Neck	265
30 Poverty & Misery: Your Prerogative!	277
31 Careful How You Quote The Old Testament!	281
32 When Bad Theology Happens to Good People	283
33 Patient No More	293
34 Don't Pray About Healing	295
35 Achsah: A True Story	307
36 Be Prepared Be Preprayed	315
37 New Testament Commandment Raise Your Dead!	319
38 Seven Miracle Power Tools to USE!	327

ᴇ Part 4 Secret Weapon ᴈ

39 The Secret to Success	351
40 Charismatics Gone Wild	355
41 Pink Slime or Filet Mignon?	361
42 Proving God	365
43 Are Tongues for Every Believer ?	369
44 Are Tongues Necessary?	375
45 Satan's Plan for Sammy	379
46 Can You Be Filled Without the Tongues Part?	381
47 Your All Access Pass	385
48 The Breakthrough Tool	387
49 The Gateway Gift	389
50 Get Power Hungry	393
51 Don't Trash Your Treasure	397
52 A Baker's Dozen Benefits	403
53 The Night Before Last	409

❧Introduction❧

As soon as I caught the healing revelation, I launched out into the deep, but no one told me about the sea monsters.

One hot Virginia summer day, my nurse friend, Sharon and I went down to our crowded apartment pool to lie out. We noticed a boy, who was normally getting his rent's worth splashing and terrorizing the lifeguards, hobbling around the edges of the pool on crutches, one foot all wrapped up.

We told him Jesus wanted to heal his foot so he could go swimming with his friends. Of course he wanted that too, so we prayed and forgot about it --until the next day when he was running on the deck, jumping, splashing and terrorizing the lifeguards.

The kid's father, who we had never seen before, hurried toward us, "Are you the ones who prayed for my son's foot?"

"Yes!" What an exciting time for this father and what a blessing we had been to him!

He pointed in our faces and threatened, "Don't you ever pray for my son again!"

We stammered a little, "But...didn't he get healed?"

Now he was stammering, "Well...y-yes, but don't you ever pray like that for my son again!" and he left us frozen a little, in the hot Virginia summer sun.

Why we should pray 'like that'

Healing may not be any more essential to your personal salvation than whether you were sprinkled or dunked, use a hymnal or overhead, raise your hands or fold them, or whether you are pre, mid, or post trib. Still, I contend that healing is core, foundational and yes, essential to the Christian faith specifically as it relates to saving the lost --which is Jesus' primary concern and should be ours as well. Healing should never have been relegated to the periphery.

The gospel writers detail more about Jesus' healing actions than any other thing he did. They also recount several instances where Jesus instructed his disciples to heal the sick. Before returning to heaven, Jesus told the remaining eleven disciples to teach the disciples from all nations (us) to obey everything he commanded them to do. This included obeying the healing commands.

Jesus exemplified for us a healing lifestyle and gave us the power to emulate it. According to God's word, we need to take responsibility for our own healing and stop being event or famous-person-dependent. Stop waiting for the Christian healing celebrities to come to town. Learn how to make God's power a daily force in your life and see how it will effect the world around you.

The difference healing makes is in the numbers of people rescued. By now, we have all heard the story about the one beached starfish among hundreds, thrown back in the surf, and how it meant all the difference in the world to that one. But what about all the others left to dry up in the sweltering sun? God does not want any to perish. Healing draws crowds...crowds who listen.

My mission is to provide a systematic but entertaining Biblical defense of the radical concept that Christians should be healed and heal others --and that healing is an essential element of saving souls. Loving the lost into the kingdom of God is the desired end, and my job is to show you from God's word that supernatural interventions are the most effective means by which that is accomplished.

An elementary analysis of Jesus' earthly agenda will reveal what the principles are, why they are important, and most importantly, how to apply them. All we need to do then, is change the way we think, the way we read our Bibles, the way we talk and especially, the way we pray.

What are the promises about healing? What are the lies we have believed as a Christian community that have kept us from healing? Once convinced of my Biblical inheritance, how do I claim it? How do I get from diseased, defeated, and destroyed, to healed, happy and helpful?

The healing promises, as espoused by the radical Jesus Christ himself, are to be fulfilled in and through us. We will explore the original prescribed method for spreading his kingdom. Divine disruptions of the natural destructive course of sickness and disease provide opportunities for the popularization of the gospel. As is recorded on many pages of the Bible, signs and wonders capture attention and draw crowds.

When the crowds heard Philip and saw the miraculous signs he did, they all paid close attention to what he said. Acts 8:6

It is your job now. He does not ask you to do what he does not give you the power to do. Instead of passively allowing the devil free reign to destroy us, let's aggressively destroy him. The mission is to teach the facts about Biblical healing because the Bible says,

My people are destroyed from lack of knowledge. Hosea 4:6

Once the truth is out, then we will get the healing, saving, delivering promises of God from your Bible into your experience.

We will go from suffering migraines to no more migraines, from asthma to no asthma, from cancer to no cancer, from chronic pain to no pain, wheelchair to walking, blindness to seeing, danger to safety, depression to joy, insanity to peace, empty womb to bouncing baby.

Because Jesus loves you.

In reading this book, I pray you will be empowered to walk in the healing and protection promises of the Bible. I want to provide you with a myth debunking guide for getting healthy, staying healthy and for healing others, as is the clear dictate of the Great Commission.

Stop waiting for that special sermon, meeting, book, anointed song or random act of supernatural kindness. Start making healing a lifestyle, not a special occasion. It takes study, time, devotion and discipline. It means being a disciple. It means taking charge, not only for yourself but for the world to which you are called.

There is not a more transformational revelation than this one that has been jumping up and down on the pages of the Bible for thousands of years.

Disease, disability, deformity, pain, premature death, depression and depravity are enemies that were forever vanquished, dismantled, dismembered and destroyed at the cross. We bear them unnecessarily.

You will be offered a captivating and Biblically sound prescription for anything that ails, from headache or cold, to cancer and terminal illness. I believe that there would be standing room only in multiple services at any given church where members were doing the 'works' that Jesus expects of them. Crowds of people, whole cities followed Jesus as a result of the miracles he did. Healing the sick, crippled and demon-possessed, by miracles which Jesus authorized and empowered us to do in his name, is the most effective evangelistic campaign ever launched.

With all of our clever programs and gimmicky soul-winning strategies, has anyone ever come up with one more successful than performing miracles?

Part One

You Should Never Be Sick

Chapter 1

Why is Healing Such a Big Deal?

I was pregnant with my second baby, and only twelve weeks along when I saw his tiny legs kicking on the sonogram screen...a three inch person fighting for his life.

Because I was bleeding heavily; my doctor had ordered me to Labor and Delivery; I was having a miscarriage. Nurses kept coming into my hospital room to check for a heartbeat. While they dutifully searched my stomach listening, I prayed silently, earnestly, "Let there be a heartbeat; let there be a heartbeat. I want this baby. Jesus, please."

The doctor explained that I must stay in bed. I asked him, "If I stay really still is there a good chance I could keep the baby?" He said that no, there was not a good chance, that it was very early in the pregnancy to lose so much blood and worse, that there was amniotic fluid mixed in. He explained that even if the baby lived, there might be something wrong with him. The doctor told me to pray -- so I did. Every time the nurse came in with a stethoscope, I prayed for a heartbeat.

Well meaning family members tried to encourage me by discouraging me from hope. Suddenly Bible scholars, they called me in my hospital room and counseled that this may be God's merciful way of dealing with a problem with my baby. Couldn't the Lord have thought of that about twelve weeks earlier?

If there were something wrong with my baby, he would just have to fix it. Another close family member refused my petition for prayer, afraid of what saving this life would look like in a full term baby. Fading phrases from a days old sermon on faith consoled me. Staying still and conjuring up every Bible verse I could think of was how I spent my days in the hospital.

Six months later I had a heavenly baby boy with super fat cheeks. It has been over twenty years now and there is nothing wrong with Joey.

I make such a big deal about healing because the Biblical principles of healing work, just as the Biblical principles of finance, marriage or forgiveness work --when they are applied properly. I make such a big deal about healing because it is under and mis-taught, and as such, has left a cavernous pit in our effectively conveying the redemptive message of Christ. Mostly, I make such a big deal about healing because Jesus does. Healing was such a huge part of his ministry on earth and a central theme of his instructions to believers, that for us not to focus on it would be a misrepresentation of scripture and an irresponsible omission in teaching the Bible. There are more accounts of Jesus healing people than any other thing he did.

There are no accounts of his unwillingness to heal anyone from anything.

There are no accounts of his "choosing" to not heal anyone from anything.

Why is healing such a priority for Jesus? Because he loves us. When you love someone, you want to rescue them from disease and peril above all else. It is all about redemption -- buying us back from the enemy, who has power to incarcerate us by our rebellion and sin. Healing the sick and disabled was both Jesus' personal passion and a specific part of the believer's marching orders in the Great Commission. The last thing Jesus told his disciples before going back to the Father was to make disciples of all the nations and teach them to obey everything that he commanded them. We represent some of these "disciples of all nations" and as such, are commissioned to "obey everything" that Jesus taught these anxious Eleven.

Then Jesus came to them and said, "All authority in heaven and on earth has been given to me. Therefore go and make disciples of all nations, baptizing them in the name of the Father and of the Son and of the Holy Spirit, and teaching them to obey everything I have commanded you." Matthew 28:18-20

In Mark's account of this, Jesus specifies the things that should accompany those who believe in him: preaching, healing and casting out demons. As disciples of Christ, we are to obey everything Jesus commanded the Eleven to obey. We have to agree with that. We know to comply with *"do not murder, do not commit adultery, do not steal," Mark 10:19*, and though we may forget it is a command, *"don't be afraid." Mark 6:51* We may not like it but we must also, *"love our enemies and pray for those who persecute us." Matthew 5:44* We obediently submit to the command, *"love each other," John 15:17* and to one like it, *"forgive, and we will be forgiven." Luke 6:17*

While we so eagerly teach obedience to the commands of love, forgiveness, prayer and every other instruction in the Bible, we as eagerly dismiss other mandates that are often from the same sermons Jesus gave. They often come from the same chapter -- but two verses down, commands like, *"Heal the sick." Luke 9:2*

The acts of God are vital to drawing the crowds that Jesus regularly did, as on the day he stepped out of a boat on a far shore of the Sea of Galilee to be met by townfulls of people. Numbering over 5,000, this *"great crowd of people followed him because they saw the miraculous signs he had performed on the sick." John 6:2*

People, after seeing miracles, assembled into larger and larger crowds. The gospel writer John was not the least bit hesitant or apologetic in recording that great crowds followed Jesus because of the miracles. John also quoted Jesus telling the disciples that if they would not believe that he is in the father because he said so, then they should at least believe on evidence of his works. He had to prove his word.

Believe me when I say that I am in the Father and the Father is in me; or at least believe on the evidence of the miracles themselves. John 14:11

The same thing happens today. Reinhart Bonnke draws hundreds of thousands, even millions to his African crusades where it is the norm and to be expected, that blind eyes, gaping tumors, deformities and every imaginable defect will be supernaturally cured.

If Jesus needed to interest an audience with miracles, signs and wonders, how much more we, who lack in his charisma and verbal finesse, need to employ this 'evangelistic technique' of delivering the sick and oppressed. After routinely gaining the confidence of his hearers by attesting to the power and love of God through supernatural acts, Jesus was able to snatch the lost from fires of eternal damnation.

That was only the beginning, because he ordained us to continue in his steps, and gave us his power to do it. He first instructed the original Twelve.

When Jesus had called the Twelve together, he gave them power and authority to drive out all demons and to cure diseases, and he sent them out to preach the kingdom of God and to heal the sick. ... So they set out and went from village to village, preaching the gospel and healing people everywhere. Luke 9:1-2...6

Then he broadened the commission to the Seventy-two.

When you enter a town and are welcomed, eat what is set before you. Heal the sick who are there and tell them, "The kingdom of God is near you." Luke 10:8-9

Coupling these verses with Jesus' last directive to his disciples, where he commissioned them to teach all disciples of all nations to the ends of the earth to obey everything that he commanded them --leaves no wiggle room for our saying that Jesus wanted apostles only to heal the sick, raise the dead and cast out demons.

The Great Commission to the apostles was not some kind of new revelation to them about their duties to preach, baptize, cast out demons and heal. These things had been established much earlier in their ministries as they watched Jesus preach, teach and perform miracles. They too, had healed the sick and had by this point grown accustomed to casting out demons. No, the emphasis was on their teaching others to do what Jesus had already taught them to do. Jesus was sending them into the world just as the Father had sent him into the world, in the same way, with the same authority and with the same job description. Jesus spoke of this to the Father before he died.

As you sent me into the world, I have sent them into the world John 17:18

Our neglect of the mandates to heal is especially disconcerting as he was so emphatic about healing in his ministry, by his example, his words, and eventually, in his death. We see that Jesus reiterated, confirmed and summed this up in the last address before ascending into heaven, just exactly what he expected from those who believe in him,

They will place their hands on sick people, and they will get well. Mark 16:18

The last address --if we are so fortunate to have the opportunity to have a last address before leaving this world, what would we say? and to whom? I get teary-eyed if I think about what I would say to my four children. It would not be different than what I heard Dr. James Dobson planned on saying to his children. Of all the years worth of lessons and books and heart to hearts with them --of all the wisdom that has poured forth from his mouth as the most nation's most prominent Christian family counselor and staunch protector of all that is sacred in society, all he wants to say to his children on his death bed is "be there."

Our final words convey what is the most important to us.

Jesus' last words to us are no different. He said the most important thing last. His assignment to us was the most pressing thing to him because he wants us all to "be there." That will not happen unless we invest ourselves in the work of Christ. As we consider the scriptures in light of this, we will not so cavalierly brush aside Jesus' charge to preach, baptize, heal the sick and even drive out demons.

Exorcism? Now that is going too far! Come and see that perhaps it is not exactly like the movies portray. Instead of basing our beliefs on what we have seen or heard or on what we have been taught by errant church leaders, experiences and Hollywood, let's base our beliefs on the bedrock of the Bible.

To Jesus, healing is front and center; it should be to us as well.... not now and then, but now as then!

Chapter 2

Church Snobs Church Snubs

Several years ago, my prettiest, funniest Christian friend who lived in a big, beautiful house with a pool, four small children and a handsome young doctor husband, suffered the pain of adultery. Her high school sweetheart and love of her life was obsessed with pornography and a homely ER nurse.

The wound was deep and raw. It was a devastation for which none of us had ever planned. She laid on her back staring at the ceiling wondering how her perfect life could explode into ruins from one simple discovery. Her baby girl, just walking, lugged in a big black book and plopped it on her mommy's tummy. Jesus would heal her. A baby could figure that out.

We are too smart to adhere to the healing teachings of Jesus. We create so many variables. Until we understand like a child, we will never get it...too simple, insulting to our intelligence. For the most part, the civilized Church ignores, distorts, modifies, minimizes or complicates healing with all kinds of clever sounding, impressive and intimidating arguments that boil down to one thing. Jesus did not really mean what he said, and he certainly did not mean for us to do what he said.

Although some of us love delving into Greek and Hebrew word studies, we should not have to have doctorates of theology to understand basic gospel truths. When we become puffed up with our own wisdom and learning, inevitably our eyes will be clouded. We are well-advised to glean correction from Jesus' outburst of thanks to God --

I praise you, Father, Lord of heaven and earth, because you have hidden these things from the wise and learned, and revealed them to little children. Luke 10:21

If it cannot be understood in a Sunday school song, especially when it comes to the most common of Jesus' activities like opening blind eyes, curing diseases and making crippled people walk, then it is probably the jaded musings of the wise and learned. Jesus in is his sermons used deep theological terms like sheep, doors, bread, fire, birds, lilies, coins, fish, demons, angels, sand, rocks and children.

We often feel that in order to move into higher levels of understanding, we need to engage in progressively more academic arguments that only the elite can understand. The Apostle Paul did not adhere to this intellectual and spiritual snobbery. He wrote to the believers in Colosse to oppose false teachers who were trying to complicate the message of the gospel.

[In Christ] are hidden all the treasures of wisdom and knowledge. I tell you this so that no one may deceive you by fine-sounding arguments. Colossians 2:3,4

The treasures of wisdom and knowledge are not found in books or professors. They are not found on Himalayan mountaintops or on the internet. From Jesus' prayer of praise, we find that the hidden treasures are revealed to the superior minds of little children. Keep it simple: sheep, doors, bread, fire, birds... What did Jesus say? What did he do? Are not those the questions which are supposed to guide us?

The simple truths revealed in the gospels regarding healing have been diluted by compromising interpretations so as to render them powerless in the Church. As a group, we have become calloused to the word of healing. Can we have a fresh start? Can we put away pre-conceived ideas, excuses, doubt, fear, speculation and accounts from friends and relatives?

Unless you change and become like little children, you will never see the kingdom of heaven. Matthew 18:3

Can we become like little children with regard to healing? Children understand theological terms like birds, lilies, coins, fish... Children understand --

Many followed him and he healed all the sick. Matthew 12:15

The Apostle Paul warns of teachers *"having a form of godliness but denying its power."* They are *"always learning but never able to acknowledge the truth."* Unlike these malevolent teachers that Paul describes in 2 Timothy 3, many teachers who advocate false healing doctrines, do so from a pure heart, albeit deceived. Paul addresses again the pitfall of corrupting and complicating simple Bible truth,

But I fear, lest by any means, as the serpent beguiled Eve through his subtlety, so your minds should be corrupted from the simplicity that is in Christ. 2 Corinthians 11:3

Be wary when someone has to go through all kinds of scriptural hoops to disprove scripture that seems rather clear, obvious and simple.

Whether erroneous teaching is motivated by sin or by lack of knowledge, there are many spiritual giants of our time who build elaborate and convincing cases against every aspect of Christ's teaching on healing. We should take care not to wander from the paths of righteousness by indulging in doctrinal disputes with people that are much smarter than we are. Whether by spiritual pride or by ignorance, we have managed in the western Christian culture, to dismiss this dynamic means by which God reaches into the hearts of men. Healing, even one healing, is effective to move masses of people toward Jesus. Paul would have us be simple minded.

Jesus is simply against sickness.

Jesus commissions and empowers us to be against sickness.

Simple.

Bread, fire, birds, lilies, coins, fish, blood...

We don't heal because we make it so hard and complicated. If it's really very complicated, then it's probably not really very important. If it's for adults only, maybe it's not Christian.

One more baby later, my forsaken friend took up her five children and recaptured her life. Jesus healed her as she embarked on her journey to wholeness as a single mom.

Even babies know Jesus heals broken mommies, broken hearts, broken bodies, broken homes...simple.

Chapter 3

Saved: Spirit Soul *and* Body?

Unique from all the rest of creation. God created humans -- spirit, soul and body. We know this because after creating the heavens and the earth with all of its dolphins, alligators, bugs, cows and tigers, he said,

"Let us make man in our image, in our likeness." Genesis 1:26

Instead of the ground's bringing us forth at God's command, the Lord proceeded to make man with his own hands, out of dirt, and blew his own breath into him. Since God said the man would be in his likeness, we can know much about God from studying this man. He walks and talks; he has a body, emotions, intellect and a will. He is creative, funny, jealous, protective, loving, amazing and strong. God is three persons, but One: God the Father, God the Son and God the Holy Spirit.

One of the few times God refers to himself in the plural is in the context of making man. He wants us to realize how much alike we are. Not only are we a model of the trinity, but each aspect of our triune nature is a little replica of God. None of the other creatures share his physical semblance, nor his mental capacities to choose, create, process, reason, discern and sacrifice. They do not converse as, or share missions with him.

Understanding that man: spirit, soul and body, is made in the image of his heavenly Father, helps us understand the full impact of the redemption that was provided through Jesus' death. God made us like him in every respect of our beings: spirit, soul and body. As the result of sin, we fell and were suddenly not like him: spirit, soul nor body. Accepting Jesus' sacrifice restores us to our former stature of God-likeness.

You can be like him again if you have *"taken off your old self with its practices and have put on the new self, which is being renewed in knowledge in the image of its Creator." Colossians 3:9*

As an act of our wills, we put on the new self and are renewed in the image of the Creator God. We are to be renewed in the image of the Creator which, as we have seen, is triune. None of the aspects of our being should be neglected in redemption: spirit soul *or* body.

We comply with the call to be renewed in the image of the Creator when it comes to spiritual and soulish issues, but emphasis on our renewal in the image of Jesus' healthy earthly body has been conspicuously absent.

Like David we have to command our souls not to forget any of the benefits of our redemption,

Praise the Lord, O my soul, and forget not all his benefits –who forgives all your sins and heals all your diseases, who redeems your life from the pit and crowns you with love and compassion. Psalm 103:2-4

This salvation is complete. It is our whole being he redeems, spirit soul *and* body.

Chapter 4
Faith Healers Faith Stealers (& De-Stigmatizing Healing)

Although not naïve enough to try and make Biblical 'faith healing' acceptable to a secular society, I am constrained to at least present it in the most scripturally faithful way so that if it offends, it will do so on its own merits, and not because of dishonest representation by those who exploit healing for personal gain.

We have abrogated the responsibility of handling healing doctrine and entrusted the work to a few famous 'specialists,' some of whom have redefined the lifesaving principles and translated them into silly antics and financial opportunity. This has been bad Jesus PR and healing has gotten a bad rap.

When healers are corrupt or healing doesn't seem to work, we protect the Lord's reputation. Instead of sticking with the only credible resource on healing, the Holy Scriptures, we go to famous individuals who make the sick into heroes with super spiritual testimonies of how much better off they are, how many people have been touched, and how much wisdom and insight they have attained --all thanks to their lingering diseases.

Instead of defending God's good name by over-compensating for fraudulent healers or failed attempts at healing with equally bad doctrines that glorify sickness, we should just get our healing doctrines from the word of God.

Still, even when handled righteously, the gospel brings offense. But, if some are offended, let it be because of Jesus' words and deeds, not because of a scandal-ridden televangelist's theatrics and abuse of truth. It is not my job to be sure no one is offended by Jesus; it is my job to be sure no one is offended by the evil deeds I might do in his name. As a result of these disturbing religious behaviors, effective healing has been thrown away. There has been some very dirty bathwater and I want to help rescue the baby.

In the 1980's, the wife of Faith Healer Peter Popoff, Mrs. Peter Popoff, obtained information from guests as they came into meetings, and fed the valuable tidbits into her husband's earpiece. She began her shifty directions to Peter, "I'm talking to you. Can you hear me? If you can't, you're in trouble," and then she slipped him the name, "Jodie Dean, Jodie Dean."

Peter routinely repeated his wife's promptings, "Jodie? Dean? Jodie Dean?"

She again spoke into his earpiece, "No, she should be right there on your right side. Okay, she lives at 4267 Masterson."

"4267 Masterson?" he revealed to Jodie, "I can see the angels of God all around your house!" Then he would 'heal' the diseases that the Lord showed him via wireless.

In 1987, Peter Popoff declared bankruptcy shortly after being exposed. The self-declared prophet is again profiting in a lucrative, multi-million dollar television ministry on the backs of the desperate poor and sick.

Because of reprobates, we have often veered into the opposite ditch, promoting Christian celebrities whose acceptance of their diseases and disabilities has given them a spiritual platform from which to teach. Their infirmities have replaced the word of healing as their teacher. Instead of the teachings of Christ, which are without exception pro-healing, they teach unscriptural concepts that limit healing and contradict the redemptive work of Christ in healing our bodies.

Jesus constantly showed us how to get rid of sickness; they constantly show us how we can thrive with sickness.

Even though we are repeatedly reminded of the tremendous witness they have because of their conditions, I have yet to see crowds of people and whole towns saved as a result of observing the courage of these sick and disabled Christian leaders. The secular infirmed are every bit as courageous as they are. They have changed the rules to accommodate their situations. Instead of speaking the word of the Lord over people who have physical needs; they say things like, "The Lord wants us to put on our thinking caps."

The Lord does not want us to put on our thinking caps; he wants us to *"heal the sick and say to them, 'the kingdom of God is near.'" Luke 10:9*

Famous Christians who are sick, and make a stand for the valor of being sick, are in no position to teach on the subject of healing, not because they remain unhealed, but because they refute the teachings of Christ. They postulate that it is not God's will, or not his timing to heal, that there are any number of reasons he may "choose" not to heal. These limitations are not found in the Bible.

No one is being hard on them because of their unfortunate situations, but because of their recklessness in discouraging others from pursuing the deliverance that clearly permeates the pages of the Bible. Because they have not been able to receive, have given up, or do not believe, is not an excuse for them to spread false doctrine. If we teach in the name of the Lord, the lessons need to come from his word, not from experience and certainly not because we went to twelve healing services and nothing happened.

Let not many of you become teachers, knowing that we shall receive a stricter judgment. James 3:1

Command certain men not to teach false doctrines any longer... These promote controversies rather than God's work --which is by faith. The goal of this command is love, which comes from a pure heart and a good conscience and a sincere faith. Some have wandered away from these and turned to meaningless talk. They want to be teachers of the law, but they do not know what they are talking about or what they so confidently affirm. 1 Timothy 1:3-7

I absolutely could not get my three year old to eat her vegetables, my 21 year old to cover her face in the sun, or my boys to stop watching Jerry Springer. Being unsuccessful in these areas is no license for my teaching that toddlers do not need veges, sun damage is fine and so is watching Jerry Springer all day. My parenting failures do not qualify me to teach child rearing classes.

Our understanding, our experience, our customs, our successes and our failures are not the standard to which we should align ourselves. The best we can do is not the best. The word of God is the only standard to which we should aspire.

When it comes to a physical malady, most people of any faith or even who have no faith, are not offended when someone says they will keep them in their prayers. Often though, those same people are offended by the 'extreme' Christian teaching that God will actually do a supernatural feat by miraculously curing them through the faith they put in Jesus Christ. How much of this negative sentiment results from the ridiculous theatrics and manipulation that imposters have called faith healing?

Is it the raw Christian healing doctrine as displayed by the life and teaching of Christ that is offensive, or is it what we associate in our modern society with healing that is offensive? If your answer is the latter, then this message is for you. All the healing promises in the Bible are for you. Do not allow someone's lifestyle or ignorant teaching steal this incredible benefit from you.

But there were also false prophets among the people, just as there will be false teachers among you.... Many will follow their shameful ways and will bring the way of truth into disrepute. In their greed these teachers will exploit you with stories they have made up. Their condemnation has long been hanging over them, and their destruction has not been sleeping. 2 Peter 2:1-3

Next to these people, Jerry looks pastoral. Don't take my word for any of this. Just abandon all of your preconceived ideas and see for yourself because --

The anointing you received from him remains in you, and you do not need anyone to teach you. But as his anointing teaches you about all things and as that anointing is real, not counterfeit — just as it has taught you, remain in him. 1 John 2:27

Use your good, Bible-based discernment to determine who has the scripturally verifiable message.

Chapter 5

More Faith? Me?! How Offensive!

Any blame for the abandonment of our healing heritage could be assigned to laziness, theological sloppiness, ignorance or false doctrine spread by teachers who may or may not be well-intentioned. Trying to sort out what or who is right in an arena of such intense dispute as that of healing is frustrating and confusing. Inevitably someone ends up mad and no one ends up healed.

No one ends up healed. Why is this the norm while it should be the exception? Jesus constantly commends people's faith for their healings. They are healed by faith every bit as much as they are saved by faith. So what is the problem with our healing apparatus? Not enough faith?

Look out! That is a charge you better never make if you like pleasant conversations with Christian people. Even if you remotely suggest a lack of faith, defenders of the infirmed-for-a-good-reason will bust a cap.

In your face proud people! My life goal is more and more and more faith....for everything.

Faith is your life line. It is through faith that you gain the promises, just like the faith heroes of old *"who through faith conquered kingdoms, administered justice, and gained what was promised; who shut the mouths of lions."* Hebrews 11:33

Whether you call it lack of faith, doubt or unbelief --it is your enemy. As offensive as it apparently can be, it is not wrong to make a case that we need more faith in the area of healing.

"Whoever loves discipline loves knowledge, but he who hates correction is stupid." Proverbs 12:1

I am corrected about doubt and unbelief when I read about my faith from the perspective of God's word. If the Lord rebukes us for lack of faith, we are in good company! Jesus was always rebuking his disciples for their lack of faith. They didn't seem offended; they seemed eager to learn.

5 Rebukes to Disciples for <u>Lack of Faith</u>:

1) When the disciples asked Jesus why they were unable to heal a man's epileptic son, he responded, *"<u>Because of your unbelief</u>; for assuredly, I say to you, if you have faith as a mustard seed, you will say to this mountain, 'Move from here to there,' and it will move; and nothing will be impossible for you." Matthew 17:20*

Jesus followed the constructive criticism with a word of encouragement for the next time. He was prepping them for success next time around.

2) Addressing the problem of worry, Jesus said to consider the carefree lilies of the field which are more beautifully clothed than Solomon in all his riches. *"If God so clothes the grass of the field, which today is, and tomorrow is thrown into the oven, will he not much more clothe you, <u>O you of little faith</u>?" Matthew 6:30*

Again, Jesus never points out a problem without offering a solution. He follows this critique of their faith immediately by giving them instructions for growth in this area.

"Therefore do not worry, saying, 'What shall we eat?' or 'What shall we drink?' or 'What shall we wear?' For after all these things the Gentiles seek. For your heavenly Father knows that you need all these things. But seek first the kingdom of God and his righteousness, and all these things shall be added to you." Matthew 6:31-34

Jesus does not fault-find to be mean. When he picks on us it's only because he wants us to do better --because he loves us and wants us to be happy, and because he knows that without faith we can receive nothing from him. This is a real dumb thing about which to be offended.

3) After hushing the windstorm that petrified the disciples, Jesus said to them, *"Why are you fearful, O you of little faith?"*

I believe this shows off the character of the special men Jesus chose to be his apprentices. Instead of looking inward by being insulted by his remark, they kept their focus God-ward and marveled at his greatness and power by saying, *"Who can this be, that even the winds and the sea obey him?" Matthew 8:26,27*

How weird if the Church were more God-ward and outwardly focused?

4) To me, the most ironic incident of Jesus' reprimanding a disciple for having small faith was when Peter exercised what I thought was the greatest act of faith. Not only did he step out of the boat into a stormy sea, but he did so going to someone who they all thought was a ghost. Peter cried into the noisy gale, *"Lord, if it is you, command me to come to you on the water!"*

First of all, Peter is the one who came up with the idea of his walking on the water; it was his initiative. Being assertive like that takes faith. Second, he could not distinctly make out anyone's voice in such a squall. He had to trust that it was not the ghost that said, *"Come."* And thirdly, when he did sink in the waves, he trusted the Lord to save him. "*Lord, save me!*"

I thought that was a great effort and amazing display of faith, but after Jesus did save him, the first words out of Jesus' mouth were not praise but, *"O you of little faith." Matthew 14:28-31*

Saving faith is just the beginning. Jesus expects much more from us than that. He has an investment of blood in us that should move us past merely personal salvation of our spirits souls and bodies to the world around us. Our focus should be outward.

5) After Jesus rose from the dead, he *"rebuked [the disciples] unbelief and hardness of heart, because they did not believe those who had seen him after he had risen." Mark 16:14*

Still, these were the special forces he sent out into the world to teach all disciples, from all nations everything that he taught them to do... by faith. He was not going to let them off the faith hook. Perhaps his big plans for them were the reason he was so hard on them.

Come on soldier, you can take it.

Yes, Jesus still expects a lot from his disciples. That includes welcoming a stinging word of admonition now and then. Sorry to disappoint those who are eager to pounce on me for this, but I am not saying, nor do I believe anyone should point fingers saying, "you don't have enough faith," or "your grandma didn't have enough faith." That is not a solution. It is not helpful and it conveys as a condemning statement.

Lack of faith (doubt, unbelief) is the problem, but the root of the problem is church leadership. The solution lies at the feet of church leadership. Grandma did great with her faith in spite of all that rogue teaching.

Since *"faith comes by hearing, and hearing by the word of God," Romans 10:17*, then an accurate diagnosis of our faith deficit points to church leadership. Our faith deficiency comes from not hearing the word of God on healing. It has not been taught, and worse, has been taught contrary to the word of God, inspiring doubt instead of faith. Bad teaching has subjected healing to emotionalism and conjecture rather than to the legal covenant that God has made with us.

First, we have to unlearn the myths and theories that were pushed as truth.

We are at such an advantage if we can raise children from infancy with Biblical truth about healing. The best place to start is to teach them plain old Bible verses – no editorializing:

By his wounds we are healed. Isaiah 53:5

He took up our infirmities and carried our diseases. Matthew 8:17

Many followed him and he healed all their sick. Matthew 12:15

It is wise to esteem God's words above all others' words. He is the only authority on the subject.

I am happy to point the finger of blame for our healing difficulties at erroneous Bible teaching, at a campaign of unbelief that has been running rampant in the Church for generations, at Christian leaders that have abrogated their responsibility to properly equip believers, and at myself for wasting too many years with these convictions in the back of a messy closet.

Chapter 6

Q. Healing? A. Yes!

Healing is an answer, not a question.

When we ask for healing, it is like asking for the butter. "Will you please pass the butter?" It is assumed the answer is yes; you are just letting it be known that you are ready for it. You are being polite. It really means, pass the butter. You know your family at the table wants you to have the butter or it would not be on the table.

If we need money, we go to the money verses. If we want them to work, we comply with them. If we need love, we go to the love verses. If we want them to work, we apply them. If we need wisdom, we go to Proverbs. If we need healing, we go to healing verses and the verses surrounding them, and the verses surrounding the verses surrounding them.

Once we have a solid grasp of healing, having understood verses in their proper context, we will not be manipulated out of our miracles by faulty interpretations. Neither will we be relegated to the sick masses, hoping ours is a winning ticket in the Jesus miracle lottery, hoping we will be picked out of the crowd by a preacher we have never met. Hoping and wishing and praying. No, healing is for everyone. It belongs to us. It is on the table.

Have you ever said anything like this?...
"I'm sick and praying doesn't work! I've prayed and prayed and prayed. My pastor prayed, my bishop, my priest, the whole church, the whole diocese, the women's Bible study, the

men's Bible study, the youth group, the care group, my Facebook friends, Billy Graham, Franklin Graham, Benny Hinn, the Pope, and still, I'm sick as a dog. God's answer is obviously no, and I'm angry."

If his answer is no, then God does not keep his promises. For healing, protection, salvation and forgiveness of sin, things that are scripturally well established as his will, they are not yes or no questions --they are things we pray for, believe for and learn to receive. Healing is a promise. We should not ask God if he will keep a promise. That is insulting to his character and false humility. We claim the promise, abiding by its conditions. For example, James says,

The prayer of faith shall save the sick and the Lord shall raise him up. James 5:15

If we pray the prayer of faith, then the Lord will raise us up. In order to be saved from sickness, there has to be a prayer. Oh no, not just a prayer, but a prayer of faith. Those are two entirely different things.

"Mommy can I have lunch?" assumes an affirmative answer. A good Mommy would never say, "No lunch for you today."

These are communications that show and affirm our confidence in him as a loving, healing, protective father who keeps his promises. The answer is implied in the questions. They are rhetorical.

First of all, healing is a promise, one that is made on dozens and dozens of occasions throughout the scriptures. *"He forgives all your sins and heals all your diseases,"* Psalm 103:3 for example.

Secondly, according to the Bible, all the promises are yes in Christ. There is no such thing as God's answering no to a request about something that he has promised. If someone calls upon the name of the Lord, they shall be saved. Healing as well as salvation is a promise that needs to be acted upon, not questioned.

For all the promises God in [Christ] are yes. 2 Corinthians 1:20

In order to pray effectively, we need to know the truth about what we praying. Without this confidence, we are like the waves of the sea driven and tossed, with no chartered path, no direction, no map --just like a lost person. We have no excuse for that kind of instability given the volume of wisdom that has been made available to us.

If any of you lacks wisdom, let him ask of God, who gives to all liberally and without reproach, and it will be given to him. But let him ask in faith, with no doubting no hesitating, no wavering), for he who doubts is like a wave of the sea driven and tossed by the wind. For let not that man suppose that he will receive anything from the Lord; he is a double-minded man (hesitating, irresolute), unstable in all his ways. James 1:5-8

What is the correct course of action then, to just keep on praying and never give up? I am a big believer in NEVER giving up, unless of course, you are headed down the wrong road. So, it depends on how and what you are praying. Think about how most people respond when they hear of your bad health, "You're in our prayers" or "We will be praying for you." Nice of them to say, but even if they follow through, how often are the prayers effective for healing --if indeed they are praying for healing and not for strength to endure a disease (as scripture never prompts)?

The only direction we are ever given with regard to sickness is to heal it and to be healed of it. Yes, he will help us to endure suffering; he will sustain us on our sickbeds. There is a verse to back that up. *"The Lord will sustain him on his sickbed."* Be sure to read the whole verse though.

The Lord will sustain him on his sickbed AND restore him from his bed of illness. Psalm 41:3

The second half of this sentence proves there is a different end the Lord has in mind to our lying in bed miserable and sick, yet sustained. The end he has in mind is to get us out of the sickbed and restored to health.

Neither Jesus nor his disciples ever glorified God by being sick or by remaining sick. They never remotely suggest that any kind of disease endurance has any kind of virtue. There is no Biblical instruction or precedent for us to pray to any other end than full recovery.

We see this again in James 5 where prayer is prescribed for affliction or trouble. For sickness though, he is more specific. James recommends not just prayer, but for elders (spiritual guides) to pray the prayer of faith that makes the sick person well, not a prayer that makes the sick be at peace with being sick. How many times and in how many ways does God have to clarify his wish, his desire, his will for our health? We need to pray his will because,

If we ask anything according to his will, he hears us. And if we know that he hears us – whatever we ask – we know that we have what we asked of him." 1 John 5:14,15

We ask according to his will. That means we need to study and seek out his will, not act like it is virtuous or insightful to be unclear about it and surrender to that. It is not even enough to know God's will; we have to do it.

Not everyone who says to me, 'Lord, Lord,' shall enter the kingdom of heaven, but only he who does the will of my father in heaven." Matthew 7:21

Someone said to Jesus, *"Look, your mother and your brothers are standing outside, seeking to speak with you."* But he answered and *said to the one who told him, "Who is my mother and who are my brothers?" And he stretched out his hand toward his disciples and said, "Here are my mother and my brothers! For whoever does the will of my Father in heaven is my brother and sister and mother." Matthew 12:47-50*

If anyone is a worshipper of God and does his will, he hears him. John 9:31

Our intimacy with Jesus is based only on first knowing, and then doing his will. If we don't know it, we cannot do it.

Our relationship with him is not according to our birth, position in society, intelligence or education. The strength of our relationship with him is based on our earnest to do his will. David was not great because he was a great king. He was great because he was obedient. God made a king from a great shepherd. He raised up David as king because he was faithful when lowly. God said of him, "*I have found David the son of Jesse, a man after my own heart, who will do all my will." Acts 13:22*

When we do not know God's will, we look for it, study and search till we find it. We may never get it all, but we can find what we need. Don't let anyone tell you otherwise. *"His divine power has given us everything we need for a godly life through our knowledge of him." 2 Peter 1:3*

We have everything we need through our knowledge of him. If we need to know and we don't know, then we need to find out. Not knowing is not spiritual, it is foolish –not wise.

Do not be unwise, but understand what the will of the Lord is. Ephesians 5:17

Do not be paralyzed by fear of doing the wrong thing. If you are operating by faith in Jesus, and you go in the wrong direction, he will grab the wheel and set you straight. Jesus will take the wheel. It is much easier to steer a moving car than one that is sitting in a garage. Just go. Do it. He can teach you along the way. If you are willing to do his will, you will find the right road --even if you have to stop and get directions every once in a while.

The God of our fathers has chosen you that you should know his will. Acts 22:14

When we seek God's will on something that is not clearly laid out in the scriptures like healing and salvation are, then we search the word of God and pray. We should pray in the Spirit because,

We do not know what we should pray for as we ought, but the Spirit himself makes intercession for us with groanings that cannot be uttered. Now he who searches the hearts knows what the mind of the Spirit is, because he makes intercession for the saints according to the will of God." Romans 8:26

Praying in your prayer language, words that cannot be understood, to express the perfect will of God, is the ultimate in effective prayer.

Do not be conformed to this world, but be transformed by the renewing of your mind, that you may prove what is that good and acceptable and perfect will of God." Romans 12:2

In order to prove his perfect and acceptable will, we need to find out what it is and not cave in to the often faith destroying cop out, "If it be thy will." That excuse is much easier than digging, studying and seeking; it is also not effective.

You have need of endurance, so that after you have done the will of God, you may receive the promise. Hebrews 10:36

This is no cake walk. It takes work, but it's worth it. To do the will of God is first to listen, then obey. It is not about sitting in a church pew chanting prayers that barely hit the rafters. So we are not going to say sluggish things anymore that weary the Lord like, "God is in control!" No more lethargic, emasculating statements like, "if it be thy will!" It would be more honest to just say, "whatever."

God is not always in control. There are little girls and boys living as sex slaves, unborn babies being stabbed in their mother's wombs and entire populations being starved, raped and tortured who would not testify that God is in control, unless he is a sadistic god. That is closer to the truth. The Bible tells us that our struggle is not against people, but against the god who *is* in control.

For our struggle is not against flesh and blood, but against the rulers, against the authorities, against the powers of this dark world and against the spiritual forces of evil in the heavenly realms. Therefore put on the full armor of God." Ephesians 6:12,13

Not only does that sound like God is not in control, but it sounds like he expects us to take control of these controlling dark forces with the weaponry he provides and his power working through us as we *"pray in the Spirit on all occasions with all kinds of prayers and requests." Ephesians 6:18*

Earlier in this letter to the Ephesians, Paul establishes that it is Satan who is the prince of the power of the air. He says the Ephesians once walked according to the course of this world, *"according to the prince of the power of the air, the spirit who now works in the sons of disobedience." Ephesians 2:2*

Paul goes on to say that we are in Christ to do the good works that he prepared for us. We have to take control back from Satan. Unless we buck up as God has instructed, engaging the enemy, he will stay in control of this dark world.

It looks like God has given us the responsibility of being in control. It is much easier to be passive and not go to battle. The problem is that the battle will rage whether you fight or not, and you could be killed or injured. We would rather God do it all, but Jesus said that he was finished. We are the body of Christ in the earth. When Jesus blesses someone, it comes through our hands, whether money, love or healing. In Jesus' name and by his might, it is we who have to take power back from Satan, the prince of this dark world.

No, God is not always in control. We dodge our obligations when we say things like that. We provide ourselves a safe escape also when we tack the Old English, "if it be thy will" onto a prayer,

There are many things in life for which we do not know God's will, but healing is not one of those. Healing, like salvation, is an abiding blood covenant promise. When Jesus uttered those famous words, "if it be your will," he followed immediately with "nevertheless," precisely because he knew God's will in this matter of his sacrifice, and was submitting his flesh to it.

The "if it be thy will" conversation shows how Jesus processed and then resolved. "Nevertheless" he relented to his Spirit, "not my will but yours (which he knew) be done."

Father if it is your will, take this cup away from me; nevertheless not my will, but yours, be done." Luke 22:42

When he said, "If it be thy will, take this cup away," his flesh, his will as a man was craving for the cup of suffering to pass, begging for a way out., but he knew what God's will was. He was wrestling in his flesh knowing full well that God wanted him to drink of the rotting poison of human depravity and disease. Was there any other way to do this? No, he was well aware of God's will; it was his destiny, the entire reason he became man. It was planned from the foundations of the earth. He was struggling out loud. We tack this on to our prayers and have convoluted the meaning to be the exact opposite of Jesus' meaning. For us it is an indication of ignorance, for him, understanding.

We use that phrase in the exact opposite way that it was given to us, as a cop out, an excuse for not knowing God's will. How insulting it is after everything he has done to make his will plain to us, through the prophets, the life of Christ, the death of Christ, the preservation of God's word and the arrival of the Holy Spirit. We still say things like "if it be thy will?" regarding issues that are right in front of our face in black, red and white. Really? We still don't know after all that?

With "nevertheless," Jesus deliberately chose what he knew to be God's will over what he knew was the will of the man he willingly stepped off his throne to become. It hurt. He suffered and died to provide our access to the Holy Spirit. He gave us a complete and perfect library of 66 books to explore and discover his perfect will for our lives. Until we have exhausted that, we should be very careful about flippantly claiming ignorance of his will. How can you do what he wants if you don't know what that is?

"God is in control" and "If it be thy will." Yes, one can back these claims citing chapter and verse, providing the verses are taken out of context. These postures taken to refute God's healing nature and laws are not Biblically sound. They are religious speak. They are among many myths to be debunked. Whether well-intentioned or scheming, advocates of these views have to convolute the scriptures to disprove what seems pretty straightforward. They indulge the ears of audiences in religious heresy with nary a single parishioner's demand for scriptural evidence. Such dogma is soaked up quickly by believers who demand no proof text and who neglect their

Bible homework. What is worse is congregations of these believers go into their communities comforting the sick with doctrines of doubt and casseroles, instead of building them up with the word of faith.

If I had a disease, I would not want people to pray for me to be patient and peaceful because they had some a-biblical inkling that God had a special cause for my pain. I would not want compassionate sympathy, but passionate warfare -- fighters that never quit. I would want them to argue with me and demand more from me. I would want them to do what the New Testament teaches --to pray the prayer of faith. Why? Because *"the prayer of faith will save the sick and the Lord will raise him up." James 5:15*

Since we are supposed to do to others what we would want done to us, I am thereby constrained to never give up on a sick person. No more tidy doctrines that excuse us from the brawl. The casserole would be a good bonus.

With all the information he has given us on this subject, with all the mysteries he has revealed through Jesus, we have no excuse to be ignorant of God's intentions about healing. We need to pray responsibly and according to his word.

But you say, "I believe in healing, but my prayers don't work!"

Still, all the prayers, doctrinally correct or not, have not made you better. Once you are convinced of the truth about healing or anything in the word, then you build your faith in that area. It is a lifestyle --your daily bread. Know this: your healing is not dependent on the number or stature of the people that pray. Your healing is dependent on the ability to receive the healing that God has already provided through the sacrifice of Jesus. It is by faith, the prayer of faith, the demonstration of faith in Jesus, that you will receive and be healed.

Yes, of course we pray, but that is not normally the missing ingredient. The missing ingredient is faith. *"The prayer of faith will save the sick, and the Lord will raise him up.' James 5:15* James provides no exceptions to this. Faith is what we need. Faith is what we lack.

Jesus never said, "your prayer has healed you" or "your prayer has made you well." He repeatedly said to people who were healed, "*your faith has healed you*" and "*your faith has made you well.*"

So, instead of more praying, begging and deal-making, maybe we need to concentrate on preparing ourselves to receive the answer that has already been given --by building our faith. This is not a passive, wait around and see what God will do stance. It is aggressive. It is an I will never give in, I will never give up position. Perseverance, God loves that about you.

So how do I get more faith?

Faith comes by hearing, and hearing by the word of God. Romans 10:17

It comes by less talking, more listening. Less complaining more reading, less conjecture, more surrender. Then when you pray, pray God's will. God's will is synonymous with God's word. Pray God's word over your circumstances and symptoms. Confess healing scriptures. Talk about healing verses, hang them up, write them down, sing them, listen to them, watch them, think about them, stick them on stuff, dream about them, eat them, drink them, act on them.

Healing is a promise. All the promises are yes. His word never fails. We might. If there are failures, they are not his. Praying for healing requires believing God will deliver on his promises. Do you believe it is always God's will to heal? Hmm. You don't know? He unequivocally promises healing...always. The better question then is: Do you believe it is always God's will to keep his promises?

Regarding healing and other promises, don't take no for an answer. No is not from the Lord. Remember,

All the promises of God in [Christ] are yes. 2 Corinthians 1:20

We have been granted access to the blueprints and materials to build our faith in Jesus so that we can believe for healing. Thus empowered, we can walk as Jesus did, healed and healing others. This is the duty of those who claim to live in him.

"Whoever claims to live in him must walk as Jesus did." 1 John 2:6

I want people to learn that their miracle is not dependent on syncing up with a power evangelist, reading the right book, attending the most anointed meeting, making the most sacred pilgrimage or having the largest number and highest caliber of people praying for them. I want people to stop praying that they will be part of the divinely lucky few who get a supernatural intervention. Healing is for the masses, not a special chosen few. Healing is meant for everyone that needs it.

[Jesus] spoke to them about the kingdom of God, and healed those who needed healing. Luke 9:11

Your qualifications for receiving healing are based upon nothing except your need. Heavenly solutions to your problems, from diseases to demons, are waiting to be delivered through your trust in the word of God. If you need healing, you are a prime candidate. It is your job to get your healing. God is not delaying, He is not making you wait. No, he is waiting for you. Go to the instructions again --in the Bible. His word is truth. Truth is a firm foundation and the most profitable way to pray.

That we pray is not as important as how and what we pray.

Chapter 7

Satan's Top 10 Lies That Bind

"Education consists mainly in what we have unlearned."
– Mark Twain

To decipher truth, the bedrock of our faith, we have to consider source and context. The most believable lies are the ones that sound like the truth, or that line up with the religious propaganda we have been indoctrinated with our whole lives. Lies are partial truth or delivered convincingly as truth. They are truths surrounded by discourses that altar the original intent.

"Mommy said I could have this cookie Daddy...." The part she left out? "...after I eat all my turkey burger."

Once an old boyfriend of mine who was the youth group worship leader justified our climbing over the fence at the Washington State Fair, "It says in Ecclesiastes to be good but not too good." Our pastor did not agree with his scriptural application.

You can justify anything if you take a verse just a little out of context. The devil is great at skewing truth to fit his subversive agenda. He quoted Psalm 91 to Jesus like a champ.

Basing my beliefs about healing on the Bible --that sounds good, but many Bible teachers argue against many aspects of healing, quoting from the same book. In order for them to make their arguments believable, they must extrapolate verses, interpreting them according to personal opinion and not according to the context in which they were found.

I was driving on I-4 in Orlando with my daughter Courtney, who was seven. She was in the front seat and my boys, Sammy and Joey, four and five, were in back. I took the last sip of my soda and set it in my lap as I turned onto the off ramp. Courtney said, "Mommy, you can throw your can out the window."

"What? Honey no, that's pollution!"

"It's okay, Mommy," she insisted.

"What are you saying? Of course that's not okay.."

She did not back down. "You really can, that sign right there says, Fine for Littering."

She failed to see the $50 at the bottom of the sign, which led her to believe the exact opposite of the sign's intent. This illustrates the fallacy of giving advice based on an incomplete assessment of facts.

Time consuming as it may be, studying God's word in its entirety and obeying it in its entirety, is the key to spreading truth --not lies. If we do not have a rudimentary understanding of God's word, from Genesis to Revelation, we can be unsuspecting recipients of bad teaching that is extrapolated from random Bible passages.

In my journey toward understanding Biblical healing, and the importance God has placed on it in our lives, I am as amazed at how many Christian experts on the subject I run into. They know all about how and when God does or, usually, does not heal people. They are all too anxious to share their insights. They have strong convictions on the subject and will not be dissuaded, whether or not they have read the Bible. Maybe they have read some or most of it, not really studied too much, but heard some real convincing sermons. They just know instinctively things like God is mysterious and God is in control. They ask questions to which I need not respond as they already have the answer. It's great. I have whole conversations without saying anything but, "uh-huh." Others, Bible scholars, senior pastors and university professors have angrily defended their Biblically justified unbelief.

Yet, even with such representation of years and fortunes spent in academia, I have never heard anyone produce a credible Biblical argument against healing. The most damaging teachings are not those that discount all possibility of miracles, healings and supernatural manifestations. That posture loses credibility with even the most ardent healing arbiters. 'God does not heal at all' is not a viable position by almost any Christian's standards. The most insidious are stances that permit healing but take exception to it in areas. But Jesus never qualified healing. He preached healing without exceptions....

The serpent was more crafty than any of the wild animals the Lord God had made. He said to the woman,

Did God really say...? Genesis 3:1

Satan's Top 10 Reasons God Doesn't Heal

This list provides a quick reference when you are attacked by unbelief in sheep's clothing.

LIE #10 "God may not heal for his own purpose; it is a mystery."

The New Testament is all about the mystery revealed. Everywhere the mystery of God is mentioned, it is always in the context of its revelation. All the treasures of wisdom and knowledge, all the secrets and fantastic mysterious plans God has in store are all accessible to us now by his Spirit that lives in us –-no longer a mystery!

"We declare God's wisdom, a mystery that has been hidden and that God destined for our glory before time began. None of the rulers of this age understood it, for if they had, they would not have crucified the Lord of glory. However, as it is written: 'What no eye has seen, what no ear has heard, and what no human mind has conceived' --the things God has prepared for those who love him – these are the things God has revealed to us by his Spirit." 1 Corinthians 2:7-10

The things we have never seen, heard or imagined have been revealed. Let's go look!

The knowledge of the secrets of the kingdom of God has been given to you. Luke 8:10

Pray also for me, that whenever I open my mouth, words may be given me so that I will fearlessly make known the mystery of the gospel. Ephesians 6:19

God willed to make known what are the riches of his glory of this mystery among the Gentiles, which is Christ in you, the hope of glory. Colossians 1:27

He wants us to seek and search, dig and explore, hunt and not say, "It's too mysterious." That is lazy.

LIE #9 "God may not heal old people because they have to die somehow."

That is an easy thing to say, until the old person is your parents or you! God's promises are not age discriminate. Being old does not disqualify Grandpa from the blessing of healing. He is not vanquished to being under the curse, where is found every disease known to man, because he is a senior. Jesus became a curse for Grandpa, to redeem him from the curse too --no matter how old he is.

Precious in the sight of the Lord is the death of his saints. Psalm 116:15

Their death is not precious because they are abandoning a body plagued with a painful, tormenting medical condition. It is precious because they are finished here and get to go home. We do not have to get sick for that to happen. That is not satisfaction in life --to experience disease or look forward to its inevitability.

Psalm 91 is a promise to everyone regardless of how long ago they were born.

He will call upon me, and I will answer him; I will be with him in trouble, I will deliver him and honor him. With long life will I satisfy him and show him my salvation. Psalm 91:16

We are promised long life with satisfaction.

LIE #8 "God may not heal a child because he needs another little angel."

Truth is once again our safety net. Venturing into such frivolous hypotheses leads to false comfort and dangerous theology. This is not a faith-builder for parents who are trusting God to heal their baby. These kind of sloppy religious sympathy card verses incite fear and doubt which are the weapons of our enemy. They should not make it to the pages of our devotionals.

Angels are not children and lost loved ones. Angels are created, non-human, androgynous, servant spirit-beings. Angels cannot become humans nor can humans become angels. They are mighty, ministering agents of God that do not experience salvation. One third of them fell to make up the demon population. Humans will judge them.

Do you not know that we shall judge angels? 1 Corinthians 6:3

The good ones are assigned to protect our children and loved ones. It is mean to tell a mother who lost a child that God needed her baby. He is not cruel. God gives life, not death. "*The Lord gives and the Lord takes away*" was one of many foolish things that Job said, and for which he later repented. Indeed the Lord does give and take away. The Bible says that he gives a full life span and takes away sickness.

I will take away sickness from your midst, none will miscarry or be barren in your land and I will give you a full life span. Exodus 23:25-26

It is God's wish, desire, choice, will for our children to thrive with us. I was curious about how it would feel to have a grand baby. I was not expecting to feel so protective over my daughter Courtney's love affair with baby Hazel. I would be full of evil if I took Hazel away from Courtney and kept her exclusively to myself. We make God out to be even more wicked because for him to 'take' a child means killing it.

We suffer more from slandering God's character than anything else, not because he punishes us for it, but because we waive our rights and privileges by doing it. According to our faith it will be unto us... God needs another little angel?

There is no redemptive power in fantasy.

LIE #7 "God may heal some by taking them to heaven."

Not only did Jesus heal to prevent death in every case, but he raised the dead when he came across those who died prematurely, those who died before they were satisfied with a long life. He raised a widow's only son right there from his coffin, Jairus's only daughter from her little bed and Lazarus from a stone tomb. He not only raised the dead but instructed believers to do the same.

Peter raised Tabitha; Paul raised Euticus.

There is no doubt that if a believer loses a battle with sickness and goes to heaven early, he is healed. We should rejoice about that, but should not make a new Bible verse out of it. It is what it is, a tragic loss, a premature death. Jesus made provision for our healing right here in this wicked world, right here where the kingdom of God has come to exploit the rotten devil.

Heal the sick, raise the dead, cleanse those who have leprosy, drive out demons. Freely you have received, freely give. Matthew 10:8

No conjured up dogma can negate this command.

LIE #6 "God may not heal in order to teach a lesson, or to discipline."

We need to be disciplined if we are doing something wrong. We also need to be disciplined in order to lead successful, productive lives. We teach and instruct our children because we love them and want this kind of life for them. Maybe we arrange some consequences for children's bad behavior because we want them to learn that, as adults, sin has its own built-in consequences: death, jail, herpes, depression, divorce

...sometimes sickness (not that all sickness is the direct result of personal sin, but sometimes). None of these consequences of sin come from God; they come from rebellion, whether our own or someone else's.

When teaching our children, we would not, even if we were able, put one of these consequences on them. We would not strike them with cancer or arrange for a disabling accident. Instead we instruct and teach. If they don't listen and obey, they may have privileges taken or more vigorous work assigned. They might get a spanking to be get a taste of the pain of sin. If the spanking exceeds low impact, high sting, causes any damage and is not motivated by love, then it borders on child abuse --not good parenting. How angry we are at child abusers; we want to kill them. I do --yet we accuse God of much worse in our sacred conversations full of accusations.

Discipline should come from God's word and the Holy Spirit in us.

For this reason I remind you to fan into flame the gift of God, which is in you through the laying on of my hands. For God did not give us a spirit of timidity, but a spirit of power, of love and of self-discipline. 2 Timothy 1:6-7

God gave us his word to instruct, reprove, convict, correct, discipline and train.

Every Scripture is God-breathed (given by his inspiration) and profitable for instruction, for reproof and conviction of sin, for correction of error and discipline in obedience, [and] for training in righteousness (in holy living, in conformity to God's will in thought, purpose, and action), 2 Timothy 3:16 Amplified

That is all we need and if it is not enough and we need to be brought to repentance for our wandering ways, then his goodness can do it.

Or do you despise the riches of his goodness, forbearance, and longsuffering, not knowing that the goodness of God leads you to repentance? Romans 2:4

If we have to learn the hard way because of rebellion, that is not God's discipline; that is consequences. Regardless, the good Lord does not need the devil's arsenal of cursed weapons to discipline us, and we would be wise to stop accusing him of such.

LIE #5 "Healing might not be God's will"

You can say it might not be God's will to heal, as long as you are willing to say that It might not be God's will to save. No Christian will say that. From a Biblical standpoint they are the same though. In the Greek, the original language of the New Testament, the word for healing and salvation is the same, 'sozo.' In English, as well as in our minds and culture, we separate healing and salvation, ascribing different qualities to two words which should really be one. They are both '*sozo*' in Greek.

Definition of *sozo*: salvation, to save, keep safe and sound, to rescue from danger, destruction or peril, to save a suffering one from perishing or disease, to make well, heal, restore to health

Who are we to pick through this list of meanings for the word salvation? It means physical healing as much as it does spiritual. You have to apply the healing aspect with the same vigor as you do the salvation from sin. It's one, big, happy all-inclusive word.

Notice all the following verses where sozo is used in the scripture, and how they illustrate the purposeful, directional, unwavering, saving/healing ministry of Christ. He was not the least bit hesitant or reticent about healing or saving anyone from anything.

Also, the verses traditionally quoted that are about saving people from hell have a much richer meaning, extending to the whole person's well-being, from now into eternity. When Jesus talked about saving people, he used the word sozo which means healing every bit as much as it means salvation.

Whoever believes and is baptized will be sozo'd (healed, saved, rescued, made whole) but whoever does not believe will be condemned. Mark 16:16

God's intent was never to isolate our spirits and souls from our bodies in salvation. We are not suppose to wait till heaven to get our healthy bodies any more than we are suppose to wait to stop sinning!

SOZO for save/heal:

For God did not send his Son into the world to condemn the world, but to sozo the world through him. John 3:17

And wherever he went — into villages, towns or countryside---they placed the sick in the marketplaces. They begged him to let them touch even the edge of his cloak, and all who touched him were sozo'd. Mark 6:56

The disciples went and woke him, saying, "Lord, sozo us! We're going to drown!" Matthew 8:25

Jesus turned and saw her. "Take heart, daughter," he said, "your faith has sozo'd you." And the woman was sozo'd from that moment. Matthew 9:22

He pleaded earnestly with him, "My little daughter is dying. Please come and put your hands on her so that she will be <u>sozo</u>'d and live." Mark 5:23

"Go," said Jesus, "your faith has <u>sozo</u>'d you." Immediately he received his sight and followed Jesus along the road. Mark 10:52

Jesus asked, "Were not all ten cleansed? Where are the other nine? Was no one found to return and give praise to God except this foreigner?" Then he said to him, "Rise and go; your faith has made you <u>sozo</u>." Luke17:17-19

And everyone who calls on the name of the Lord will be <u>sozo</u>'d. Acts 2:21

If we are being called to account today for an act of kindness shown to a cripple and are asked how he was <u>sozo</u>'d... Acts 4:9

Salvation is found in no one else, for there is no other name under heaven given to men by which we must be <u>sozo</u>'d. Acts 4:12

And the prayer offered in faith will make the sick person <u>sozo</u>; the Lord will raise him up. If he has sinned, he will be forgiven. James 5:15

It is difficult to build any case against God's willingness to heal when that is all Jesus did. It is even more unreasonable when we notice that in his own language he used the same word for healing and saving. Following his clear advise and actions is the best way to determine his will. For healing and saving, there was no wavering, doubting, no preventing, no suspending, no modifying, no caveat, no exception, no exclusion. He just sozo'd everyone from everything....unless unbelief stopped him.

Because sozo means healing and salvation, try substituting 'salvation' for 'healing' in Satan's Top Ten Excuses. This is an effective way to expose heresy that has worked its way into mainstream Christianity. Let's try it....

LIE #4 "God may not heal (save) in order to be glorified through the sickness (sin)."

To glorify God through sickness, is another commonly parroted unscriptural excuse for failure to see God's promises manifested. This is not the person you want to minister to your sick body in a hospital bed. There is no Biblical basis for saying God is glorified in sickness. Whenever there is talk of God's being glorified in or through sickness, it is in the healing of the sickness and not maintaining the sickness. How arrogant and insulting to suggest someone has to stay sick to best glorify God. Jesus taught his disciples that God gets glory, not by sickness, but by healing sickness.

My husband thinks scrap metal is glorious. Is it because 50 year old lockers and rusty dryers look cool piled in his truck? No. It's because of the cash he gets for adding to the big heap of twisted metals at the scrap yard. The glory of scrap? cash. The glory of sickness? healing.

Jesus corrected the disciples about a man born blind. They thought the blindness was the result of either his sin or his parent's sin.

"Neither this man nor his parents sinned," said Jesus, "but this happened so that the work of God might be displayed in his life." John 9:3

This happened so God could get glory --in the healing that was just about to happen. You could say Jesus was happy to encounter these sick eyes --so he could heal them!

Toward the end of Jesus' earthly ministry, Jesus heard that his good friend Lazarus was sick. It was another bad situation in which Jesus saw an opportunity for God's glory. He said,

This sickness will not end in death. No, it is for God's glory so that God's Son may be glorified through it. John 11:4

According to our new fangled theology, this would mean that Lazarus would not die but would glorify God in a lingering illness, giving him the blessed opportunity to show everyone how much he believed in God, in spite of the fact that God would not heal him. He would be such a grateful victim. At least he had his salvation. He would be healed in heaven. Oh wait! Salvation means healing! Confused.

No. This thinking is chaotic; no child could ever understand such wacky rationales. Jesus knew when he said that the sickness was for God's glory, that he was going to restore Lazarus to perfect physical health. Obviously, the glory comes in the restoration. That is a miracle. Glorious.

After Jesus told them to remove Lazarus' grave stone, Martha again argued with his healing will (desire, plan). He said to her,

"Did I not tell you that if you believed, you would see the glory of God?" John 11:40

If you believe, then you will see the glory.. There is no glory in being sick. This is the glory:

Jesus called in a loud voice, "Lazarus, come out!" The dead man came out, his hands and feet wrapped with strips of linen, and a cloth around his face. Jesus said to them, "Take off the grave clothes and let him go." John 11:43-44

LIE #3 "We have to wait for God's timing."

We would never say that salvation is according to God's timing, but we do it with healing all the time. It makes no sense because all sozo (healing/salvation) is according to individual will, not God's will. His will has already been established and clearly revealed. He wants everyone to be sozo'd (saved/healed) Also, God has already finished the work of redemption. It is up to us to reap the benefits.

The only one who has a decision to make is you.

Sozo (healing/salvation) is ours. The work for it has been completed. We take it by faith. It is not something we have to wait for.

It is as if you were hungry with no money. A friend told you about a wild apple tree down the road whose branches were heavy with giant red fruit. How unreasonable if you were to say, "I will eat the apples --in God's timing."

The apples are already there. It's not up to God to deliver them, he already did. You have to go get them. There is no timing. Either you pick and eat the apples or not. It might be hard to find the tree or climb the tree. You might need a friend to help you get high enough to reach the fruit.

He himself bore our sins in his body on the tree (cross) so that we might die to sins and live for righteousness, and by his wounds you <u>have been</u> healed. 1 Peter 2:24

You were healed over 2000 years ago. The fruit is on the tree. How do you like them apples?

LIE #2 "God may not heal (save) so the sick can share in Christ's sufferings."

Many Christians get tripped up here because they do not realize there are two very different kinds of suffering in the Bible, with two very different kinds of solutions, the kind that is God's will and the kind that is not.

1) *Suffering That IS God's Will*

There are several promises in the Bible indicating that we would and should suffer persecution. All of Paul's famous sufferings were persecutions, not sicknesses. Even if sickness were among Paul's sufferings, as many teach, then he was healed, because whenever talking about his persecutions, he also says things like, *"and out of them all the Lord delivered me."*

He assures that Christians will be persecuted.

All who desire to live godly in Christ Jesus will suffer persecution. 2 Timothy 3:11-12

The things that Jesus suffered were persecutions, not sickness. Jesus warned,

If the world hates you, you know that it hated me before it hated you...If they persecuted me, they will also persecute you. If they kept my word, they will keep yours also. John 15:18...20

2) *Suffering That Is NOT God's Will*

Suffering sickness, pain and disability is not God's will (his desire, his wish). We know this because:

A) Jesus, who is our model and example, was never sick, infirmed, disabled or injured from having accidents.

B) Jesus spent his ministry going around and healing every instance of sickness and disability he encountered. There was never a time that he either caused someone to be sick or chose to leave them that way.

C) We know also that suffering disease is not his will (his desire, his wish) because Jesus atoned for sickness every bit as much as sin.

He was pierced for our transgressions .... and by his wounds we are healed. Isaiah 53:5

D) Jesus' commission to believers summed up the goal of his life's work and sacrifice, which was to save and empower humanity to spread his kingdom in the sin and sickness eradicating way that he did. Jesus told the Father,

As you sent me into the world, I have sent them into the world. John 17:18

The fact that he was a picture of health, that he went around healing everyone, that he was punished to provide healing, and that he installed us to continue in his healing footsteps, proves that it is his will, his desire, his wish and his good pleasure to heal -- period. Without exception, when Jesus is said to encounter anyone suffering any kind of sickness, disease, infirmity or disability, he makes it go away.

People brought to him all who were ill with various diseases, those suffering severe pain, the demon-possessed, those having seizures, and the paralyzed, and he healed them. Matthew 4:24

"Lord," he said, "my servant lies at home paralyzed and in terrible suffering." Jesus said to him, "I will go and heal him." Matthew 8:6-7

A Canaanite woman from that vicinity came to him, crying out, "Lord, Son of David, have mercy on me! My daughter is suffering terribly from demon-possession." Then Jesus answered, "Woman, you have great faith! Your request is granted." And her daughter was

healed from that very hour.   Matthew 15:22, 28

"Lord, have mercy on my son," he said. "He has seizures and is suffering greatly".... Jesus rebuked the demon, and it came out of the boy, and he was healed from that moment.   Matthew 17:15, 18

Simon's mother-in-law was suffering from a high fever, and they asked Jesus to help her. So he bent over her and rebuked the fever, and it left her.   Luke 4:38,39

There in front of him was a man suffering from dropsy .....taking hold of the man, he healed him and sent him away.   Luke 13:2, 4

[Publius'] father was sick in bed, suffering from fever and dysentery. Paul went in to see him and, after prayer, placed his hands on him and healed him.   Acts 28:8

First, we need to learn to discern the two kinds of suffering. Then we need to work on responding correctly. One is to be endured and the other removed.

LIE #1 "God may choose not to heal (save)"

There is no talk by God the Father, Son or Holy Spirit of choosing not to heal anyone ...ever.

Oh but what about in the Old Testament when God smote with all kinds of plaques and destruction!? The rebels and enemies of God in the Old Testament often came under God's judgment. They were under the curse and all its associated plaques because of their rebellion. We too were under that curse, subject to every vile disease associated with it, until Jesus was judged in our place. Since he redeemed us from the curse of the law, we are not subject to its punishments.

People often make the mistake of saying that the Old

Testament shows God as judgmental and the New Testament shows him as merciful. That is fine, except that he is the same God in both. He is as judgmental now as he was then, and was as merciful then as he is now.

The difference now is that Jesus took our judgment --which only makes a difference to us if we receive this gift of grace, of forgiveness. Forgiveness cancels the debt of sin which leads to eternal death. Grace gives us the power we need over sin so we are not its servants anymore. Grace is not permission to sin; it is power to overcome sin. There is wrathful, eternal judgment awaiting those who do not choose to be saved from sin.

Jesus did not get judged in our place so we could sin without repercussion. He did it so he could give us power over sin, sickness and eternal damnation. With that power, with that grace, we are free from sin to no longer live in it or suffer the consequences of it.

So, the curse is still active in the earth even though its power has been destroyed. We are born into sin and under the curse, or God's judgment. We have to choose to be under the blessing. The choice is black and white and easy to understand in the Old Testament catalogue of blessings and curses, Deuteronomy 28. I often do a check-up in that chapter. If I have any symptoms listed in the curses, I get busy to get rid of them.

I may not have chosen any particular cursed disease or famine, but it is my responsibility to choose to come out from under that curse through the cross of Christ.

God is not choosing to save or heal anymore. He already did that when he allowed his son to be violently murdered for us. Salvation was provided universally, but is chosen individually. The choice is up to us.
If you are in Christ, you are under the blessing. His life in you

gives you grace --the power to live free from the bondage of sin and rebellion. If you are not experiencing a life of blessing, which in Deuteronomy 28 research you will find is a life of health and prosperity, then let the work begin. I did not say you will be conflict free, but you will be a purposeful, happy and healthy person living under the blessing.

God already chose the blessing destiny for us. God does not spend his time now sitting around choosing this and that for us. God provided a way for us to be under the blessing. If we accept his offer, we get all the blessings of health, safety and provision. He does not nitpick through and stingily dole them out according to his fancy that day.

I have set before you life and death, blessing and cursing; therefore choose life. Deuteronomy 30:19

Choose for yourselves this day whom you will serve. Joshua 24:15

The onus is on us to choose, so next time you hear someone say, "God may choose to not heal you," you tell them that it's too late because God's word says,

By his wounds we have been healed. 1 Peter 2:24

He already did it. All that kind of talk does is stop your onward march to claim your God given, blood bought, Deuteronomy 28 blessing.

If someone picks your name out of a bowl as the grand prize winner of a new car and calls you up to claim your prize, you do not have to accept it. You can stay in your seat until he draws out another name.

The only thing God chooses to do is sozo (save/heal) us. He calls everyone, wishing that none should perish, the Bible teaches over and over.

Many are called but few are chosen. Matthew 20:16

He chooses those who answer the call. He wants that to be everyone. That is the end of his choosing. The rest is up to us.

This day I call heaven and earth as witnesses against you that I have set before you life and death, blessings and curses. Now choose life, so that you and your children may live. Deuteronomy 30:19

Chapter 8
❧☙
God Bless It!!! *&%#*^%*$@!!!

They're only words.

When Lucy was four, we were waiting up late one night for Daddy, trying to find something appropriate on tv. We stopped on a popular adult cartoon. How bad could it be really? After about 30 seconds the mom said she burned the damn cinnamon buns.

"Oh! Okay! Let's change that!"

When Lucy asked why, I explained that the mommy was saying bad words --so she asked, "What's wrong with cinnamon buns?"

Okay so that will not scar anyone, but --we can do so much damage with our mouths, often innocently. And, innocent mistakes can be just as dangerous as hostile attacks. Innocently, I reached into the backseat to give my then two year old, Courtney, a bite of my yogurt bar (yogurt bars are so mid-eighties), causing me to swerve, mow over a mailbox and smash the hood of my then new car.

When I was nine, I innocently left my bedroom window open on a chilly afternoon. Later, my sunny yellow parakeet was not perched on her little swing. Instead, she was lying all stiff at the bottom of the cage. I killed Peep. I did not consider or I was not aware of the stupidity of my behaviors. They were innocent albeit dumb mistakes, and innocent or not, they had consequences.

Innocently, we speak words of death, "I am dead tired, I could die I love him so, he is accident prone." The intentions are innocent enough. If called out on it, we belittle any notion that the words spoken so flippantly carry any power. Yet the Bible says,

Death and life are in the power of the tongue. Proverbs 18:21

I am still working with the baby of the family. We bundled Lucy in a giant towel after bringing her up from the beach at dusk. A ferocious thunderstorm was still far enough across the ocean that we could sit on deck chairs to admire it. Warm and dry, resting from her day's play, she expressed her coziness, "It feels good...till you get struck by lightning."

After I finished laughing at my tiny blonde powerhouse, I corrected her. "Honey, we don't get struck by lightning in this family."

This is not just a matter of being jealous over my positive confession theology. Being wrong in this area can have dangerous results, resulting in unnecessary pain and suffering, and often, pre-mature death. If I am accused of silliness, so be it. If I err, it will be on the side of life and health, not death and disease.

Am I going a little too far with this? People that think so have no evidence that I am wrong.

Do I think that tired person will surely drop dead? No, but, like sin, when it is fully matured, words can bring death.

Eventually words of death and cursing give birth. Pay attention to the dark mantras people speak over themselves, and the eventual consequences that materialize.

Like blessing, cursing people is an act of prayer. Don't think for a minute that Satanists, witches and practitioners of Voo Doo don't pray. They pray curses over people religiously, just like we pray blessings. Blessing is speaking words of approval and encouragement. No man will argue that praise and adoration does not lift his spirits while criticism and disapproval are painful and depressing.

When we bless, we highly esteem and respect; we invoke divine care for protection, preservation, healing and favor. It makes the recipient feel happy, valuable and loved. It is encouraging, energizing and motivating. It is good and bears good fruit. It initiates a wave of blessing that passes to others. The words from our mouths cause giant things to move and happen, whether good or bad, from blessing or cursing. Our words set things in motion.

James uses these analogies to drive this point in Chapter 3:

1) *We put bits in horses' mouths that they may obey us, and we turn their whole body.*

2) *Look also at ships: although they are so large and are driven by fierce winds, they are turned by a very small rudder wherever the pilot desires. Even so the tongue is a little member and boasts great things.*

3) *See how great a forest a little fire kindles! And the tongue is a fire, a world of iniquity. The tongue is so set among our members that it defiles the whole body, and sets on fire the course of nature; and it is set on fire by hell.*

Like a little bit steers a horse, a small rudder turns a ship, a tiny spark starts a forest fire; I have Biblical evidence that the stupid, harmless <u>little</u> curses we speak do matter. These are some of the reckless, thoughtless things you should not say, things you would never hear Jesus say:

You make me sick!
That makes me sick.
I'm an idiot!
You're an idiot.
He's an idiot.
This is killing me.
I'm gonna kill myself.
He's going to kill someone.
I'm dying to do that.
I'm going crazy.
Cancer is in my family.
Heart disease runs in my family.
Alzheimers runs in my family.
Allergy season is coming.
You're gonna give me a heart attack.
You're gonna wreck!
Flu season is coming.
I'm getting a cold.
You're getting a cold.
Break a leg.
You're going to crack your head open.
You're gonna get hit by a car.
It's all down hill from here.
I'm coming down with something.
I'm getting a sore throat.
I'm getting a migraine.
You're a headache.
I have always had this and I always will.
He will never walk again.
I will never be able to have children.
After 40 it all goes down hill.
You are a pain in the neck.
She's so sickly.
Somebody stick a fork in my eye.
I can't get pregnant.
My husband is impotent.

We justify talking this way because we are just speaking the truth or joking around. Reiterating a problem not only does nothing to fix it, but endorses its position in our lives. We are reckless if we affirm the right of vermin to live in the house. If there is a rat in the kitchen, then acknowledge it, but don't stop there; don't adjust your life to live with it. Use all your words and energy to get it out! Maybe you are "getting a headache." You can apply your faith to that inevitability or you can apply your faith (and words) to the higher truth that Jesus took away your pain and sickness on the cross.

You are not "catching," but "throwing away" a cold. You are "getting rid of" a headache.

Surely he bore my pain (headaches). Isaiah 53:4

This is what the Proverbs says about our negative words.

Reckless words pierce like a sword but the tongue of the wise brings healing. Proverbs 12:18

Pleasant words are a honeycomb, sweet to the soul and healing to the bones. Proverbs 16:24

Death and life are in the power of the tongue, and those who love it will eat its fruit. Proverbs 18: 21

If you are suffering any condition or situation listed under the curses of Deuteronomy 28, and they're all there, then remember that Jesus rescued you from the power of the curse.

Christ redeemed us from the curse of the law by becoming a curse for us, for it is written: Cursed is everyone who is hung on a tree. Galatians 3:13

Following are things you should say because they are the powerful things that God, our example, says:

If you doubt that God will heal you —

No matter how many promises, God has made, they are yes in Christ. 2 Corinthians 1:20

God is not a man, that he should lie nor a son of man, that he should change his mind. Does he speak and then not act? Does he promise and not fulfill? Numbers 23:19

If you are smitten by an incurable disease --

I will take away sickness from among you. Exodus 23:25

I am the Lord who heals you. Exodus 15:26

The Lord will keep you free from every disease. Deuteronomy 7:15

If you are fearful of sudden disaster --

He will command his angels concerning you to guard you in all your ways. Psalm 91:11

If you are worried that you will be assigned a sickbed for some strange divine appointment --

The LORD will sustain him on his sickbed, and restore him from his bed of illness. Psalm 41:3

If you are worried God will never heal you --

He took up our infirmities and carried our diseases. Matthew 8:17

By his wounds you have been healed. 1Peter 2:24

When you are uncertain because someone asks you to pray --

They will place their hands on sick people and they will get well. Mark 16:18

The prayer offered in faith will make the sick person well. James 5:15
One of Patrick's best friends flew for the sheriff's department. His baby boy was almost one when his helicopter crashed into a black Florida swamp in the middle of the night. Such tragedies are much harder to take when the victim is as great a father, husband and son as Chris. We know he went straight to heaven. Since that time, Patrick has often reminisced, "Chris used to always say, 'When it's your time to go, it's your time to go.'" I would never try to make a case that this was the cause of his accident. Nevertheless, we cannot afford to indulge these kinds of lies, innocuous as they may seem.

This pop culture philosophy, "When it's your time to go, it's your time to go," is in contradiction to the teachings of Christ. It endorses a submission to fate, instead of a determination to stand on the promises of God's protection, deliverance and long life.

It is not only the bad things we do say, but the good things we do not, like --

If you make the Most High your dwelling – even the LORD, who is my refuge, then no harm will befall you, no disaster will come near your tent. For he will command his angels concerning you to guard you in all your ways; they will lift you up in their hands, so that you will not strike your foot against a stone. Psalm 91:9-12

These promises to us are to be appropriated by us through our believing them. *If* we make the Most High our dwelling, *then....*

These promises, as with any promises in the Bible, are conditional. Making the Most High our dwelling, our habitation, our home, does not happen as the result of a prayer we said once, or twice or ten times. It is a lifestyle.

We cannot expect to experience all the incredible promises God makes to us by resigning ourselves to mindsets that oppose his word. Often Christians say things like, "We never know when the Lord will take us home!" Wait a second. What about the promises of protection?

"Because he loves me," says the Lord, "I will rescue him; I will protect him, for he acknowledges my name. He will call upon me, and I will answer him; I will be with him in trouble. I will deliver him and honor him. With long life I will satisfy him and show him my salvation." Psalm 91:14-16

The Lord promised that if we make him our dwelling and love him and acknowledge his name that he would do these things:

1) Rescue
2) Protect
3) Deliver
4) Grant Long Life

Since everything we receive from God is conditioned upon our faith, *"The promise comes by faith." Romans 4:16*...then should we not deliberately engage God's word --which brings faith?

Faith comes by hearing, and hearing by the word of God. Romans 10:17

No more saying, "He'll never walk again" or "You're gonna give me a heart attack." I do not let one of my favorite people see the smoke billowing out of my ears when he says, "I'm getting a migraine and there's not a damn thing anyone can do about it." True that. Probably not. Thankfully, our salvation trumps the dumb sayings and philosophies we coddle. But let's get rid of the junky beliefs and language. Let's be very strict about what we embrace as truth when it comes to life, safety and health. It may be true that you are sick. It is also true that Jesus took that sickness away. The latter overcomes the former.

Jesus' mother Mary said at the conception of her son,

May it be to me as you have said. Luke 1:38

Do we want it to be done to us as he has said.? Or do we want it to be done to us as we have said? Wow, sometimes I hope it is not done to us as we have said. What about as the doctor has said? Jesus did not say, "you have macular degeneration; you're going blind," or "you have six to nine months without treatment, seven to twelve with it….feeling miserable."

Scoff on scoffers. Whether we flippantly joke about things which lead to death, or resign ourselves to a medical condition, we do not align with God's word. What we say is what we believe in our hearts.

Out of the abundance of the heart his mouth speaks. Luke 6:45

Announcing things without really meaning them, "I have early onset alzheimers" which I have jokingly said, is an indication that we do not believe in the power of our words, nor the necessity to discipline our mouths.

He who guards his mouth and his tongue keeps himself from calamity. Proverbs 21:23

We do not understand the power God has invested in us to change our circumstances by his powerful words in our mouths. We cannot have it both ways. Who will sort out what we mean and what we do not?

A wise man's heart guides his mouth. Proverbs 16:23

Our ambivalence about the power of our words undermines us. We should be saying to a menacing mountain, "Move!" Jesus said the mountain would move just as we told it to. Practice on the rolling hills, maybe some little mounds first... a bump. I had a bump on my ankle for the longest time, years not months. It started getting bigger and bigger till it looked like cauliflower. When Patrick called attention to it, I called it a mole-kinda-thing because warts are gross and embarrassing, unfeminine and witchy. He believed me. Beauty secrets girls.

There would have been nothing wrong or sinful with getting wart remover and it would have worked. Instead, I took the opportunity to practice my mountain moving faith, and it was gone in days not weeks. I believe the little stuff is important training ground for our faith, to keep away big stuff and get rid of it in other people's lives. I have gotten pretty good at bump moving faith. Lucy had one in her mouth for as long as she could remember. We told it what to do and in less than three days she realized it was gone, whatever it was. I had a long time bump on my lip that a doctor advised me to have removed. I did…Doctor God.

My friend Jenny appreciates medical treatments of any sort and was complaining of a nuisance ailment one day. She knew about the power of Jesus for healing but was not active about it. I told her about my wart removing faith and she became indignant. "If Betsy can rebuke a wart into oblivion, then certainly I can do the same for this!" and she did.

Start by saying things like:

My youth is renewed like the eagles. Psalm 103:5

He sent forth his word and healed me; he rescued me from the grave. Psalm 107:20

He is the LORD, who heals me. Exodus 15:26

Many followed him and he healed all their sick. Matthew 12:15

Instead of mimicking phrases we have heard, thought or deduced, let's determine to repeat only the words of God. If you have an injury or ailment of some kind, be careful about how you talk to it, or about it. We can unwittingly curse ourselves. Sometimes we think a curse is a bad word. It is, but so much more. It is applying anger and condemnation in an already bad situation. "This #&^%$ job, that *$%#^! bank, these $#!%$&@ people, my *&*%@#$ head!" These further damn us. If I am in a pit, how will it help to further entrench me in an unfortunate circumstance with a bad attitude and its accompanying reinforcing words?

The most important time to have a positive attitude and the words to go with it, is when things are negative! In our humanity we default to cursing at bad things. If we want to change circumstances, we need to intentionally bless, infusing the situation with positive words. The words themselves are powerful. Do the words "I love you" carry power? How about "You are ugly" or "I hate you"? Words are not magic but they are powerful.

When used properly, they can actually be the catapult from which you are launched into a better situation. You will benefit from the fruit of your lips if they stay in the realm of goodness, love and blessing.

Death and life are in the power of the tongue and those who love it will eat its fruit. Proverbs 18:21

If we love and are kind with our tongue, we will eat the good fruit that grows from it. Speaking words of life, love and healing --that is how God works. On the first day of creation he spoke light into darkness, order into chaos.

The worlds were framed by the word of God, so that the things which are seen were not made of things which are visible. Hebrews 11:3

God speaks healing to sickness, joy to depression, liberty to the demon possessed, life to the empty womb. We have been given the same heritage of power in our mouths. We are warned about the force of our words because God entrusts us to have the same effect on negative situations that he has.

Bad words are bad medicine. They might not be the F-bomb. They may be words of doubt or even compassionate sounding words that encourage the acceptance of a cursed condition. They may even sound positive, "It's not so bad; a sore throat is better than a migraine!" Maybe we are trying to have a good attitude by saying things like "I'll take diarrhea over constipation any day." Any kind of deference to a curse is a curse. Do not yield to curses by speaking curses. Don't talk nicely about curses. Curses are not our friends. There is nothing good about tumors, bumps, boils, paralysis, pain, madness, blindness or confusion.

The word of God is *"health to a person's whole body." Proverbs 4:22*

It is good, effective medicine when you apply the word with faith. If, instead of God's word about your body, you say things like "this trashed knee" or "I have a bad back," and that is all you say, do not expect to get better. You don't have to deny that you have a problem, but instead of constantly reinforcing the problem by referring to your bad back say, "Back, according to 1 Peter 2:24, by his wounds you have been healed."

Take that medicine. Speak life, blessing and healing over your noncompliant body. God wants you whole. You pray for your body the way Jesus and the disciples did. Talk to it. Command it.

Do it like this:

(insert any injury or malady)

<u>Leg</u> you are healed in the name of Jesus Christ.

<u>Leg</u>, you conform to the word of Almighty God, that declares by the wounds and beatings of his Son Jesus Christ you are whole. (Isaiah 53:5)

<u>Leg</u>, be made completely strong and healthy according to the healing promises of the holy scriptures, for he sent his word to heal them. (Psalm 107:20)

<u>Leg</u>, you bow your knee in submission to the will of God concerning you, that this repair is a benefit that you do not forget. (Psalm 103:2,3)

<u>Leg</u>, your Maker is the Great Jehovah Rapha, the Lord who creates and heals and don't you forget it! (Exodus 15:26)

<u>Leg</u>, you are my leg and in Jesus' name, I command you to submit to the word of God and be made strong! (Acts 3:6)

This confession teaching brings a lot of reproach. Some people think I've gone off the deep end, but they'll have to admit I've gone off the deep end with lots of kids who testify to supernaturally healed body parts.

Chapter 9

Saved *and* Healed in The Atonement

Sounds religious. Not a great attention grabber for the masses. The atonement provides reconciliation of God and humans through the gruesome, sadistic beating and slaughter of Jesus Christ.

Okay, so if that is the definition of atonement, what does it mean to you in this 21st Century cyber world you live in? How does this doctrine impact your life? But first, I want to encourage you to study these next few chapters with diligence. Read them, digest them, consider them, let the revelation download. I promise if you do, beside becoming a certifiable BetsyB.tv theologian, the devil will have nothing on you. You can do this -- the reward will be so gratifying!

"Recipe for success: study while others are sleeping; work while others are loafing; prepare while others are playing, and dream while others are wishing." –William A. Ward

How the atonement impacts us, is not necessarily how it can and should impact us. That is what I am determined to change. There are many areas of dispute among Christian denominations, but when it comes to the essential doctrines of the Christian faith, there is unity. Otherwise, it is not Christianity. From Baptist to Catholic, from Lutheran to Assemblies of God, Christians cannot afford to compromise on such fundamentals as the Virgin Birth, the Sinless Perfection of

Christ, the Resurrection, the Trinity and the Atonement. They should set aside peripheral spiritual issues that do not impede the all-important relationship to Christ. Whether we dunk or sprinkle, use hymnals or projectors, sit in pews or folding chairs, wear suits or robes, celebrate Halloween or Harvest, speak in tongues or in response, silently concur or shout amen to preachers or preacherettes, we love God and each other. Right?

Although I do not believe that understanding healing as God fully intended for us is essential for our salvation, I do believe that our often gross misunderstanding of it paralyzes the Church's ability to most effectively spread the kingdom of God on earth.

Healing is cast aside as an area of denominational dispute, too controversial and divisive to be worth our while. As the most overlooked and under valued facet of our salvation, we are deprived of the fruitful results of the most generative evangelism known to man. The force for change that even one healing can exert is evident in the 1st Century through the ministries of Jesus and the first disciples. Healing is to be implemented by us in conjunction with the preaching and teaching of repentance from sin, as was represented by Christ. Freedom from sin and sickness are the benefits we have as a result of his atoning work at Golgotha. Jesus died to provide these benefits for us –so we could follow his example and engage them likewise. Unfortunately, the doctrine of healing as modeled by Jesus is not an area of unity in the Church.

Jesus went through all the towns and villages, teaching in their synagogues, preaching the good news of the kingdom and healing every disease and sickness Matthew 9:35

The miraculous effects of this routine practice were also routine, also not acknowledged throughout the Modern Church.

When the crowds heard Philip and saw the miraculous signs he did, they all paid close attention to what he said. With shrieks, evil spirits came out of many, and many paralytics and cripples were healed. Acts 8 6-7

They heard Philip, but it was not until they saw the miraculous signs Philip did, that they paid attention. No, they paid close attention. Not only did they pay close attention but a few verses later, they believed Philip as he preached, and were baptized. They were saved after they paid close attention, because of the works! Works work! Wild horses couldn't drag me away!

They work together: preaching, teaching and healing (healing of soul and body).

They work together: preaching teaching and salvation (salvation of soul and body).

They go together. Healing and salvation are indistinguishable from the standpoint of the Bible. From the original languages to the Old Testament prophesies, to the example of Jesus and the disciples, we should all be persuaded that healing and salvation are one and the same, intertwined, inseparable and originating from the same place --Golgotha, "The Place of the Skull." It was the mount of death, sin and sickness. I want us to leave our evil deeds, proclivity to wickedness, diseases and disabilities there.

Not acknowledging the healing work Jesus did for us on the cross equates to not appreciating everything he did there. Sure, it would have been enough if he had only provided for the forgiveness of our sins.

There are two problems with excluding physical healing in such a scenario:

1) He heals because of his love for us. Any good father would go to any length to heal his sick baby. There is no getting around God's character. God is love.

2) He heals because healed people are easily convinced of his love. It is the best way of spreading his love. Healed people jump around and shout out about it.

We have separated physical healing and salvation in our Christian culture by ascribing different names, guidelines and requirements for what is the one concept, represented by the Greek word sozo. Making this one word into two, healing and salvation, was the first mistake.

While salvation is a universal, free gift of God to be received by any one who will --healing, we say, is not necessarily a universal free gift of God to be received by any one who will.

By tinkering around with the simple message of Christ on healing, Christians have thrown many wrenches into the growling engines of the rescue-boat that Jesus built. We are still afloat, but using paddles in a muscle boat that has two 500 horse power engines.

We do not want to handicap our ability to rescue people by keeping the *John 3:16, "God so loved the world that he gave his one and only Son that whoever believes in him should not perish but have everlasting life."* and throwing away the *1 Peter 2:24 "and by his wounds we have been healed."*

King David was unaware of this distinction between salvation from sin and sickness when he wrote,

Forget not all his benefits- who forgives all your sins and heals all your disease. Psalm 103:2,3

We will see that both sin and sickness are dealt with equally in the scriptures about the atonement. David recognized that God healed him and saved him as part of the same benefits package. By the command of the Holy Spirit speaking via the pen of David, we too are commanded to remember all his benefits: the forgiveness of all sins and the healing of all diseases. This verse makes it impossible to consider the first part of the sentence, forgiveness of all sins, as universally true, while taking exception to the second part of the sentence, the healing of all diseases.

Both have to be appropriated by faith. The first half is as true as the second. Healing of all diseases is *as* legitimate as forgiveness of all sins. It is the same sentence! We are not at liberty to qualify one half of the sentence to the exclusion of the other.

Speaking of liberty and half-truth, what if a presidential candidate praised the Founding Father's words in the Declaration of Independence, "We hold these truths to be self-evident, that all men are created equal, that they are endowed by their Creator with certain unalienable Rights, that among these are Life, Liberty and the Pursuit of Happiness," but with some reservations and multiple arbitrarily imposed restrictions about the Liberty part.

He might lecture, "While Life is definitely an unalienable right, Liberty is not always for everyone. Bondage can serve in teaching valuable lessons; slavery makes a people stronger."

No matter his intellectual qualifications, such revisionist musings are not acceptable. How silly that would be, and yet we do it with the scriptures all the time when we separate the benefit of his healing all our diseases from the benefit of his forgiving all our sins. David does not consider the forgiveness of all sins to be of a different magnitude than the healing of all diseases.

Neither does the New Testament distinguish salvation from sin, and healing from sickness like we do. The authors of the New Testament were entirely unfamiliar with the now popular notion that "Jesus Saves" and "Jesus Heals" are two different things with two sets of rules, the latter being complex with lots of variables.

Jesus illustrated the difficulty in segregating healing from our complete salvation --spirit, soul and body, when he 'fixed' people. He fixed their sickness and/or sin problems. It was the same thorough fix every time. The only thing that differed from person to person was which aspect of a person's being was affected: the spirit, the mind or the body. In many cases, as with the Canaanite woman's demon-possessed daughter, it was all three. *"Her daughter was healed." Matthew 15:28* from suffering in her body, her mind and her spirit.

This complete salvation is made possible because of the atonement. Jesus' sacrificial torture and death, gave us access to freedom for our spirits, souls and bodies from the decay of all sin and every disease. Payment was made in full. How much freedom we experience, though, is a different matter and depends on either our willingness or reluctance to believe and receive.

Jesus' sacrifice, his atoning work on the day of his death, is a contractual, historical event, and we are the beneficiaries. We claim the benefits with faith. The atoning work for our healing and salvation is secured in the covenant God made with us that horrible day in his wounds and blood at a place called Skull. Why we use the Latin derived 'calvary' instead of 'kranion' or 'skull,' which is the direct translation for the location of Jesus' crucifixion, is a mystery, except that it helps veil the savagery of his murder.

Lilies and a silk draped over a smooth cross? No, a sadistic execution devise on a mount of darkness and unparalleled evil. Why does it matter? Everything that happened on that horrible Friday of literal thick, black darkness happened for death, death to wickedness, death to bondage, death to disease and death to death. None of cursed things rose with Jesus when he did, so we have no business to either live amongst the damned things or make place for them in our doctrines or bodies. We need to be respectful of what Jesus endured at the Place of the Skull --and leave them there.

Our benefits as believers are according to the effectiveness of God's blood sacrifice, and our acceptance of that sacrifice. Human postulating and speculation about healing blocks the free gift of healing. Believing fuels healing.

As foretold in Isaiah's prophesy of the atonement at the Place of the Skull, and often overlooked by Christians, both sin and sickness were dealt the same death blow. The fact that Jesus' substitutionary sacrifice incorporated our souls and bodies is the reason we are within our rights when we stand against the forces of sin (which destroys souls) and disease (which destroys bodies). Furthermore, in honor of Jesus' human sacrifice, it is our duty to stand against sin and, as unequivocally, to stand against disease.

Little Hakan

This works. Being convinced of this brings conviction. Conviction makes a stout heart that will not yield to a lie. Once you are convinced that God destroyed disease, it will change your life. The signs and wonders of his love that can be displayed through your life are without limit.

A boney Plot Hound puppy with big glassy tear drop eyes lay still on my boys' couch; all his siblings had been put to sleep. He was next until my sons, Sammy and Joey adopted him from the shelter. They named him Hakan, which means fire. We laid hands on him and rebuked death and pneumonia but still he would hardly eat or drink. He coughed and coughed.

Is there really a premise for dog healing? I believe so. Jesus put away the curse of disease from this earth, having himself become a curse.

I found a promise that our young animals would live and not die. In summary, he would keep us free from every disease, our crops, our children and our animals.

None of your men or women will be without children nor any of your livestock without young. The Lord will keep you free from every disease. Deuteronomy 7:14-15

For several days Hakan stayed in the same sickly condition, then worsened. In spite of this, every night, sisters and nieces believed. The vet advised immediate (expensive) hospitalization for intravenous hydration and nutrition. The boys thought they might have to put him to sleep, but took him home and continued to nurse him instead --and we continued to pray. Downhill he went. The boys said he was dying. I reminded them to repeat God's word about Hakan's situation and not the medical or circumstantial prognosis.

"Hakan, you will live and not die according to the fact that the curse of disease has been removed from the earth and according to Deuteronomy 7 which declares you to be free from disease."

The next day when I called, Joey said he was better. After a couple days, he was chunking up. He made a happy puppy, miraculous recovery without the prohibitively expensive medical intervention. Praise the Lord.

The Prophet Breaks It Down

It becomes natural to stand defiantly in the face of sickness when you understand the ramifications of the atoning work Christ accomplished on the day of his death. Isaiah's prophesy in Chapter 53 is the core for understanding the complete message of salvation. This foretelling of Jesus' sacrifice provides an end to every argument, the death blow to every attack. It is fixed truth.

We are out of order to modify or customize the scriptures to fit our situations or understanding. We should change our words to align with God's words instead of trying to change the obvious meaning to line up with our ideas and circumstances.

For I am the LORD, I change not. Malachi 3:6

As Isaiah 53 foretells Christ's death, it is undeniable that physical disease and sin are established forever as atoned for. The inflexible facts are:

Surely he took up our infirmities and carried our sorrows, yet we considered him stricken by God, smitten by him, and afflicted. But he was pierced for our transgressions, he was crushed for our iniquities; the punishment that brought us peace was upon him, and by his wounds we are healed. Isaiah 53:4-5

Let's break down this revolutionary passage so we can shake the sluggish, hibernating and comatose in ourselves first. Study this passage so you can understand it and educate others.

Break Down of Isaiah 53:4-5

1) He took up our <u>infirmities</u> (sicknesses, 'cholly' in Hebrew)
2) He carried our <u>sorrows</u> (pain, 'makob' in Hebrew)
3) He was pierced for our <u>transgressions</u>.(evil deeds)
4) He was crushed for our <u>iniquities</u> (injustices)
5) He was punished for our <u>peace</u> (safety, soundness in body, welfare, health, prosperity, 'shalom' in Hebrew)
6) By his wounds we are <u>healed</u> (to heal, physician, 'rapha' in Hebrew)

Notice that the first four are impediments which Jesus removed from us. These are the things he saved us from. The last two are the replacements, what he saved us for. After he cleans out the junk, we get the good stuff.

In spite of the clarity of this foundational doctrine of the Christian faith, some oppose God by imposing qualifications on healing that they would not dare impose upon salvation.

After so long praying unsuccessfully for my crack addict, would I throw up my hands and resign him to the damned? I could justify my giving up on him by saying, "Alas, it is not always God's will to save." My spiritual stamina may have run out, but that does not change God's desire to save, no exceptions allowed. It is not his will that any should perish. According to the atoning work of Christ, described in Isaiah 53:4-5, it is no different with healing ––no matter how tired we are of pounding heaven.

With this knowledge, we no longer have the prerogative of saying about a cancer victim, "It may not be God's will to heal her" anymore than we could say, "It is not God's will to save her."

Breakdown of Parts 1 & 2 of Isaiah 53:4-5
"Sickness and Pain"

Surely he took up our infirmities and carried our sorrows.

When Isaiah said in verse 4 that the Lord took up our infirmities and carried our sorrows, was he referring to spiritual infirmities or physical? Did he just mean emotional sorrows?

He was talking especially about physical infirmities, diseases and pain. In subsequent phrases he thoroughly covered soulish and spiritual depravity and sin.

The Hebrew word for infirmities is 'cholly' and also means sickness. The Hebrew word for sorrows is 'makob' and also means pain. These Hebrew words clearly mean physical disease and pain, as indicated by their use as such throughout the rest of the Bible. For example,

"And the Lord will take away from you all sickness (cholly)" Deuteronomy 7:15

The stance that somehow we are only guaranteed spiritual or mental health cannot be validated from scripture.

But you can forget the ancient languages! If Isaiah were speaking only of 'spiritual disease,' then Matthew in Chapter 8 of his gospel would not have referenced this particular prophesy as the one Jesus was fulfilling when he was healing everyone's physical sicknesses and physical demon-possessions at Peter's house. A child could understand this.

By Matthew's translation of Isaiah 53:4 from Hebrew into Greek, we know Matthew thought it was about physical illness. He translated the Hebrew makob (sorrows/pains) to diseases. This reflects his understanding of Isaiah 53:4...

When Jesus came into Peter's house, he saw Peter's mother-in-law lying in bed with a fever. He touched her hand and the fever left her and she got up and began to wait on him. When evening came, many who were demon-possessed were brought to him, and he drove out the spirits with a word and healed all the sick. This was to fulfill what was spoken through the prophet Isaiah: "He took up our infirmities and carried our diseases (from Hebrew 'makob' meaning pain/sorrow)" Matthew 8:14-17

Matthew diffuses any argument that somehow Isaiah meant only spiritual disease by consigning only physical healing to the fulfillment of this prophesy.

Mark's version of the same event says Jesus healed 'various diseases.' It is interesting that the proponents of 'spiritual healing' only, cannot prop up their theory with a single specific incident in these passages. There is nothing specifically mentioned other than physical cures to exemplify the fulfillment of this most heralded Messianic prophesy. No doubt there were people healed of all sorts of spiritual and emotional maladies, but if you had to exclude an aspect of salvation, and you don't, it would have to be 'spiritual healing.' My point is to expose the absurdity of this so called Biblical insight.

If anything, it seems like the Bible over-emphasizes the physical healing aspect of our salvation, almost as if God knew we would be so hell bent on neglecting it.

The number of physical healings that are described in the gospels dwarfs the number of salvation testimonies. By the logic we use to dismiss healing, we could more easily dismiss salvation. After all, Matthew considered Isaiah's Atonement prophesy to be fulfilled by physical healings to the exclusion of even one specific example of 'spiritual healing' from sin.

Of course, no Christian would attempt to make the silly argument that 'spiritual healing' or salvation from sin and hell is not as universally, uncatagorically and unequivocally provided as healing from physical sickness and disability is. Yet, the examples we have been given are predominantly, almost exclusively, physical healings.

Clearly, Matthew describes a host of physically sick and fevered people, as well as those suffering physical and mental trauma from demon-possession. Where he writes the phrase *"healed all the sick,"* he uses the Greek word 'kakos' for sick, which means to be ill. It is used elsewhere in the New Testament for diseases and physical infirmities. There is no way around the fact that Jesus heals. Making it true for you personally is another lesson.

Break Down of Parts 3 & 4 of Isaiah 53:4-5 "Sin and Other Human Depravity"

He was pierced for our transgressions, he was crushed for our iniquities

Reading further into Isaiah's prophesy, we as Christians have no argument with Jesus' being pierced for our transgressions (evil deeds), or crushed for our iniquities (sins).

There is consensus among Christians that Jesus died for all the sin of every sinner. We will learn that in the same way that people elude the benefits of such forgiveness, they also miss out on the benefits of healing.

Break Down of Part 5 of Isaiah 53:4-5
"More Than One Peace To Peace"

The punishment that brought us peace was upon him.

Neither do we have a problem with the Biblical contention that he was punished for our peace, that is unless we look at the full spectrum of the meaning of the Hebrew word for peace, 'shalom.' The peace Jesus bought for us by his mutilation and humiliation was much more than tranquility.

Shalom means welfare, safety, wealth and prosperity. Our peace is soundness in body and is a guaranteed benefit. Jesus earned it for us. Why do we think he went through all that

We need to proudly wear our healing and soundness in body as a badge of honor.

Break Down of Part 6 of Isaiah 53:4-5
"FACT: You Are Healed"

...and by his wounds we are healed.

This one little Bible verse can all by itself squash, with all the power punch of heaven, any argument any man can erect against any aspect of healing. Facts can be irritating little things.

So if you are not convinced yet, Isaiah finishes verse 5 with *"by his wounds we are healed."* The Hebrew word for 'healed' here is 'rapha' meaning to heal, to make healthy and physician. Rapha is used elsewhere in the Old Testament for physical healing, like when God says, *"I am the Lord that <u>heals</u> you." Exodus 15:26* or you may have heard it, *"I am Jehovah Rapha, the Lord who <u>heals</u>."*

This is where we got the name for God, The Great Physician.

No matter how you cut it, rapha equals bodily health. Over 50 times, rapha is used for undeniably physical conditions, *"If the sore is unchanged so far as the priest can see, and if black hair has grown in it (as opposed to yellow), the affected person is <u>healed</u>."* Leviticus 13:37 They are rapha'd, nice and healthy.

On every occasion where rapha is used in the context of personal physical healing as opposed to figuratively of a land or people, it is exclusively physical healing for physical impairment or abnormalities, never emotional or 'spiritual disease.'

In the New Testament, Peter, like Matthew, acknowledged the healing of physical disease as prophesied by Isaiah. Matthew referenced Isaiah 53:4 to explain the miraculous manifestations of the day, while Peter quoted from the next verse, Isaiah 53:5 to explain his understanding of the Atonement and its consequences of salvation and healing. Peter recalls the death of sin and sickness, both as being vanquished at the cross. All we need was given to us that day.

He himself bore our sins in his body on the tree, so that we might die to sins and live for righteousness; by his wounds you have been healed. 1 Peter 2:24

The notable difference in Peter's rendition of Isaiah 53:5 is that he used the past tense, *"by his wounds you have been healed."* It is a done deal. It's a wrap. It's finished.

Again, the party crashers press on into 1 Peter 2:24 by again claiming that Peter was speaking of the more important 'spiritual healing.'

But the Greek will not allow it.

Where Peter writes *"you have been healed,"* he uses the word 'iaomia' (to cure, heal and make whole). It is the word used to describe the physical healings of paralysis, chronic bleeding, leprosy, disabilities, palsy (paralysis of part of the body that has uncontrollable tremors), dropsy (swelling caused by fluid in the body tissue), fever, dysentery, demon-possession, all kinds of diseases, the oppressed --and in one verse only, the broken-hearted.

Not a compelling case can be made for spirit only healing in 1 Peter 2:24. Instead, it just gives further credence to the fact that our redemption absolutely encompasses our physical bodies.

7 Words That Can Change the World

The seven words, *"By his wounds you have been healed."* 1 Peter 2:24 are some of the mightiest in the universe. There is nothing left to do about your healing. The jury is not out. The decision has been made; the price has been paid. If you want it, you have to take it.

In Isaiah 53:5 *"We are healed."*

In 1 Peter 2:24 *"You have been healed."*

Apply these verses to overcome every obstacle that impedes you from your healing. None of the arguments that put conditions on healing can stand up to this. It is non negotiable.

If you get a bad medical report, you can cling to your Auntie's word that God may not always heal, or you can cling for dear life to God's word, *"by his wounds I have been healed."*

"God does not always heal." If you choose to believe that neo-proverb, fine. Not me, I choose *"by his wounds I have been healed."*

"God wants this sickness to teach you a lesson." Oh wow! I guess the lesson is that he wants me healthy because the word is, *"by his wounds I have been healed."*

"God wants you to be patient and wait for his timing to heal you." Well how awesome! Because his timing is 2000 years ago. So, when the symptoms rage, you can pick, "it might not be God's timing" or you can pick God's word, which teaches that as long as we are sick, we are not yet in God's timing. Why?

Because he already healed us —past tense. You will know you are in God's timing when you are well. Now is the time of salvation. You were healed a long time ago —*"By his wounds you have been healed."*

"It may not be God's will to heal," cannot stand against *"by his wounds I have been healed."* It's too late to change his will.

Okay so hold on a second. He might not want to heal me, but he already did heal me? Since I cannot find a verse about God's perhaps not wanting me to be healed, I think I'll stick with *"by his wounds I have been healed."*

Any doubts the devil or anyone else can throw at you, will not penetrate the fortress of Isaiah's prophesy. Matthew and Peter's expansions of Isaiah 53:4-5 further disable any attempts to subvert what Jesus did for you, and what he wants you to do in response: actively believe.

In light of all the torment Jesus endured on the cross because of us, it is our duty to be as intolerant of sickness as we are of sin. Having a thorough understanding of this historical fact is critical in our implementation of our healing heritage as Christians. The defeat of sin and sickness is the foundation of the gospel message and the ammunition for our assault on the thief who has stolen our inheritance. We want it all back.

It is wrong to factionalize God's treatment of sin and sickness with man-made philosophies. "We cannot always understand everything God is doing!" they insist. True, we cannot understand everything, but, when it comes to healing, that is an excuse to remain apathetic. God has been explicit in his instructions and expectations with regard to healing. Healing is not a subject about which God has been the least bit mysterious.

There is no other issue that Jesus spent more time on. We have ample information and the accompanying power to get the job done. He left a detailed shopping list and a gold card with our names on it.

The Bible does not provide the text from which we morph Jesus' healing ministry into an esoteric, intellectualized, nebulous healing ministry that an average brain cannot grasp.

He was clear enough in his teachings about sin and forgiveness. We do not need to make them analogous. Gospel accounts are not analogies; they are moments in history that were painstakingly recorded so we could know what Jesus did, why he did it, how he did it, and how to transmit those actions to successive generations --until his return. Only the parables are analogous, which Jesus did not leave open to interpretation, knowing how we would botch them.

I am amazed at the lengths to which sick people go to give purpose and meaning to their physical plights. Beauty for ashes! It is so simple. We need to stop trying to make our ashes beautiful. Only beauty is beautiful. He wants us to trade in the ashes, not learn to accept and appreciate the ashes. Disease is the ashes, nothing about disease is beautiful. It is ruin and rot and listed with great specificity under the curse.

Beauty for ashes, that is what he offers. Give Jehovah Rapha your ashes. He promises beauty in return. Cancer is not beautiful. Freedom from cancer is beautiful. He does not want us to praise him for the ashes. He wants us to praise him for the trade. I pray this message will be delivered to you not by persuasive words of wisdom but by revelation of the Holy Spirit!

When Jesus died, sin and sickness died with him. Only Jesus rose. They did not. When we begin to grasp the enormity of what he did for us, we will not be as cavalier about sin or sickness. They are dead. The devil does not want us to know it!. Because I am in Christ, sin and sickness are dead in me too.

Arthritis, you will not be raised in me.

Cancer, you have no resurrection.

Diseases that rage in our children, you are dead!

The atonement of Christ speaks of the beating and crucifixion of Jesus, whereby he took the power of death, hell and your grave away from Satan. It is vital to your success and prosperity to understand the contractual ramifications of this event.

The non negotiable components of Isaiah 53 will change life as you know it.

Chapter 10

Two Damned Doctrines

You've come so far.
Don't back out now.
Discipline those Bible study muscles!
Train yourself.
Become a specialist.
Put forth effort.
Separate yourself from those who surrender to enemies.
Become courageous.
Save people.

"Few men are born brave. Many become so through training and force of discipline." -Publus Flavus Vegetus Renatus

You will not regret a moment of this study struggle --for the trophy of lives rescued! It will get you over those restrictive barriers:

Beware of two modern day heresies that have been slithering around under pews and at the feet of Christians since the 1st Century when Paul and friends had to battle them.

The first they called Gnosticism. Centuries later, Martin Luther called it Antinomianism: anti (against) nomos (law) or against the law, law breakers. Now they call it 'Once Saved Always Saved,' Saved by Grace (or Faith) Only, or 'Eternal Security.' It means you don't have to abide by God's moral law to get into heaven. Instead of being free from sin, you are free to sin without fear of repercussion. Instead of God's grace giving you power to not sin, it gives you permission to sin. It just means:

say the 'Sinner's Prayer,' mean it, and, although most do not recommend it, you can live however you want.

Second, and in the opposite corner, are the 1st Century Judaizers. Throughout history, their theological diversions have been promoted by legalists. Presently, they demand allegiance to rituals, practices, rules and penance to assuage guilt. They replace a personal relationship to God with actions, traditions and ideas. Today this is Legalism, Saved by Works (or Deeds) Only --Big Religion.

Neither extreme is stern about sin. They are both hospitable to sin that leads to death, and so steal the fuel that churns our supernatural engines: righteousness. These false doctrines dull the adventure and thrill by excusing permissiveness.

The Early Church was replete with miracles. We are not. Why isn't the Modern Church as fluent in miraculous signs and wonders as the Early, 1st Century Church? Because the Early Church was A) intolerant of false doctrine and B) intolerant of sin.

Does that mean only those who have sound doctrine and no sin can experience a miracle? No, miracles are especially for unbelievers and sinners who know nothing about such theological issues. Miracles are the most effective means of saving people, numerically speaking --Biblically speaking. But, for a believer to move in and perform signs and wonders, he must A) have sound doctrine and B) live a righteous life.

Because of these two damned doctrines, we have become tolerant of both false doctrine and sin. Sinning from time to time, and repenting, is not the same as deliberately violating God's laws as a lifestyle. Everyone knows the difference between a lifestyle of pursuing righteousness and a lifestyle of violating God's moral laws. You are not fooling him. It is the difference between having sex with your boyfriend from which you truly repent, and living with him. If he really loves you, he will take you to the altar before he takes you to bed. That is obeying God's law --laws that are there for your happiness and protection. What girl would not prefer above fornicating, to be so highly honored that the love of her life would not have sex with her until she was his wife? Ephesians Chapter 5 for that.

These heresies --winking at sin and shrugging at grace, clog our heavenly power receptacles for miracles. Either of the two ditches will impact the eternal destinations of the people who are duped into believing them. Worse, populations of people remain doomed and damned when the supernatural power of the Church is stifled by marginalizing holiness and justifying sinfulness.

From the birth of the Church, leaders have been warring against these same spirits of error, no matter what masks they lurk behind. In either case they are vehicles that ingratiate sin.

Saved by Grace (Faith) Only	**Saved by Works (Deeds) Only**
Gnosticism	Judaizers
Antinomianism	Legalism
Once Saved Always Saved	Reliance on Religious Rites
Eternal Security	Big Religion

Ironically, in neither of these popular camps is sin dealt with as severely as it is in the Bible. The God of the Old and New Testaments is the same; he is the Judge and the Merciful. The only difference is that in the New Testament, Jesus is judged and punished instead of God's people. The requirements of keeping the morals of the Mosaic Law of the Old Testament are more, not less valid under the New Testament. Yet, those of the Saved by Grace (Faith) Only camp boast of not being under the law to the extreme of not having to keep the moral law! Jesus fulfilled the Law and the Prophets so it would be possible for us to do so --in him! We are still obligated to keep the moral laws that were the motivation of the civil and ceremonial laws of the Old Testament. We can only do that by his power in us.

On the Saved by Works (Deeds) Only/Legalists/Big Religion side, it was the Judaizers of the 1st Century who were the culprits of demanding that Old Testament customs and ceremonies, which only housed the moral law, were kept. They tried to make new Christian converts obey Hebrew ceremonial laws which had been fulfilled in Christ. Jesus completed the need for those as he himself became the house, the temple, the place of worship. All the symbolism and ceremony pointed toward him.

Now that he is here, we are only required to follow and obey him! It's a new day. He fulfilled all the requirements. Our only duty is to love him, and if we love, we obey.

Demanding adherence to the civil and ceremonial laws of the Old Testament would be like forcing a teenage girl to write on a scroll with a feather dipped in ink and send it by a courier via pigeon or donkey --instead of texting. She would be stifled, frustrated and unsuccessful in this day and age, were she forced into old ways of communicating. It would be impossible for her, and she just wouldn't do it. Yet many of our Christian denominations have sets of rites and rituals they have devised that have to be followed, so they say.

Legalism is religion's made up rules. By following them, we strain impossibly to obtain a connection to God and be saved, ease guilt or satisfy our souls. We set ourselves up to fail. Why? Legalism is based on works only, doing things to make up for our failures, and depending on our spiritual superiors. There can be no real satisfaction or peace.

A-biblical traditions divert from the real power that belongs to every believer. The source of hundreds of these church traditions, like praying for the dead or priesthood celibacy, is lust for money and power. Celibacy was instituted by church leaders who did not want priest's property passed to their children, but instead wanted it to go to the church. Now, many just accept celibacy as godly because it is robed in sacred tradition, albeit corrupt. Praying for the dead started as lucrative business as well for the Catholic Church, when the faithful could buy loved ones time out of hell.

Many Pentecostal preachers rape their television audiences and congregations by promising healing and prosperity for seed gifts of a thousand dollars. They say they are not doing that, but they are. This modern tradition has also become a sacred cow. Never seen that in the Bible. But I did see Ruth get rich because she was nice to her mother-in-law, David get rich because he killed a giant, and Solomon get rich because he prayed for wisdom. Sure seems like the key to blessing is obedience to what God says to do --giving money is only one of thousands of ways to obey God.

The greed and lust for power at the top of the religious pyramid of any denomination cannot be dismissed. Legalism demands a mediator between you and God. No human from any church, can fill that role or replace your need to stand alone before God.

There is one God and one mediator between God and men, the man Christ Jesus. 1 Timothy 2:5

Only Jesus is ordained to mediate between you and God. Modern day Christian priests in a role of Church leadership are really operating in ministry offices like pastor, teacher or apostle. They are priests, yes, but no more so than you or I who are believers. The role of a priest as a mediator between God and man was done away with as part of the Old Testament law and prophets. From several passages in the New Testament, we are taught the priesthood of all believers.

You are a chosen people a royal priesthood a holy nation. 1 Peter 2:9

We are under the New Covenant, whereby Jesus Christ himself has become our High Priest, and every believer a priest of God whose duty it is to bring reconciliation to the lost.

Jesus the last High Priest, was himself the last sacrifice. All the millions of Old Testament sacrificial lambs, goats and bulls died to foreshadow him. All the priests foreshadowed him. We need no more priests and no more sacrifices. He is it. We do not need anyone to give us a list of things to do to erase our sins or make up for them. Penance is not Biblical. Good works come as a result of being with Jesus, not as a means to get to him. Ministers should guide and encourage. They should not lord over, but serve the saints.

Yes, if you are a believer, then you are a saint. You *are* a saint; you don't *pray* to saints. We, living saints, pray only to God, and to no man or woman. It is witchcraft to pray to the dead. This is a non negotiable tenant of the Christian faith. Many who want to continue in sin are duped into thinking they can still get into heaven by habitually saying they are sorry and by getting a list of little punishments they can self-inflict, and duties they can perform to pay for sin. Like a drug, this will provide guilt relief until the next sin fix. And the cycle continues....

If we lean toward being Saved by Grace (Faith) Only, Eternal Security and Once Saved Always Saved errors, we are unfaithful to God because our flesh discovers another cover for sin. As with Legalism, we appease our consciences by saying sorry, over and over and over. But this time because of grace, sin is erased. We don't have to do anything. Right?

Except that Jesus never said to say sorry. Saying sorry alone, without accompanying change in behavior, leads to false security, a deception that all is well and that sin is absolved. We mock God when we say we are sorry but have no real intention of doing anything about it. He is not stupid.

Do not be deceived, God is not mocked; for whatever a man sows, that he will also reap. For he who sows to his flesh will of the flesh reap corruption, but he who sows to the Spirit will of the Spirit reap everlasting life. Galatians 6:7

If you keep sowing seeds in your flesh (sinful nature), you reap corruption. Saying sorry doesn't change that. Merely listening to the word, without doing it, is tantamount to self-deception. We deceive ourselves into thinking we are safely saved.

Do not merely listen to the word, and so deceive yourselves. Do what it says. James 1:22

Nether confession, nor sorrow, nor penance purges sin. Penance is not repentance. Penance determines to pay for sin; repentance determines to stop sin.

The Old Testament manner of dealing with sin is a good visual. The high priest would place his hands on the head of a live goat and transfer the sins of the people onto it. Jesus our now High Priest, does this:

Aaron shall lay both his hands on the head of the live goat, confess over it all the iniquities of the children of Israel, and all their transgressions, concerning all their sins, putting them on the head of the goat, and shall send it away into the wilderness. Leviticus 16:21

Confessing the sins over the goat would not be enough. The sin-burdened goat had to go into the barren wilderness, far away from the people. The sins had to leave the area.

In order to stay out of these two pits, grace only or works only, maintain a relationship with God through Jesus, obeying the moral law by his power in you, not because you have to, but because you want to. The secret is grace fueling works. It is burdening the goat with sin *and* sending it into the barren faraway places. Let's see...

We get saved and then we stop sinning. If we are truly saved then our heart's desire is to not sin. Surely our flesh may crave sin, but in our spirits we strive against it. Do we want our spouses to stay faithful because they have to, constrained by marital law, or because they want to, constrained by love? It is the free gift of grace that enables us to live free from the law of sin and death. Let Jesus live his life in you. You cannot do it without his grace.

Grace is freedom from the laws and regulations of religious institutions and systems that are set up in vain to connect people with God. Only Jesus, the man/God can do that. Because he is here, we no longer need the Old Testament customs and practices. The OT laws housed the moral code. Now Jesus does. We don't need a man-made temple anymore, but we need the new one, the person of Jesus.

Paul explains this to the Romans after telling them that no matter how great their sin is, God's grace is more. Where sin increases, grace much more increases. But, he warns against a dangerous conclusion --that grace makes sin permissible.

What shall we say, then? Shall we go on sinning so that grace may increase? By no means! We died to sin; how can we live in it any longer? Or don't you know that all of us who were baptized into Christ Jesus were baptized into his death? We were therefore buried with him through baptism into death in order that, just as Christ was raised from the dead through the glory of the Father, we too may live a new life.

If we have been united with him like this in his death, we will certainly also be united with him in his resurrection. For we know that our old self was crucified with him so that the body of sin might be done away with, that we should no longer be slaves to sin --because anyone who has died has been freed from sin.

Now if we died with Christ, we believe that we will also live with him. For we know that since Christ was raised from the dead, he cannot die again; death no longer has mastery over him. The death he died, he died to sin once for all; but the life he lives, he lives to God. In the same way, count yourselves dead to sin but alive to God in Christ Jesus.

Therefore do not let sin reign in your mortal body so that you obey its evil desires. Do not offer the parts of your body to sin, as instruments of wickedness, but rather offer yourselves to God, as those who have been brought from death to life; and offer the parts of your body to him as instruments of righteousness. For sin shall not be your master, because you are not under law, but under grace. Romans 6:1-14

Your freedom in Christ is not freedom to sin. Your freedom to sin is equivalent to your freedom to go to jail.

Paul thought putting away the moral laws was an absurd interpretation of what he was teaching and yet, we have credentialed, respected pastors and professors teaching that you should, but do not have to, keep the moral law if you want to go to heaven.

It would be a terrible spouse who whores around all over town and then expects to enjoy all the benefits of marriage. No, the marriage covenant is broken. False teachers contradict Jesus and the apostles by teaching that it doesn't matter how you live as long as you have at some point said The Sinner's Prayer, which is also not in the Bible. Just say "I do" and then get a girlfriend –see how that goes over.

The sacrifice of Jesus transferred God's power into our lives where the animal blood of the Old Covenant could not. Because Jesus died, rose from the dead, went back into heaven and sent the Holy Spirit to live in us, his house, we are without excuse for sin. The Grace Only people have no excuse not to walk in holiness. If they do walk righteously, they have no business teaching others that they don't have to do the same. Confusion in this area has split what should work together into two broken pieces. One errs on the grace only side while the other, works only.

It's not grace or works. It is grace and works, grace and moral law (deeds/works). We need grace so we can do the moral law. We need both, not one or the other. Balance. The only thing God tells us to choose between is life and death, blessing and cursing. We don't choose among living things, among good things. We want all the living things, all the power of grace and all the good fruit of good deeds --all the blessings and none of the dead things.

Rat or Demon?

Courtney and my grand-baby Hazel spent the night at our house last night, not because her firefighter husband was on a routine 24 hour shift, but because their walls are open to the attic for repairs. Courtney thought she heard the sound of scampering nails across the wood floors in the playroom. She didn't want to be alone with the baby in bed when the rat that Dustin saw in the back yard earlier that day, came snooping around in the comforter.

Sitting on my couch she mused, "I'd rather have a demon than a rat; I know how to get rid of those."

Haha but we don't have to choose among dead things. We should put up with neither rats nor demons. We should put up with neither hell nor sin. We can have all the good stuff with God.

Pridefully, one boasts about his working of miracles while another thinks he needs no miracles because he has taken the higher road of love and compassion. In the famous Love Letter, Paul said.

Follow the way of love and eagerly desire spiritual gifts, 1 Corinthians 14:1

Paul did not say follow love or gifts. God wants you to have both. He wants you to have it all, things that are meant to work together --salt and pepper, food and water, day and night, love and miracles, grace and works.

Works are proof of the grace. No works indicates no faith. No grace yields no good works. The grace is the gas. The works is the car. Without each other they are both useless. You are the driver. God fills your tank with grace and YOU drive the car.

Proponents of the Once Saved Always Saved, Eternal Security, Grace Only mess admit that we are agents of free will, able to choose whether we serve God or not, but if we do decide thus, via a fervent prayer, suddenly we become robots --unable to lose the reward of heaven no matter how apostate or wicked our ways, no matter how vehemently we turn our backs on God. Of course that is ridiculous.

Anyone can choose to follow and be a Christian as well as change his mind, lose interest or even hate God and his heaven. They aren't going there and we aren't doing them any favors by telling them they are. If we really love them, we will tell them the truth so they can have a chance of being ultimately saved.

Whether through the 1st Century Gnostics, the 16th Century Antinomians or the Modern Eternal Security bunch, this grace cheapening devil always finds a way to creep into the Church in some kind of religious garb. From the time of the Early Church Fathers until now, Christians will continue to blow the whistle on this Pied Piper.

True freedom is not the power to do whatever you want. The Bible teaches that adherence to the moral law is the path to true liberty.

Some political parties promote personal freedom to the point of legalizing drugs and prostitution. The countries that have adopted such policies are indeed infested with illegal drugs and prostitution, but also with higher incest rates, addiction and thriving child sex trades. The people are slaves to all ther "freedoms."

Whom the Son sets free (from sin and death) is free indeed. John 8:36

Jesus gave us power to be free from moral decadence --because God still judges sin! We need to be found spotless in Jesus to avoid judgment. If we are in sin, we are not in him. The whole entire message of the gospel is liberation from sin and sickness. Of course, if we do not want to be free, and many do not, Jesus is of no use to us. We will have to pay for our own sin, here and in hell.

If we deliberately keep on sinning after we have received the knowledge of the truth, no sacrifice for sins is left, but only a fearful expectation of judgment and of raging fire that will consume the enemies of God. ....

How much more severely do you think a man deserves to be punished who has trampled the Son of God under foot, who has treated as an unholy thing the blood of the covenant that sanctified him, and who has insulted Hebrews 10:26,27,29

All the time you hear, "Well you don't know his heart" or "Only God knows my heart." While that is true, it does not mean all is well. The assumption here is always that the heart is good, despite some outward negative manifestation. Jesus said we could not judge a person, but that we could judge his fruit. There is no indication that Jesus wanted us to be in the dark about other people's character. The fruit tells.

By their fruit you will recognize them. Do people pick grapes from thornbushes, or figs from thistles? Likewise every good tree bears good fruit, but a bad tree bears bad fruit. A good tree cannot bear bad fruit, and a bad tree cannot bear good fruit. Every tree that does not bear good fruit is cut down and thrown into the fire Thus, by their fruit you will recognize them.

Not everyone who says to me, "Lord, Lord," will enter the kingdom of heaven, but only he who does the will of my Father who is in heaven. Matthew 7:16-21

Interesting that Jesus directly links good fruit with doing what he says, not just saying something, like a prayer. Only those who have visible, useful fruit of obedience go to heaven.

Whether called Gnosticism, Antinomianism, Eternal Security, Saved by Grace Only or at the opposite extreme, Saved by Works Only, the Judaizers, Legalists, and Big Religion bunch, none require repentance (change). The most basic gospel message is REPENT of evil deeds. Nowhere in the Bible does it say we will be judged based on our hearts. Ultimate judgment is made according to a person's deeds and not their heart or intentions. Yes, God looks at the heart --and knows that if it is good, there will surely be good fruit.

Repentance is about changing direction. Not always does it speak of what we would think of as traditional sin. Sometimes we need to repent of thinking like victims. If we need healing, deliverance or financial help, we must stop praying like victims and losers. Change your mindset in order to have effective prayers. Pray like victors and winners. People name kids Victor, not Victim.

In my healing conferences, I teach the word, the word, the word, because it is by the word of God that we build our faith. I have no intention of changing that, but what about when we are in the word and we have no breakthroughs?

That was me at one time --okay many times, always wailing the Psalms of David, "WHEN! O Lord will you deliver meeeee!?!" and that was it. It was a good start, but you see, after David went to battle, the songs of victory came. I forgot about those.

We know that sorrow endures for a night but joy comes in the morning. Morning after mourning.

It's not wrong to mourn, in fact it is a good and necessary step through the process of grief. If we get stuck in mourning, it leads to depression, not joy in the morning. All the steps are important. Denial, sadness, anger, acceptance, forgiveness --we need to move through a spectrum of emotions and stages for a healthy, balanced life of joy and peace.

It takes initiative and struggle. It takes perseverance and faith. The minute we give up and give in to our sin, circumstances, sickness or losses, we are beat.

Religion that pats your back when you sin, or on the other side, gives you a list of things to do to pay for it, does nothing to promote salvation or success. Only repenting, confessing and forsaking the behavior leads to salvation.

In the same way, we have to get off the couch about healing, relationships, finances and any other areas in which we are stuck. It is not by osmosis that we inherit the promises, breakthroughs and victories; it is by obedience. It is showing our faith by our works.

You are not a victim anymore. You are a victor, not because your body feels good, your bills are paid or because your circumstances have changed, but because you are standing on God's promises of healing and provision. Your conquering mindset, knowing who you are in Christ, will change the way you pray and fight. By this pro-activity, and not by permitting sin and evil, you will get the healing, the provision and the relationships that belong to you.

Remember when you face an enemy, use your sword, God's word. Swing aggressively, knowing that you are in Christ who has already won the battle. He has already healed you and already provided for you. He is just waiting for you to go take your Promised Land!

Moral rules, not religious or ceremonial rules, protect you.

How about the moral law of obeying laws imposed for protection? If I continually disobey the red traffic light, I will eventually die, along with whichever innocent riders I have in the car. If I disobey the moral law of paying my dinner check, then I hurt the server who will have to pay my bill, not to mention my kids and myself if I end up in jail. If people disobey the moral laws of marriage by indulging in extra-marital sex, they will suffer heartache, loss, loneliness, feelings of worthlessness, depression and perhaps, disease.

God is not playing games with us. He is not mocked. If you say you believe, he expects you to act like it – and he died so you could.

Not everyone who says to me, "Lord, Lord," will enter the kingdom of heaven, but only he who does the will of my father who is in heaven. Many will say to me on that day, "Lord, Lord, did we not prophesy in your name and in your name drive out demons and perform many miracles?" (Did we not do all the actions and works you require?) Then I will tell them plainly, "I never knew you, depart from me you evil doers!" (law breakers) Matthew 7:21

Jesus considered all their works to be evildoing, lawbreaking because they were performing religious actions and not living righteous lives. Indeed, he looked at their hearts, wicked hearts, and reckoned their deeds wicked. They missed the grace through faith in him, and skipped to the superficial acts and deeds part. They needed both to avoid ultimate rejection.

Away from me you evildoers! Matthew 7:23

'Evildoer' comes from the Greek 'anomia': lawlessness, iniquity, disobedience, sin, an utter disregard for God's law. It is the condition of being without law, whether by ignoring or violating. Being contemptuous of law is not equivalent to freedom. It is the path to incarceration.

Where did we get the idea that freedom in Christ is freedom to sin without repercussion? This will land us in a bottomless pit.

The ones who went into the fire were the lawless ones, not the ones who refused say the Sinner's Prayer. Grace is misunderstood to mean that now, because Jesus died for our sins and he forgives us, we can sin without consequence. The opposite is true. Grace is what he freely gives us so we can have the strength and power to do good and be good in him. It is evil to teach that grace is a license to sin. Although many pastors will not admit it, that is what they do when they tell followers that no matter what they do, they cannot lose their salvation.

Grace is not a sin permit.

For certain men whose condemnation was written about long ago have secretly slipped in among you. They are godless men, who change the grace of our God into a license for immorality. Jude 1:4

If we claim to have fellowship with him yet walk in the darkness, we lie, and do not live by the truth. 1 John 1:6

If we are in sin, we are living a lie. Jesus is the truth. Satan is the liar.

He who does what is right is righteous, just as he is righteous. He who does what is sinful is of the devil, because the devil has been sinning from the beginning. The reason the Son of God appeared was to destroy the devil's work. 1 John 3:7

When we boast about not being 'under the law,' we are correctly saying we are not under the punishment of the law since we have inherited the righteousness of Jesus Christ. We mean that we are not under the requirements of civil, traditional and ceremonial law that were all fulfilled in Christ.

The moral principles of the law are still valid. They manifest as fruit of the Holy Spirit in us. If anything, the moral requirements of the law are more strict for Christians than they were under the Old Testament system. Not only must we not murder, we cannot even hate. Not only are we forbidden to fornicate or commit adultery, but we cannot even lust about it.

But I tell you that anyone who looks at a woman lustfully has already committed adultery with her in his heart. Matthew 5:28

This is all impossible without his perfect love and life in you.

Jesus in you is the only way you can make that trip to heaven anyway.

10 Red Flags of Saved By Grace Only Heresy
(Eternal Security, Once Saved Always Saved, Gnostic, Antinomian)

1. Anyone who believes that Christians are not obliged to obey the moral division of the Law of Moses

2. Anyone who believes that Christians are not obliged to obey the commands of Christ and the Apostles

3. Anyone who believes that Christians are not obliged to obey any law

4. Anyone who sets the 'leading of the Holy Spirit' in opposition to obedience to God's word

5. Anyone who sets grace in opposition to obedience to any written word of God

6. Anyone who believes that their spirit is saved, but their body, and what they do with it is not important to their eternal life, because of grace.

7. Anyone who uses Christ's forgiveness to excuse or justify their sin

8. Anyone who thinks they will go to heaven on the basis of a prayer alone and not their lifestyle, choices and actions.

9. Anyone who thinks that believing in Jesus, without a life that reflects such a belief, will secure them a place in heaven.

10. Anyone who believes that being sorry for sin is the same as repentance.

10 Red Flags of Saved by Works Only Heresy
(Legalism, Big Religion)

1. Anyone who believes their good deeds will make up for their sins or bad deeds, works, actions or thoughts

2. Anyone who thinks they can pay or be punished to expunge their sins, evil deeds or disobedience to God's law

3. Anyone who believes they will go to heaven by being a good person outside of faith in Jesus Christ

4. Anyone who thinks if they just say they are sorry for their sins, they will go to heaven

5. Anyone who thinks they will go to heaven if they engage in certain religious acts or rituals including baptism, communion, penance, church attendance or choir membership

6. Anyone whose conscience is appeased when they see someone committing worse sins than themselves

7. Anyone who does not know that it is by grace we are saved through faith in Jesus Christ, evidenced by good works

8. Anyone who thinks there is anything they can do to replace repentance (a complete abandonment) of sin

9. Anyone who uses Christ's forgiveness as insurance that they can sin freely as long as they confess their sin regularly

10 Anyone who depends on a religious institution to raise them from the dead after their funeral

Too complicated? All you need to be saved is REPENT !

Chapter 11

Stop Saying Sorry!

Repentance (not being sorry, not a rote prayer, not fessing up) is the only safety net for true eternal security.

What is repentance? Christians are called to be free from sin, not just sorry for sin. Everyone in hell is sorry. Being sorry is only a first step.

We should steer away from destructive behavior and go on to maturity, *"not laying again the foundation of repentance from acts that lead to death."* Hebrews 6:1

God wants us to repent because he wants us to be successful and happy. The destruction and pain that result from sin may still not be enough to convince some sinners to repent.

The rest of mankind that were not killed by these plagues still did not repent of the work of their hands. Revelation 9:20

This destruction will come as judgment for continued rebellion, not so that people will be convinced to finally repent. By this point in the future, God will have provided many invitations and warnings for people to avoid these judgments --through repentance.

We are not to commiserate with darkness by praying judgments (curses, punishments, negative consequences) into loved ones lives in order to somehow provoke them to repent. It is by his goodness that God implores people to repent.

Do you show contempt for the riches of his kindness, tolerance and patience, not realizing that God's kindness leads you toward repentance? Romans 2:4

That is why we should not pray for bad things to happen to people so they will wake up and repent. This makes it less fun to pray for enemies, "Lord pour out your goodness, mercy and blessings on those rotten idiots!"

The primary call of God's word is to repent, for the sake of our health, success, happiness, relationships, prosperity and effectiveness in this world. The timeless message echoes from the past...

<u>John the Baptist</u>
"Repent, for the kingdom of heaven is near." Matthew 3:2

<u>Jesus</u>
"Repent, for the kingdom of heaven is near." Matthew 4:17

<u>The 12 Disciples</u>
They went out and preached that people should repent. They drove out many demons and anointed many sick people with oil and healed them. Matthew 6:12,13

<u>Peter</u>
"Repent, then, and turn to God, so that your sins may be wiped out, that times of refreshing may come from the Lord." Acts 3:19

<u>Paul</u>
"First to those in Damascus, then to those in Jerusalem and in all Judea, and to the Gentiles also, I preached that they should repent and turn to God and prove their repentance by their deeds." Acts 26:20

"Prove their repentance by their deeds."

Saying sorry is talk; it is not good enough when there is a problem. Godly sorrow incites change. A hotel bell hop once told me that he saw a man in the gift shop buying flowers to take home to his wife after having a lady whore in his room just the night before. If his wife knew about it, I doubt that the lovely arrangement would help. He was planning on keeping his dirty little secret, and flowers would appease his conscience. Flowers for penance --there was no hope for ultimately saving the marriage unless he changed his behavior.

He needed to prove his sorrow by his deeds, and those would not include more adulterous sex acts followed by bouquets and bon bons. This repentance thing is not rocket science.

How many times did John the Baptist, Jesus and all the disciples who wrote the New Testament call on anyone to say sorry? Zero.

How many times did they call on us to repent? Over 50 times.

Saying sorry and being sorry, even really meaning it, like so many wife beaters, child abusers and drug addicts do, is the sacrament of religious heresy.

I did not want my weeping alcoholic father to hug me and beg forgiveness. I wanted him to stop drinking vodka. I learned to stop enabling alcoholics when I stopped allowing them to wipe their consciences all over me by saying they were sorry. Leave your alcoholic in his vomit. Jesus won't let him keep getting away with tears and hugs.

Heresy is religion that provides sanctuary for sin. The lies appear holy. Say your sorry every time you sin, and grace covers it, or pay for your sin with confession, rote prayers and good deeds.

Neither are repentance. Neither change behavior.

Sorrow sits in an open cell; repentance walks out.

The Apostle Paul was happy with his baby, the Corinthian Church, because they exhibited healthy stages of repentance. Their being sorry was not what he was happy about. It was where the sorrow took them that made him happy.

I am happy, not because you were made sorry, but because your sorrow led you to repentance. For you became sorrowful as God intended and so were not harmed in any way by us. Godly sorrow brings repentance that leads to salvation and leaves no regret, but worldly sorrow brings death. 2 Corinthians 7:9-10

Godly sorrow produces change, repentance. It is repentance then that saves, not sorrow! If you do not plan on changing, then it is better not to even say you are sorry. Why?

Normally, after a man beats his wife, he is sorry, sometimes tearfully so. He may be really, really sorry and the woman knows it --which is why she keeps giving him chances and chances and chances, making her friends and family wildly crazy. But, because his is not godly sorrow that leads to repentance, or change --his sorrow is a liar, coercing her into deeper and longer relationship.

The collateral damage is her kids. The cycle spirals downward to worse trauma. His sorrow deepens as the violence gets worse. His episodes of grieving and gifts of sweetness to her become the love and affirmation fix she needs to endure another assault. She and her husband feed off each other's unhealthy appetites. His sorrow and her falling for it, leads them both, and their children, into a codependent spiral of ruin. Worldly sorrow postpones the change that leads to eternal life.

See what this godly sorrow has produced in you: what earnestness, what eagerness to clear yourselves, what indignation, what alarm, what longing, what concern, what readiness to see justice done. 2 Corinthians 7:11

Do you want to know if someone has godly sorrow?

With 2 Corinthians 7 as a guide, these are some things to watch for:

Signs of Godly Sorrow

1. Repentance, change of direction, abandonment of sin
2. Earnestness, serious intent to take action
3. Eagerness to be cleared
4. Indignation, anger aroused by the injustice to others
5. Alarm
6. Longing
7. Concern for others
8. Readiness to see justice done

And are you dealing with some unhealthy sorrow?

Signs of Worldly Sorrow

1. Flowers and candy as penance
2. Tears, sincere regret
3. Depression and self loathing, focus on self
4. Kindness and affection
5. Feeling sorry for oneself
6. Self destructive behavior
7. Refusal to seek help, blame shifting
8. Deal making
9. Repeated offense
10. Intentional, deliberate sin....and this leads to death

If we deliberately keep on sinning after we have received the knowledge of the truth, no sacrifice for sins is left, but only a fearful expectation of judgment and of raging fire that will consume the enemies of God. Hebrews 10:26-27

From "Sorry man" to Superman

So we are not under the law of sin and death. The law of sin and death is the curse. We are not under the law (the curse, punishment, judgment) because we are not subject to its punishment. We met all its requirements through Jesus and now we live with him in a constant relationship of cleansing and growing in our spirits, minds and bodies. We are working together with him.

We are not under the law (of sin and death) because we obey God's law (his moral instruction for our happiness by the power of the Holy Spirit) We can do now what we could not do before, obey, because of his Spirit in us.

So our command is not to constantly say we are sorry and beg forgiveness. It is to follow Jesus and live by the Spirit, who will take care of all of our mess. We sure can't.

Live by the Spirit, and you will not gratify the desires of the sinful nature. For the sinful nature desires what is contrary to the Spirit. They are in conflict with each other so that you do not do what you want. But if you are led by the Spirit, you are not under the law. The Spirit leads us out from under the law (of sin and death) to a life of righteousness. and not sinfulness:

The acts of the sinful nature are obvious: sexual immorality, impurity and debauchery; idolatry and witchcraft; hatred, discord, jealousy, fits of rage, selfish ambition, dissensions, factions and envy; drunkenness, orgies, and the like. I warn you, as I did before, that those who live like this will not inherit the kingdom of God.

It is Jesus' Spirit in you that produces the fruit you want.

But the fruit of the Spirit is love, joy, peace, patience, kindness, goodness, faithfulness, gentleness and self-control. Against such things there is no law.

And this is the bottom line:

And those who belong to Christ Jesus have crucified the sinful nature with its (evil) passions and desires. Galatians 5:16-24

God knows you cannot do it alone. If your fleshly, sinful desires rise up, don't just lie down and take it. Concentrate on walking in the Spirit. Let him empower you for the fight because the stakes are too high:

Do you not know that the wicked will not inherit the kingdom of God? Do not be deceived: Neither the sexually immoral nor idolaters nor adulterers nor male prostitutes nor homosexual offenders nor thieves nor the greedy nor drunkards nor slanderers nor swindlers will inherit the kingdom of God. 1 Corinthians 6: 9-11.

It is not those of us who sometimes fall or stumble in sin that are in trouble; it is those who maintain a lifestyle of sin in one of these areas. Some prayer they may have said at some point along the way doesn't have a thing to do with their end.

The cowardly, the unbelieving, the vile, the murderers, the sexually immoral, those who practice magic arts, the idolaters and all liars - their place will be in the fiery lake of burning sulfur. This is the second death. Revelation 21:8

Paul and James pitted against each other?

The Saved by Faith people and the Saved by Works people would seem to have Paul and James at odds with each other. Once again, this can be chalked up to taking scriptures out of context. Actually, the two men couldn't have agreed more.

Nevertheless, the first group quotes Paul:
It is by grace you have been saved, through faith – and this is not from yourselves, it is the gift of God – not by works, so that no one can boast.

Saved by grace? True, but that is only the beginning...

For we are God's workmanship, created in Christ Jesus to do good works. Ephesians 2:8-10

So we are saved by grace, a free gift, so that we can do good works. We go to the grocery store so that we can feed our families. The first is no good without the last. The purpose of the grace is the works.

The second group likes James:

A person is justified by what he does. James 2:24

Justified, saved and made righteous by works? Yes, that is what it says. See how bluntly James explains how grace and works are so interdependent:

What good is it, my brothers, if a man claims to have faith but has no deeds (righteous behavior)? Can such faith save him? James 2:14

By this rhetorical question, James highlights the absurdity of a man's thinking that faith with no accompanying action could save him. He illustrates his point:

Suppose a brother or sister is without clothes or daily food. If one of you says to him, "Go, I wish you well; keep warm and well fed," but does nothing about his physical needs, what good is it? In the same way, faith by itself, if it is not accompanied by action, is dead. James 2:15-17

James dispels the rumors about how we do our Christianity.

Someone will say, "You have faith, I have deeds." Show me your faith without deeds, and I will show you my faith by what I do. James 2:18

His obvious point is that if you believe in the one true God, it will necessarily have to materialize in your life. Otherwise, your belief is no different than that of demons.

You believe that there is one God. Good! Even the demons believe that – and shudder. James 2:19

James recalls how Abraham had to show his faith in God by what he did in lifting a knife to sacrifice Isaac.

His faith and his actions were working together, and his faith was made complete by what he did. James 2:22

God credited Abraham to be righteous, after he proved his faith.

You see that a person is justified by what he does and not by faith alone. James 2:24

James concludes the matter by saying:

Faith without deeds is dead. James 2:26

In other words, if you want to be saved, you can't have one without the other. What do the lack of good morals and deeds have to do with the Church's near absence of miracle working power?

Remember we mentioned that miracles were so commonplace in the Early Church partly because of the intolerance of sin?

In the 21st Century, Charismatics get psyched when the subject of the 'dunamis' power of God comes up. Dunamis is the Greek word for the miracle working, supernatural power of God, available to us by the Holy Spirit. Charismatics understand its relevance to the impartation of healing. This they know, but there is something some of them do not. Remember, the Early Church was intolerant of false doctrine *and* sin. What does dunamis power have to do with sin? Everything.

Dunamis is...

1) Power for performing miracles
2) Moral Power and excellence of soul

Jesus exerted moral power every bit as much as he did the dynamite supernatural signs and wonders power. Moral power or virtue, which speaks of quality of character is another translation for dunamis. Virtue and Power can be used interchangeably.

When the woman who had been bleeding for twelve years touched Jesus' robe --he said he felt virtue come out of him. Some translations say power. Both are correct. Virtue, moral power and miracle working power are actually the same. If virtue is missing, miracle power is diffused.

You cannot have one without the other. And to you religiously proud who think you are exempt from performing miracles because you take the higher road of holiness and moral power above all others –you're only halfway there! Christians have libraries full of excuses as to why they should not, cannot and will not participate in the supernatural manifestations that Jesus and the disciples modeled. They stubbornly defend their positions. They oppose the stance of Paul who boasted to the Church in Thessalonica about his dunamis displays...

Our gospel came to you not simply with words, but also with power, with the Holy Spirit and with deep conviction. You know how we lived among you for your sake. 1 Thessalonians 1:5

and to the Church at Corinth....

I will come to you very soon, if the Lord is willing, and then I will find out not only how these arrogant people are talking, but what power they have. For the kingdom of God is not a matter of talk but of power. 1 Corinthians 4:19-20

We have determined that God's power includes both moral and miraculous power. Walking in this power is so important because it is why people are attracted to Jesus. That is a mission upon which we can all agree.

And the whole multitude sought to touch him, for power (virtue) went out from him and healed them all Luke 6:19

Multitudes followed after Jesus, not necessarily always because of his good morals and holiness, but because of the miracles resulting from the dynamic force he exuded. His moral excellence fueled that fire power. It was the secret to his awesome displays.

Miracles are necessary proof of Jesus. Watch out for the spiritual pride that boasts of such great faith that it needs no proof. Jesus thought we needed proof. When John the Baptist's disciples came to Jesus to ask if he was the One who was to come, Jesus told them to go back to John in prison with some evidence.

Go back and report to John what you have seen and heard:
1) The blind receive sight,
2) the lame walk,
3) those who have leprosy are cured,
4) the deaf hear,
5) the dead are raised,
6) and the good news is preached to the poor. Luke 7:22

Five out of the six evidences that Jesus gave to prove he was the 'One,' were about healing, only one about preaching. Where is our emphasis today?

Jesus did not even expect the *"greatest man who ever was born of woman"* to believe without some proof. Who do we think we are that our capacity to believe is so superior to that of John the Baptist? Moreover, who do we think the unsaved masses are?

They are not even interested in this deaf mute God they think we have. God wants to be noticed, and apparently he thinks miracles are a good way to accomplish that.

When Jesus walked in our dirt, God proved his persona by miraculous manifestations, with no apologies. If Jesus the Great God-Man needed to be accredited and proven to the people by miracles, how much more do we need them to show his presence!

You men of Israel, listen to what I have to say: Jesus of Nazareth was a Man accredited and pointed out and shown forth and commended and attested to you by God by the mighty works and [the power of performing] wonders and signs which God worked through Him [right] in your midst, as you yourselves know Acts 2:22

Remember that if they wouldn't believe Jesus without the supernatural proof, they are not going to believe us either, not in the numbers. When Philip preached, the people heard him, but it wasn't until they saw some things, that they really paid attention and reacted.

When the crowds heard Philip and saw the miraculous signs he did, they all paid close attention to what he said. With shrieks, evil spirits came out of many, and many paralytics and cripples were healed. Acts 8:5-7

How can we draw a great big crowd?

A great crowd of people followed [Jesus] because they saw the miraculous signs he had performed on the sick. John 6:2

Come on church evangelism committees, do we think we are going to come up with a more effective attention getter? Paul's words should be on the tombstone of every Christian:

My message and my preaching were not with persuasive words, but with a demonstration of the Spirit's power, so that your faith might not rest on men's wisdom, but on God's power. 1 Corinthians 2:4-5

Our words should always be backed up and reinforced by action.

If we are to be taken seriously by God and man, then just saying that we are sorry, just saying that God is powerful, and just saying Jesus loves you --is not enough.

Chapter 12

False Humility & Self Sacrifice

Being a good moral person of strong Christian character is touted by some as more honorable than doing miracles or receiving miracles. Ok, yes, maybe if it were a choice between the two, but it is not.

Suffering disease and enduring pain has become to some, a measure of spiritual maturity. It is not. We are expected to at least try working like Jesus did, instead of just lying down and taking it. This kind of passivity among the Israelites, who had been living in the Promised Land for years, is the reason Joshua asked them,

How long will you wait before you begin to take possession of the land that the Lord, the God of your fathers has given you? Joshua 18:3

It is more honorable to obey heavenly orders to fight enemies like sickness, having mercy on none, than it is to sacrifice our health to them. Jesus sacrificed himself so we could have victory over such enemies. We do not honor him by ignoring this. We get no heavenly brownie points by neglecting our responsibility to practice miracle working faith.

Some years ago in the case of my son, Joey, it was forgetfulness, or not thinking of some kind. Imagine that from a teenager. One night, he called me from north Florida, where he and his brother Sammy, pro rollerbladers, were ending a skate tour. Joey told me he had a dream that Sammy became paralyzed, a very real concern for boys who skate off roofs and down stadium rails 20 feet over concrete wearing only their helmets of salvation. The nightmare scared him so much, he told God to let him be paralyzed instead of Sammy.

"Joey!" He must have known I would yell, knowing what a stupid prayer that was, "You never make deals like that. It's making a deal with the devil. You know better than that!"

"I know Ma," he conceded and continued his report.

Skating the next day, he made a hard landing on a death drop and bruised his heels badly. He could not walk. His skate friends were his crutches wherever they went. After leaving a pizza place, they put him in a shopping cart, pushed it in the restaurant and left. All night when they stopped at skate spots, the carload of skaters would blow out the doors (to get footage before security came around) --and forget him sitting there. And whatever other things skaters do to their best friends.

For two weeks after the boys got home, Joey crawled around the house, unable to stand. Once I had to step over him because he was lying on the kitchen floor holding open the refrigerator door, looking for something to eat.

I thank God Joey's disability was temporary. He ventured out on his own to test the power of his words and prayers. Still, Satan has never been allowed to cause any lasting damage to my kids. It is also a comfort to me that God hears my continual prayers for my kids and that the devil does not have access to hurt them or do any real damage to their minds or bodies.

I know other people who made deals with the devil who were not so 'lucky.'

Marie, a woman who attended one of my healing workshops, was grieving the pre-mature death of Anne, her best friend. A couple years previous, Marie had been stricken with an unwarranted fear that she had a rare type of breast cancer that does not manifest in detectible lumps. She had no symptoms or family history that would indicate she was sick --except for this sudden, irrational fear. Medical tests proved her wrong, but in the meantime her close friend Anne, out of compassion and concern, told Marie not to worry because she had prayed that she would get it instead. These couple years later, Annie was dead --from this exact rare form of breast cancer.

One of my daughter's friends had a girlfriend who used to say upon leaving the house, "Kiss me before I leave -- I might die in a car wreck today." And one day, she did.

A distant family relative, an active, healthy woman, used to always say that she wanted to really live it up with athletics and adventures because she just knew for some reason that someday, she would end up in a wheelchair. Not many years later in her 40's, she was diagnosed with a degenerative disease that put her in a wheelchair.

Usually the people who think this kind of thinking is silly have not examined similar cause and effect in their lives and in the lives of those around them. The mouth is a mighty powerful thing. Making negative pronouncements and this kind of deal making is in Satan's territory. It is working according to the rules of the curse of sin and death.

Praying for Sammy's safety and protection, according to Psalm 91, that no harm or disaster would come near him, that God would command his angels to guard him in all his ways -- would have been the right thing to do after Joey's dream.

Praying for the safety and health of a loved one is the correct reaction to a dooming vision or warning dream. It should not be received as an inevitability or prophesy for the loved one, or as commission to sacrifice yourself!

Part Two
When Suffering is Wrong

Chapter 13

I'd Rather Be Healed Than a Hero

The reason the Son of God appeared was to destroy the devil's work.
1 John 3:8

We too are to destroy, not be destroyed.

While she lived in New Mexico, my mother was president of the Española Animal Shelter. She had a staff whose mission it was to rescue, love and hopefully, adopt out as many animals as possible before they had to be euthanized. Education was also a priority for staving off ignorance about domestic animals. This proved to be an area that needed more attention. One night, some animal loving ignoramuses broke into the shelter and opened all the cages, 'freeing' 50 household dogs into the wild mountain terrain of New Mexico.

What would await them? Venomous snakes, coyotes, cold, hunger, dry river beds, loneliness, not cozy warm blankets, not yummy dog food, not treats, not visiting kindergarteners, not scratches behind the ears...

Some of the volunteers got word of the break in and hurried out onto the dark remote highway. Worried about the misery their furry friends would have to endure, they pulled up to the front of the still dark shelter. All 50 dogs were waiting for them under the portico. Every single one was accounted for.

Having good intentions and loving so passionately does not make us right. Our hearts are not always very good guides.

The law breaking animal rescuers justified their actions by their own feelings and judgments. What seemed right was not right. What feels or seems right is not reliable impetus for determining a proper course of action. What God's word says is right, and is the only reliable guide, feel like it or not. Even if it means keeping a playful puppy temporarily in a cage while we pursue lasting freedom for him on the sofa of an adoring family. A true rescue may take some diligence, patience and dedication.

We err by deferring to our feelings in our healing doctrine as well. When we have not been able to conquer disease in someone, instead of persevering in the truth, we take matters into our own hands, and we let the dogs out. It's a premature rescue.

When we have not seen their healing, we give up short of the promise. It seems right and kind to validate their suffering by ascribing uncommon valor to them, to make theirs a mission of suffering instead of healing. We pray and fail. We try to heal and fail, so, out of need for some kind of resolution or relevance, we turn suffering into a job well done, something to be admired and a source of inspiration. Some even grant sufferers hero status in order to legitimize God's apparent unwillingness to answer the pleas for healing. In this way we also justify our own inability to heal. We give up on God's word. We give ourselves an out. For some satisfaction of freedom, we let the dogs out.

The tendency to fabricate lofty purpose for the sick can be motivated by pride, ignorance, frustration, exhaustion or, as commonly, by genuine compassion. Nevertheless, sickness is not God's purpose for them. Anyway, most sick people would rather be healed than heroes.

We might think we are doing a service to trapped animals by letting them out of their cages. But, instead of going into a doomed situation, the best thing for them is to stick it out, to continue to trust the shelter rescuers for their very best outcome, adoption.

Releasing the animals seems like a compassionate thing to do, but it is giving up hope for their rescue. Encouraging honorable resignation to staying sick is nothing but an excuse to quit trying and to quit the quest for understanding. It is nothing but a cop out for those who cannot make the principles work.

Their philosophies make for touching greeting card poetry but are not the fodder from which disease and demons come out. If there is failure with regard to healing, it is an opportunity to learn and grow, to go up --not give up. We do not want to miss these chances to learn. Instead of saying, "This didn't work." We ask, "Why didn't this work? What can I learn from it? How can I fix it?" We find a way to help bring families to adopt the strays. We do not just let the dogs out.

Jesus' disciples did not squander the opportunities to grow that were provided to them courtesy of their failures. This included their failures to heal.

When the disciples could not heal the epileptic, Jesus did. Just because they were unable, the disciples did not assume that it was not God's will for them to heal an epileptic boy. They did not conclude that God had a bigger plan for the boy, that his father would grow and learn through the challenges with his son, that the boy would glorify God through his demonic condition. No, the disciples went to the living word of God for answers and further understanding.

They asked Jesus, *"Why couldn't we drive it out?"*

Jesus told them why. *"Because you have so little faith."* Matthew 17:19-20

They were not insulted and incensed at this criticism. Actually they were encouraged and challenged. They realized that they could do better. Doing better would mean that children would end up healed instead of burdened with lessons about the benefits of their oppression. The disciples' question to Jesus in the wake of the failure to accomplish their goal should be a standard for Christians.

"Why couldn't we do it?"

Don't you think God was happier with the humble, self-examining approach of the disciples, rather than if they had been ready with quippy religious slogans and excuses to protect their status among the people? or even to protect God's status?

Yes, it was a rebuke, but sweeter than honey. If I am driving full speed toward a cliff, I want a rebuke! Yell at me! Criticize my driving; correct me! God's rebuke is better than kisses from an enemy.

"Wounds from a friend can be trusted, but an enemy multiplies kisses." Proverbs 27:6

The enemy cheers, "Faster, faster!" in our mad dash for the cliff.

With a rebuke comes life saving direction. Jesus immediately directed them to a solution. Have mustard seed size faith. Do not doubt in your heart.

If you have faith as small as a mustard seed, you can say to this mountain, "Move from here to there," and it will move. Nothing will be impossible for you. Matthew 17:20

There is no reason to be offended that we need more faith. Even the twelve disciples, who had already themselves been healing and casting out demons by this point, needed more

Let's just at least admit that we gave up and leave it at that, instead of justifying our failure by abandoning the sufferer to the gloomy assignment of touching lives through his misery.

Giving up and doing nothing else under the guise of a phony suffering for Jesus theory is not God's desire for us. It is the antithesis of Jesus' earthly ministry, one that is characterized by constantly relieving the suffering and oppression of everyone he encountered. By contradicting Christ's life and teaching on healing, we have left ourselves and loved ones at the mercy of coyotes and snakes.

God has established healing laws which are walls that protect and save, not obstacles to overcome and do away with in order to make sense of our healing failures. Entire books are written to present every imaginable argument against healing. It is not for today, not for this person, not for that disease, not the right timing, not universal, not God's best, not, not, not. Just say no to not. All his promises are yes.

Instead of creating these kinds of logic based excuses, would it not be better to stubbornly apply the rather pedestrian laws and principles of healing, and then enjoy the outcome of health?

Would it not be a better use of time to keep practicing and working the principles, than to keep explaining them away just because we cannot get them to work?

If we strictly adhere to God's word, we will not ignorantly, albeit with good intentions, release his children into dangerous territory. Learning to heal should be as much a part of our journey to wholeness as our learning to give, forgive, love, save and overcome sin. In any of these other areas do we have license to give up or modify the rules?

The fragrant prose we sometimes recite regarding the sick on behalf of the Lord, contrasts his ruthless man-handling of disease.

Jesus does not want us to pity the sick; he wants us to deal pitilessly with sickness. What kind of Christian would you want praying if an illness were to seize you?

Chapter 14

Christian Suffering Isn't Being Sick

Otherwise known as "suffering according to God's will," we cannot confidently believe for healing if we are unsure of the purpose of our suffering. What if we are supposed to embrace it?

The Biblical definition of faith is *"being sure of what we hope for and certain of what we do not see." Hebrews 11:1*

Faith is the assurance and certainty of what we hope for, but cannot yet see. When we are sure and certain, there is by definition no doubt.

When I had a job teaching cardio dance, every other Friday I could use my debit card because the YMCA automatically deposited a paycheck in my bank account. Even though unseen, I was sure it was there to be drawn upon --based on the good word of my employer. There was no doubt or worry because of the contract between the YMCA and me. If only I could be so confident and worry free in acting upon the contract between Jesus and me. This is the kind of assurance and certainty for which I will put up a good fight.

But, if we doubt healing and think instead that there may be a valid spiritual reason or need for suffering sickness, then we cannot be sure about healing; we cannot be certain that we have the healing we hope for. If our certainty and assurance is tempered by the least bit of an allegiance to an imaginary virtue of suffering disease for Jesus, then we have doubt. Jesus warns about this saboteur in an illustration about the faith he wants us to have.

If anyone says to this mountain, "Go, throw yourself into the sea," and does not doubt in his heart but believes that what he says will happen, it will be done for him. Mark 11:23

Instead of consoling and pampering those who doubt, let's help them to vilify and get rid of it. Doubt is the enemy.

But when he asks, he must believe and not doubt, because he who doubts is like a wave of the sea, blown and tossed by the wind. That man should not think he will receive anything from the Lord; he is a double-minded man, unstable in all he does. James 1:6-8

"By his wounds I have been healed from this fibromyalgaiuuuuhhh... (wait for it) unless you have another reason for my suffering Lord." This prayer got off to a great start but dive bombed fast. Funny, the first part was scripture and the second was not.

This 'suffering' mess needs to be cleaned up. The confusion about suffering comes from some verses that are misunderstood, like this one where Peter talks about those who are suffering.

Those who *"suffer according to God's will should commit themselves to their faithful Creator." 1 Peter 4:19*

How do we know that we are not suffering cancer according to God's will? This possibility makes it seem like our softness toward infirmity is justified. It is not.

The misunderstood 'Christian suffering' issue is one of the biggest impediments to people in their quest to be physically whole. It is often expressed as 'sharing in Christ's sufferings,' 'taking up the cross,' 'glorifying God in weakness that he might show himself strong.'

All of these Biblical references are phrases taken out of context. This random assemblage of otherwise powerful scriptures is often the basis of a casual study of Biblical suffering. When skewed this way, these verses easily discourage healing. Their misuse has become the modern creed for healing, the repetition of which inspires apathy in battle and faith in inevitable failure.

This confusion can only be cleared up when it is realized that there are two kinds of suffering in the Bible, one to be extinguished, the other to be expected.

Chapter 15

No Trouble With Trouble

Oh fun. Let's consider Christian suffering that is to be expected.

In fact, we should all be doing it! This is the suffering often confused with suffering terminal illness, paraplegia, and every other possible dreaded diagnosis.

The kind of suffering we are expected by Jesus to endure is persecution. It comes as result of living in the word as opposed to living in the world. Jesus spoke of this kind of suffering often, as if he assumed we were aware that it should be part of the Christian lifestyle. He was always very clear about it.

How do we know that the suffering about which Jesus forewarned comes because of the word? He said so.

In his story of the sower scattering seed (the word), the person who received it with joy, but had no root, fell away. He fell because of the suffering of persecution that came with the word. Jesus said this apostate only lasted a short time since he was unable to endure, having no root.

When trouble or persecution comes because of the word, he quickly falls away. Matthew 13:21

This to-be-expected kind of suffering becomes a common theme for believers in the New Testament. And then there is Paul's thorn. If you have not heard of Paul's thorn, you will as soon as you try to believe for healing. For discouragement in regard to obtaining a healing promise, Paul's thorn is a favorite. This argument will here be challenged and I believe satisfactorily discredited.

Paul's suffering will no longer contradict his stalwart stand on physical healing and deliverance. More importantly, that thorn will no longer provide believers with ammunition to sabotage miracles.

Christian suffering that is God's will, is always in the context of, and equates to Christian persecution: hatred, insults, false accusations, malicious speech, rejection, beatings and martyrdom.

"Gosh," you may say, "I'd rather be a little sick."

Actually, great honor accompanies those who endure such sufferings. Suffering persecution is what happens to believers by other people who are hostile toward Jesus Christ. It comes as a result of the Christian's good works and unrelenting, unabashed testimony.

Suffering sickness comes as a result of sin in the world, indiscriminately attacking the good and evil. There is not inherent spiritual honor in getting sick. Muslims, Buddhists, members of every world religion and atheists suffer sickness as courageously and inspiringly as Christians do.

My courageous Christian father-in-law, Hank, won his war against hell when he left this world, but his battle with cancer was a devastating defeat. There was no glory in his suffering to death. God does not want us to go to an early grave. We are not expected to endure graciously such a journey. Death is the enemy.

The last enemy to be destroyed is death." 1 Corinthians 15:26.

God promises, *"with long life I will satisfy him and show him my salvation"* Psalm 91:16

Crawling tumors stole my father-in-law's dignity, strength and chance to see his only grandchild, Lucy, turn four. He departed this life pre-maturely, leaving behind his beautiful wife, Tammie. Cancer was not God's plan for this American Naval Hero and Beers family patriarch. There is still a bitter sting in our hearts, and at family gatherings. And yet, his legacy of love is still with us as Tammie and Lucy carry on like little best friends forever in the home that Hank built. And there is the promise, we will all meet again.

A sick Christian clinging to faith in Jesus Christ should not be used to justify the phony doctrine that God uses sickness for his glory, or as a means by which the sick believer can show spiritual fortitude. Faith in Jesus is just as beautiful in a healthy Christian. Hank's faith was as precious with Lucy in his lap reading a book, as it was when he was condemned to a hospital deathbed.

In the Book of 1 Peter, the apostle majors on the subject of suffering. Although he is often misquoted by those who try to find-the-blessing-in-sickness doctrine, the letter was written to encourage believers in Asia Minor who were suffering persecution, not sickness. The trials they were undergoing were slander and abuse for bearing the Name, not for bearing sickness.

Peter reminded the believers about why these sufferings (persecutions) had been happening to them.

Though now for a little while you may have had to suffer grief in all kinds of trials. These have come so that your faith – of greater worth than gold, which perishes even though refined by fire – may be proved genuine and may result in praise, glory and honor when Jesus Christ is revealed. 1 Peter 1:6,7

Trial by persecution refines us and glorifies God.

Even though the theory has been adopted by modern Christendom, no Bible verse can be found to indicate that trials by sickness come to refine us or glorify God. The healing is what glorifies him, not grin and bear it endurance of sickness.

To some it sounds mean to say that, but to the debilitated one, it sounds great! I bet he would rather glorify God through his deliverance --and a safe bet that he would prefer to be refined by Jesus' inspired word and even a swift kick from persecutors, than by his disease. This is a hopeful message to the sick and disabled.

Sickness comes as a result of this sin polluted world we live in. We might learn and grow in the course of being sick, but that is not the purpose for which it was sent. And God did not send it. God sent his word to teach us and refine us.

All scripture is inspired by God and is profitable
1) for doctrine,
2) for reproof,
3) for correction,
4) for instruction in righteousness. 2 Timothy 3:16

I think it's funny how some Christians are so offended when their healing faith doctrine is reproved or corrected, or when they are offered instruction about healing. I would much rather be corrected or instructed by God's word than by sickness.

God teaches us by his word to avoid sickness and consequences from rebellion. In the same way I want my daughter to learn by my instruction, "Don't run down that long set of cement stairs with those big flip flops on!" If she does not listen and obey, she will probably get a scraped something. God provides us the same discipline opportunities that we do for our children, preferring we listen and obey.

I don't give Lucy a gross knee infection so she will be sure not to run down the stairs in oversized flip flops. Stupid.

It is no secret though, that obedience to the word invites persecution. Persecution which refines us and glorifies God comes because of the word, as we saw in the parable of the sower.

Sickness comes, not because of the word, but because of this world. It comes because of the devil and death that reign here.

There is nothing good about sickness, not one thing.

Chapter 16

Glorifying God in Suffering? Hmm...

Whenever an incident of glorifying God through sickness is chronicled in the New Testament, it is always in the context of the *healing* of the sickness, not the *endurance* of it.

Imagine if you explained a sick person's predicament to many Christians, as Jesus explained Lazarus' misfortune to the disciples...

This sickness will not end in death. No, it is for God's glory so that God's Son may be glorified through it. John 11:4

The sickness is for God's glory; that's what the Man said.

Many now would assume that it would be Lazarus' awe-inspiring endurance of prolonged sickness, not to end in death, that would glorify God. The suffering servant would remain faithful for his long life of misery. It would be a lingering one, as is described in the curses... Jesus promoting curses for his glory.

This is how easily so many Christians, by means of such neo-orthodox healing doctrine fabrications, automatically default to God's *not* healing. Even though the issue of healing is clearly defined in the life and times of Christ, and even though prolonged illness is never espoused by him as good or necessary for any reason, much of the Church gravitates like a bowling ball to the unscriptural rationale that God is glorified through sickness.

In the sickness of Lazarus, God's glory did indeed come --when Lazarus was called from the netherworld and to perfectly restored health! What a big scene that caused. What increased fame that miracle brought to Jesus. What persecution that instigated. If there is any suffering according to God's will in a story about a sick person, you can count on it coming *after* the healing.

Can a sick man be filled with the glory of God? Of course! Is God being glorified through his sickness? No, God is being glorified through the man! He is glorified in spite of the sickness.

God is glorified through his children, sick or not.

Wicked people and tyrants get sick. There comes no glory through their sickness even when they handle it with dignity and thankfulness.

God is not glorified through them, whether they are sick or not.

If nothing else, we are masters at concocting all kinds of superfluous meaning to scripture and the otherwise easy concepts scripture teaches. God is glorified in overcoming, defeating and destroying death and the disease that leads to it. Death and disease are the enemy to be destroyed, not utilized. Yet we are purpose driven in the quest to make better sense of sickness. If there is any way to accommodate illness, we will find it. The first disciples, at first, were no different.

On the occasion that Jesus noticed a man who was blind from infancy, the disciples, in deference to their powers of reason, tried to categorize and scrutinize the disability instead of simply confronting it. The disciples asked Jesus about the reason for a man's blindness.

"Rabbi, who sinned, this man or his parents, that he was born blind?"

Jesus answered, "Neither this man nor his parents sinned, but that the works of God should be revealed in him." John 9:1-3

Jesus clarified for all time the purpose of the blindness: Was it working patience in the blind man or his parents? Punishment for sin? Punishment for generational sin? No. The purpose of the blindness was to reveal the works of God, which he forthrightly showed to be healing. After all, the Son of God came to destroy blindness.

Jesus has no ulterior motives in healing you. He just wants the works of God to be revealed in and through you. What are those works?

For this purpose the Son of God was manifested, that He might destroy the works of the devil. 1 John 3:8

The works of God are to destroy the works of the devil. When God's works occur --guess what? God is glorified to multitudes. The news spreads like wild fire.

The people were amazed when they saw the mute speaking, the crippled made well, the lame walking and the blind seeing. and they praised the God of Israel. Matthew 15:31

It is when they saw these miracles happening that they glorified God.

Immediately he stood up in front of them, took what he had been lying on and went home praising God. Luke 5:25

When the crowd saw this paralyzed man instantly healed, they glorified God.

Then he went up and touched the coffin, and those carrying it stood still. He said, "Young man, I say to you, get up!" The dead man sat up and began to talk, and Jesus gave him back to his mother. They were all filled with awe and praised God. Luke 7:14-16

When the large crowd in the funeral procession saw the miracle, they glorified God.

Recently, I stood at the casket of a dead man and whispered with all the authority I could muster, "Young man I say to you get up." He did not. I have a lot of work to do.

Although in our culture that may seem like an extreme evangelistic behavior, calling people out of coffins in funeral home parlors, we will later look at some raising the dead scenarios that are good first steps, and do not seem so crazy.

Time and time again, Jesus illustrates his famous words, uttered at the beginning of his ministry, *"Unless you people see miraculous signs and wonders, you will never believe." John 4:48*

When we are ministering (signs and wonders) to unbelievers, it is our faith, not necessarily theirs, that will effect the change, resulting in their praise to God.

A woman was there who had been crippled by a spirit for eighteen years. She was bent over and could not straighten up at all. When Jesus saw her, he called her forward and said to her, "Woman, you are set free from your infirmity." Then he put his hands on her, and immediately she straightened up and praised God. Luke 13:11-13

It was not until the woman experienced this miraculous change to her back and posture that she glorified God.

One of [the ten lepers], when he saw he was healed, came back, praising God in a loud voice. Luke 17:15

When the formerly leprous man saw what happened, he glorified God.

Jesus stopped and ordered the blind beggar to be brought to him. When he came near, Jesus asked him, "What do you want me to do for you?"

"Lord, I want to see," he replied.

Jesus said to him, "Receive your sight; your faith has healed you." Immediately he received his sight and followed Jesus, praising God. Luke 18: 40-43

When the blind man saw, he both followed and glorified God.

Any investigation of the accounts of God's being glorified in association with disease or disability reveals one common denominator: God's glory was a reaction to the destruction of a work of the devil. Since there are no recorded incidents of God's being glorified by someone's continuing in their sickness, or by their being refused healing for any reason, it is accurate to conclude that God is not glorified through sickness, but through the healing of sickness.

We can see in the Bible that God does not seek glory through his children's suffering disease, but that he does get glory through his children's suffering persecution.

So, suffer persecution like a good soldier. Don't go looking for it; it will find you.

And . . . rage mercilessly against suffering disease or disability.

Chapter 17

So You Think You're a Martyr

What does suffering persecution look like?

It can be physical, mental or spiritual attacks, including slander and false accusations and, in some cases, death.

But, our faithful endurance under fire will bring glory to God, even through the mouths of pagans--

Live such good lives among the pagans that, though they accuse you of doing wrong, they may see your good deeds and glorify God on the day he visits us. 1 Peter 2:12

Instead of correcting the record, defending your reputation, getting mad, being surprised, blogging, spending hours on the phone and plotting juicy vindication --just suck it up, endure it, bless the liars and relish secretly that you are Teacher's pet. He will commend you. He will be glorified through you.

If you suffer for doing good and you endure it, this is commendable before God. 1 Peter 2: 20

The kind of suffering about which Peter is talking comes for doing what is right, not for inadvertently contracting some infection. He commends believers for doing good and enduring the consequential harassment, not for being sick and enduring it with a good attitude.

Having aids or cancer does not make anyone a hero. Good deeds and unselfish acts of valor make heroes. An attack does not make a hero. Whenever did a war hero attain such a status by yielding to an attack of the enemy? No, he was decorated for beating his enemy back or for refusing to give in to a tormentor. And healthy friends and family —-it is YOU who may be the ones to do the fighting for your stricken loved one.

Peter's emphasis is on the Christ motivated deeds of the people and the resulting persecution. Doing good encompasses taking a stand for Jesus, doing good deeds in his name and abstaining from sin by his power. This brings God glory and infuriates the wicked. We pray their rage proceeds their salvation.

Even if you should suffer for what is right, you are blessed. 1 Peter 3:14

Your job is just to do good and keep a clear conscience, *"so that those who speak maliciously against your good behavior in Christ may be ashamed of their slander. It is better, if it is God's will, to suffer for doing good than for doing evil." 1 Peter 3:16-17*

My responsibility to be in Christ doing good, requires constant attention, leaving no available time for judging perpetrators of hate and no time for vindicating myself or making sure everyone plays fair. God's enemies will never be ashamed of their vitriol because of my cunning use of biting phrases. Even though I can mount a vicious verbal attack, I need to leave conviction to the Holy Spirit.

Peter majors on the subject of Christian persecution, inciting believers to continue to do good in spite of abuse. Doing good also means abstaining from bad, not sinning.

Since Christ suffered in his body, arm yourselves also with the same attitude, because he who has suffered in his body is done with sin. 1 Peter 4:1

This passage teaches that we partake also of the suffering of Jesus by not sinning. This passage has nothing at all to do with suffering sickness as is often thought, but everything to do with our denying the flesh's lustful gratification, by the momentary pleasures of sin which end in death. Peter explains that the suffering of our bodies, which occurs as we forbid their carnal cravings, results in being finished with sin. Since the consequence of sin is destruction, arming ourselves with the attitude Jesus had of suffering in the body (not allowing it to fulfill it's lusts) frees us from the accompanying death.

As a result, the believer does not live the rest of his earthly life for evil human desires, but rather for the will of God. For you have spent enough time in the past doing what pagans choose to do – living in debauchery, lust, drunkenness, orgies, carousing and detestable idolatry. They think it strange that you do not plunge with them into the same flood of dissipation, and they heap abuse on you." 1 Peter 4:2-4

Not only does your body suffer the denial of unholy desires, but you reap the disdain of those who indulge their own bodies in damning activities. Such suffering or persecution is to your eternal credit. You are glorifying God, showing him off, making him look good, protecting yourself from inevitable heartache and ensuring your own ultimate happiness. And you are winning souls.

As for your example, the ones who are the most hateful are often the ones who end up the most grateful.

The believers that Peter addressed were undergoing harsh persecution, the kind of cultural persecution that intensified to what Peter himself would come to experience, barbaric torture and murder. Such were the sufferings that Christ endured.

Jesus was never sick or disabled, but he was ruthlessly tormented by those who hated him. These are the sufferings of Christ which we are to share.

Dear friends, do not be surprised at the painful trial you are suffering, as though something strange were happening to you. But rejoice that you participate in the sufferings of Christ, so that you may be overjoyed when his glory is revealed. If you are insulted because of the name of Christ, you are blessed, for the Spirit of glory and of God rests on you. If you suffer, it should not be as a murderer or thief or any other kind of criminal, or even as a meddler. However, if you suffer as a Christian, do not be ashamed, but praise God that you bear that name. 1 Peter 4:12-16

The suffering of these Christians was administered by men as a punishment for their faith. Insults, false accusations, beatings and martyrdom... it is a ridiculous reach to imply that these Christians were getting sick as a consequence of their stand for Jesus.

The way they got into this persecution predicament in the first place was by doing good. Peter cheered them on, as it would continue to bring God glory and advance the kingdom.

Those who suffer according to God's will should commit themselves to their faithful Creator and continue to do good. 1 Peter 4:19

The disciples in Asia Minor were suffering abuse by enemies whose goal it was to destroy Christianity. This letter was about not surrendering to the persecutors. This does not have anything remotely to do with being sick. Even if it did, Peter assures them of their restoration! There is nothing in this letter to suggest that Peter encourages believers to stay or continue to be sick for Jesus.

Be self-controlled and alert. Your enemy the devil prowls around like a roaring lion looking for someone to devour. Resist him, standing firm in the faith, because you know that your brothers throughout the world are undergoing the same kind of sufferings. And the God of all grace, who called you to his eternal glory in Christ, after you have suffered a little while, will himself restore you and make you strong, firm and steadfast. 1 Peter 5:8-10

So, even if one does not honor the intention of the writer and does not respect the historical and Biblical context which demands our understanding this letter in terms of Christian persecution, even if the sufferings were sickness, the sickness ends up healed. Notice again verse 10,

And the God of all grace, who called you to his eternal glory in Christ, after you have suffered a little while, will himself restore you and make you strong, firm and steadfast.

If someone were to misunderstand the suffering in Peter's letter to be a medical condition of any degree, he would have to see that this same medical condition, terminal or not, "after a little while" would go away, and that God himself would do it.

Nevertheless, Peter was speaking to them on a subject about which he had lots of experience. Peter and the other apostles were honored to suffer for the Name of Jesus.

The Sanhedrin called the apostles in and had them flogged. Then they ordered them not to speak in the name of Jesus, and let them go. The apostles left the Sanhedrin, rejoicing because they had been counted worthy of suffering disgrace for the Name. Acts 5:40-41

"...Dum de dum, we were flogged." No, the apostles were flogged in lieu of killed. They were not paddled like we spank our children. Floggings were whippings that in the culture of the 1st Century Rome, often brought the punished to the brink of death. Some died soon after, others were traumatized by the loss of an eye or too much blood.

The apostles were experiencing some of what Jesus had recently undergone. They were honored to be disgraced because of his life and work in their human bodies. These were the sufferings of Christ. Surely they remembered his warning,

If they persecuted me they will persecute you also. John 15:20

They felt blessed to have been persecuted for righteousness. With the evidence of trauma in their skin, the apostles could relate to what Jesus said to the crowds...

Blessed are those who are persecuted because of righteousness, for theirs is the kingdom of heaven. Blessed are you when people insult you, persecute you and falsely say all kinds of evil against you because of me. Rejoice and be glad, because great is your reward in heaven, for in the same way they persecuted the prophets who were before you." Matthew 5:10-12

Suffering for being a Christian ranges from being called a fanatic or Jesus freak, to being paraded into a coliseum of lions as the deafening cheers of an excited audience enjoy the mutilation of your children. Christian persecution spans being overlooked for a promotion to watching your only son be doused with gasoline and set on fire. These accounts are offensive and unpleasant for us, but much more so for those who have to experience such atrocities. Why are they important to a study on healing?

I believe that studying legitimate Christian suffering in whatever degree it may occur will guard us from being flippant about crediting every trial we undergo as 'suffering for Jesus.' Differing problems demand different solutions. Being snickered at for wearing an 'I ♥ Jesus' t-shirt is a different problem requiring a different solution than having a sore throat. The former is suffering persecution which calls for a sweet smile or shoulder shrug. The latter is not persecution, but sickness, requiring a Biblically prescribed aggressive response. Sickness provides an opportunity to believe and obey, and then to see God glorified by the ensuing healing. Jesus taught rejoicing for persecution and healing for sickness. If you want to glorify God with your sore throat, here is how:

▶ Say *"He sent his word and healed me." Psalm 107:20*
▶ Say *" The prayer of faith will make me well and the Lord will raise me up." James 5:15*
▶ Say *"No weapon forged against me will prevail." Isaiah 54:17*
▶ Say *"It is Jesus' name and the faith that comes through him that has gives this complete healing to me." Acts 3:16*

Christian's suffering persecution must not be confused with suffering disease. Unimaginable horrors have been inflicted upon those who bear the name of Jesus. These are in a different category altogether from the ravages of disease upon Christians, diseases which can be as fierce, but for which God has provided recourse in Jesus' wounds.

Christian persecution which can ultimately end in martyrdom is its own category. The writer of the Book of Hebrews lauded the heroes of old who chose life by choosing death.

Women received back their dead, raised to life again. Others were tortured and refused to be released, so that they might gain a better resurrection. Some faced jeers and flogging, while still others were chained and put in prison. They were stoned, they were sawed in two; they were put to death by the sword. They went about in sheepskins and goatskins, destitute, persecuted and mistreated – the world was not worthy of them. They wandered in deserts and mountains, and in caves and holes in the ground. Hebrews 11: 35-38

These were not people suffering disease; they were suffering persecution. These believers, looking forward to Christ, were targeted and attacked for their faith.

So how do we reconcile the sufferings of believers at the hands of their persecutors with the promises of Psalm 91 --and so many of the other promises for safety and protection upon which we should rely?

If you make the Most High your dwelling, even the Lord who is my refuge, then no harm will befall you no disaster will come near your tent, for he will command his angels concerning you to guard you in all your ways. Psalm 91:9-11

How do we fully trust in these verses that promise our exemption from harm and disaster, in light of the evil, harm and cruelty visited upon some saints? It is hard enough to fully trust these promises in light of all the bad diseases and accidents that affect Christians. The promises of Psalm 91 and every other of the good and thoroughly reliable healing and protection promises of God are conditional, as are all the promises of God. They are conditioned upon our faith and obedience. Trusting plus obeying equals blessing, a fulfilled promise.

- If we forgive, then we will be forgiven.
- If we are friendly then we will have friends.
- If we give then we shall be given unto.

If the Spirit of him who raised Jesus from the dead lives in us, then the Spirit who raised Christ Jesus from the dead will also give life to our mortal bodies through his spirit who lives in you." Romans 8:11

- If you abide in him...
- If you seek him...
- If you open the door to him...

I cannot think of a greater blessing than God's dispatching security forces with supernatural powers to guard my children. If we make the Most High our dwelling he will command his angels concerning us to guard us in all our ways...*if*. As with any of the promises, if I want it, then I have to accommodate the stipulations.

Okay so what about protection from the persecution?! What about the martyrs? Were they disobedient? Of course not.

Persecution and martyrdom are different from sickness and accidents. Persecutions, unlike cursed diseases and injuries, are to be part of our lives. Even still, Paul insisted that the Lord delivered him from all his troubles and persecutions.

Even though the cause may be different –pain --whether from persecution, sickness or injury, was atoned for by Jesus in his wounds and blood. Pain was atoned for.

A woman does not make a stand for Jesus when she surrenders to terminal disease without a fight. She does not sin --of course not. But, we have no right to set her up for failure by loading her up with notions of cosmic purpose that do not exist. Let's fight for her in her weariness. God sent his word to heal terminal disease. She makes a stand for him when she accepts and obeys his promise and provision --and she gets her life back. If she is too weak, then we need to stand!

A woman does indeed make a stand for Jesus when she surrenders her body to flames because she refuses to say, "Jesus is not Lord."

When a man with a gun to his head, silently surrenders to a bullet because he will not pledge allegiance to another god, he is a martyr. He gives his life like the ancients, who *"refused to be released, so that they might gain a better resurrection."* Hebrews 11:35

In Jesus' death, he atoned for sin and disease. We are duty bound to be respectful of this, applying the blood and wounds to our lives so that we can thrive --living free from sin and sickness.

As for persecution, God's grace is sufficient. What seems intolerable to us, is tolerable by sufferers of persecution, because God gives them the grace, the heavenly adrenalin that gets them through it. Of course, we should not provoke or incite persecution, but neither should we dread persecution that will naturally come as we engage in the works that Jesus did.

Anyone who has faith in me will do what I have been doing." John 14:12

And we should pray for the deliverance of our persecuted brothers and sisters around the world who have it so much worse than we.

It is not a hard distinction to make. Disease never makes a martyr, only a victim. Only persecution makes a martyr. How unattractive and embarrassing to act like martyrs when we are sick.

In cultures where Christian persecution is not intense, it is easier to muddle the scriptures. Christians would be less likely to throw all kinds of human sickness and suffering into the same pot where they are exposed to real persecution. If Christians in the United States had experiential knowledge of intense persecution, they would not equate contracting a staph infection from grandma's nursing home with decapitation for refusing to deny Christ.

Clearly, from an open hearted study of the Bible, Jesus has provided escape for infection through his atoning sacrifice. Having MRCA is not suffering for Jesus; it is an attack against which Jesus armed us.

The barbaric acts against God's anointed are persecutions through which God is glorified and his grace is sufficient. We read in the Book of Acts that right before Stephen was stoned to death, his murderers saw that his face looked like an angel's. Luke records that Jesus stood to his feet to honor Stephen during his mob execution.

[The religious mob] were furious and gnashed their teeth at him. But Stephen, full of the Holy Spirit, looked up to heaven and saw the glory of God, and Jesus standing at the right hand of God. "Look," he said, "I see heaven open and the Son of Man standing at the right hand of God."

At this they covered their ears and, yelling at the top of their voices, they all rushed at him, dragged him out of the city and began to stone him. Meanwhile, the witnesses laid their clothes at the feet of a young man named Saul.

While they were stoning him, Stephen prayed, "Lord Jesus, receive my spirit." Then he fell on his knees and cried out, "Lord, do not hold this sin against them." When he had said this, he fell asleep. Acts 7:54-60

God's grace was sufficient. My grandfather told me that he believed God took the pain of martyrs. I believed him then because he was my grandpa. I believe him now because I have consulted God's word. I do believe that God anesthetizes the pain of martyrs in their deaths, first because of the fait accompli of the cross. When Jesus took away our sicknesses, according to Matthew 8 and Isaiah 53, pain went too.

Surely he has borne our griefs (sicknesses, weaknesses, and distresses) and carried our sorrows and pains. Isaiah 53:4

Jesus healed those who were in severe pain as part of his earthly ministry. Also, to back up these assertions is the experience of Stephen. While being pummeled with rocks, what should be one of the most excruciatingly painful and violent deaths, he is articulate, "Lord Jesus, receive my spirit," and again, "Do not hold this sin against them." The behavior of this and other martyrs historically, is an unnatural reaction to torture.

We read about the glee of the disciples at having been whipped and beaten for the Name. Although we do not need to enlarge on Biblical history, it is worth noting that historical records of martyrs fortify the position that the pain of martyrdom is dulled or removed.

In his book, Fox's Book of Martyrs, John Fox chronicles the savage acts committed against Christians. Missing are anguished screams of torment. Instead, he documents behavior of victims that is incompatible with the hellish agonies inflicted on their flesh. These unnatural reactions to what anyone watching would consider unbearable, make it clear that God delivered. Some heathen witnesses became jealous of the deliverance that the martyrs experienced in the throws of torment and death. Ironically, this phenomenon made the era of martyrs under the Roman emperors and religious leaders into a time of unprecedented Church growth.

*At the martyrdom of Faustines and Jovita, brothers and citizens of Brescia, their torments were so many, and their patience so great, that Calocerious, a pagan, beholding them, was struck with admiration, and exclaimed in a kind of ecstasy, "Great is the God of the Christians!" for which he was apprehended and suffered a similar fate. *1*

*Under this persecution, "Germanicus, a young man, but a true Christian, being delivered to the wild beasts on account of his faith, behaved with such astonishing courage that several pagans became converts to a faith that inspired such fortitude." *2*

God was glorified in observable grace. It manifested in the honorable endurance of excruciating pain and torment of immovable Christians. The cruelties of the persecution under Marcus Antoninus AD 162 were such that *"many of the spectators shuddered with horror at the sight and were astonished at the intrepidity of the sufferers."* They were courageous and unalarmed --impossible responses considering the conditions. *3

The historian Fox admitted in his own writing that tortures to which many of the Christians were put exceeded the power of his words to describe. Still, in many accounts, executioners grew weary and unsatisfied in their butcherings because of the lack of intended impact on their victims.

Blandina, a Christian woman of weak physical constitution was suspended on a piece of wood fixed in the ground, and exposed as food for the wild beasts. At that time by her earnest prayers she encouraged others who were in the same situation. None of the wild beasts would touch her so she was remanded to prison.

*She was again brought out but this time with a boy of fifteen, Ponticus. The constancy of their faith so enraged the multitude that neither the sex of the one nor the youth of the other were respected, being exposed to all manner of punishments and tortures. Being strengthened by Blandina, he persevered unto death; and she, after enduring all the torments heretofore mentioned, was at length slain with the sword. *4*

In AD 251, Quintian, the governor of Sicily became enamored with Agatha a beautiful and chaste girl. He put her in the hands of the whore madam Aphrodica who could not influence her to give up her virginity or prostitute herself. When she claimed to be a Christian, the governor took revenge on her for not satisfying his desires.

*Pursuant to his orders, she was scourged (whipped with leather and pieces of metal and glass) burnt with red-hot irons, and torn with sharp hooks. Having borne these torments with admirable fortitude, she was next laid naked on live coals, intermingled with glass, and then being carried back to prison, she there expired on February 5th AD 251 *5*

In AD 257, The Emperor Valerian, a madman began presiding over his persecution of Christians. When he encountered the defiance of a minister of the gospel Lawrence, he cried, "Kindle the fire – of wood make no spare. Hath this villain deluded the emperor? Away with him, away with him: whip him with scourges, jerk him with rods, buffet him with fists, brain him with clubs. Jesteth the traitor with the emperor? Pinch him with fiery tongs, gird him with burning plates, bring out the strongest chains, and the fire-forks, and the grated bed of iron: on the fire with it; bind the rebel hand and foot; and when the bed is fire-hot, on with him: roast him, broil him, toss him, turn him: on pain of our high displeasure do every man his office, O ye tormentors."

Fox continues to write that after many cruel handlings, God tempered the fire.

It became not a bed of consuming pain, but a pallet of nourishing rest.
*6

Sebastian, an officer of the emperor's guard at Rome, refused the pagan practices demanded of him by the emperor. As a believer he would not participate in idolatrous rituals whether burning incense to false deities or taking oaths in the name of Roman idols. Accordingly, he was ordered to be taken to a field and shot to death with arrows. After the punishment was executed, some Christians took his body to prepare it for burial, but perceived signs of life. They moved him to a safe place and aided him in his recovery. John Fox records,

As soon as he was able to go out, he placed himself intentionally in the emperor's way as he was going to the temple, and reprimanded him for his various cruelties and unreasonable prejudices against Christianity. As soon as Diocletian had overcome his surprise, he ordered Sebastian to be seized and carried to a place near the palace, and beaten to death; and that the Christians should not either use means again to recover or bury his body, he ordered that it should be thrown into the common sewer. *7

A woman named Lucina found Sebastian's body and buried him in the catacombs, the repositories of the dead. Journalism does not often afford the emotional and relational information that we crave. Would a stranger risk her life to rescue Sebastian from rotting in a sewer ? Was Lucina in love with Sebastian? We do not know. What we do know is that they both escaped the ravages of hell.

Sebastian is a celebrated martyr because he was fearless in the face of his murderers and devoted unto death to his faith in Christ. The courage and conviction that carved Sebastian's memory on antiquity certainly launched him into eternity. These qualities on pain of death are a testament to the submission of a man to the mighty work of Christ.

In many lands, Christian persecution is and has been rampant. Peter and Paul having lead epic lives, died in the fallout of the insane Emperor Nero's persecution of Christians. The Historian Philip Schaff describes the conditions for Christians under the rule of the sadistic Roman Emperor Nero.

*There began a carnival of blood such as even heathen Rome never saw before or since....A 'vast multitude' of Christians was put to death in the most shocking manner. Some were crucified, probably in mockery of the punishment of Christ, some sewed up in the skins of wild beasts and exposed to the voracity of mad dogs in the arena...Christian men and women covered with pitch or oil or resin, and nailed to posts of pine, were lighted and burned as torches for the amusement of the mob .It was in the fallout of this that Peter and Paul gave their lives for their Savior, probably within a year of each other. *8*

For it has been granted to you on behalf of Christ not only to believe on him, but also to suffer for him, since you are going through the same struggle you saw I (Paul) had, and now hear that I still have. Philippians 1:29

And so it continues, modern persecution around the world is under-reported but just as chilling. Believers are axed, filleted, bludgeoned, doused in gasoline and set on fire. In dark morning hours, Christian villages are waking to screams of mothers whose babies and children are being torn from their arms. Whole families are driven into the wilderness leaving burning homes behind them, if not first scattered by massacre.

Do we stand idly by when this is happening to our brothers and sisters around the world? No! We should be praying and giving for the martyrs, for their safety and deliverance, and we should never give up. We do not want to be persecuted, but when we are, we should not be surprised. And if they are doing it to my brother, my baby, my friend, they are doing it to me.

God help me to be faithful to pray for them and worthy to count them as my family. May I understand what others around the world are having to endure while I enjoy safety and comfort. They understand much better than I the words of the disciple Luke,

We must go through many hardships to enter the kingdom of God. Acts 14::22

It is crucial that we identify our enemies, that we correctly discern our hardships. Is our trouble from sin? We need to fight that to the death. Is our problem disease? We fight it to the death. Evil spirit? Fight to the death. Disability? Fight to the death. Bad husband? Don't fight to the death. Bad job? Pray and work hard. No job? Pray and volunteer. No money? Pray, work hard and give to the poor. Nagging woman? Pray.

The persecutions we undergo in America starkly contrast in severity to those we read about in history and around the world. Nevertheless, at whatever level, persecutions exist.

In fact, everyone who wants to live a godly life in Christ Jesus will be persecuted, 2 Timothy 3:12

If everyone just loves us all the time, if we live to constantly please man, maybe we are doing something wrong. Maybe we are too worried about what others think of us. Maybe we fear the opinion of a person more than God's.

Fear of man will prove to be a snare. Proverbs 29:25

We have 2 choices:
1) Fear of man which brings the wrath of God
2) Fear of God which brings the wrath of man

Which do you choose?

It may be hard to serve God sometimes, but I would argue that it is harder not to do so. Also, I intend in no way to diminish the heroism of persecuted saints by saying that Jesus, in the person of Holy Spirit, is nigh to take away pain, having met pain's demands on the cross. The remarkable valor with which sufferers handle themselves is a supernatural stamina that can only be received through unbroken devotion to God. This powerful endurance is the manifestation of grace that is ours through the atoning work of Christ:

Surely He has borne our griefs (sicknesses, weaknesses, and distresses) and carried our sorrows and pains [of punishment]. Isaiah 53:4 Amplified

He carried our pains.

When God's special girl is tied to a wooden steak, when the kindling is arranged at her feet, when crowds jeer as she is slapped and smeared with pitch because she will not recant, can she call on the promise of Isaiah 53:4?

Is she still among those for whom Jesus carried away pain?

Can she count on him when the fire begins to crackle around her ankles?

Is God like a son of man, *that he should change his mind? Does he speak and then not act? Does he promise and not fulfill?"* Numbers 23:19

The flames crawl up the legs of daddy's princess and leap onto her face. She whispers, "Jesus is Lord and there is no other." Angels wisk her away.

We will all have stories about what God has done for us. Our persecutions will hopefully never compare to those we have discussed but still, you will have your own testimonies. Here is one of mine...

Chapter 18

My Kidnapping Testimony

A man's enemies will be the members of his own household.
– Jesus Christ, Matthew 10:36

News Services, API
The FBI said today that at least 11 people face kidnapping and extortion charges in the abduction of 2 sisters who are from Sterling, Virginia. Among those arrested were the women's mother and her second husband. According to an account published by the Detroit Free Press, Betsy Chase (Beers) 21, and her sister, Whitney, 18, reportedly had been detained and forced to undergo 'deprogramming' in a home in Bloomfield Township, a wealthy Detroit suburb, over the Christmas holidays...

It all started with a headache, my ten year old brother Joey's. Actually, he used to get a lot of headaches. I was visiting my mother, stepfather, and two younger brothers, Sammy and Joey in Michigan. In a few days I would fly back home to Washington DC where I lived with my father, step-mother and my best friend who happened also to my sister, Whitney. There is nothing better than being best friends with your sister.

But for the time being, I was in Michigan sitting with my little brother Joey on the couch, our backs to a window that looked out to the lake. He was upset because his head really hurt. I covered his sandy brown hair with my hands and prayed for the headache to leave. I knew immediately from the stunned look he gave me that the pain was gone. Naturally, he wanted to understand why and how this happened, so we went upstairs and sat on the guest bed where I showed him some enlightening verses. Our Bible fun was cut short when my mom marched into the room, "What are you doing?!"

Next I was downstairs, sitting in the kitchen on the fireplace hearth inches, not feet, from my very large, very rich step father, Bob. How I wished I could scooch my seat away from his, especially as he leaned into me with inflamed eyes, "You are not Jesus Christ!" I had never really thought that I was Jesus Christ, but Bob was suddenly making me feel kinda like him.

If the world hates you, keep in mind that it hated me first. John 15:18

Did anyone even care that Joey's head was better? The apparent concern was instead, that an unsophisticated, uneducated born-again, had access to power that the "Lord Larson," as his bio-daughter dubbed him, did not have. He forbad me to speak about Jesus, healing, or the Bible to anyone else in his house again.

I said, "Please take me to the airport."

The year passed and things from a thousand miles away seemed more peaceful with our mother. Whitney and I thought that her obsession with our Christianity, and with the Assemblies of God Church we were attending at the time, had faded. So, during the following Christmas holiday, we flew to my mother and Bob's new house in Michigan hoping, as usual, for a fresh start and to keep the friction to a minimum - as much as was in our power. It was amazing how well received we were, to the point where we were dancing around in the newly furbished exercise studio to a Christian band we loved. Wow!

Whitney and I would not realize until later that this trip would connect to odd events that had occurred in Sterling, Virginia, the suburb of Washington DC where we had very recently moved. Once, for example, a creepy guy that showed up at Whitney's Pizza Hut waitressing job was exceptionally inquisitive about our church and wanting to attend. She felt sorry for him. Sure enough, he came to a Bible study and acted remarkably strange. When it was his turn to read a passage, he stumbled and sputtered as if he were somewhat illiterate.

We did not know he had been sent to spy on us.

Would he report back about the cultic behaviors of the followers' "dancing in the spirit", practicing the "laying on of hands" or eschewing pre-marital sex? We did not know about all the planning and secret meetings with Parent's Underground. We did not know about all the others that had been flown into the Detroit airport for this holiday season.

Still unaware of anything amiss, our work-out session was over and it was time to go to dinner, On cue, Whitney and I got in the backseat of Bob's car. We wondered why he was driving toward the old house on the lake, the one where Joey was healed from that nuisance headache. We were told it was in order to pick something up. Okay.

It was a surprise to be welcomed at the side door as the house was supposed to be vacant. The strangers led us in, my mother and Bob followed closely, probably just in case we were spooked and wanted to perhaps get something out of the car or run like the wind.

We were invited to sit at a big table, Whitney and I obviously the focus of the gathering. Books and papers were piled everywhere. Among them was my missing diary that recounted my freshman college days when God hunted me down, and other secrets about boys and mushy stuff I didn't want my mother and a counsel of self-appointed judges to read. It was analyzed well to prepare for this meet and greet. I would never see that personal journal again.

Great! Just when it seemed all the endless assaults and challenges to every single thought we thought had ceased, here came the big one, the inquisition. I tried to be extra compliant so we could get it over with and go to dinner. I did not want to be right; I just wanted to get away from these people!

I looked around the room. All three ways out were blocked by men lying or standing. People seemed to be everywhere. Apparently we were not going out for dinner. After pointless exchanges, I was ushered to the second floor, and Whitney to the basement, still under the pretense of our having a choice in the matter. I would be agreeable in order to speed up the process and get out of there, even go to the stupid upstairs so they could "show me something."

The something was a movie in one of the bedrooms about kids in cults, even though I was 21. They should have shown me a movie about grown-ups in cults. I would like to have shown them one about grown-ups holding people against their will. After burning out from all the aggressive interrogation, I saw it was getting dark and I just wanted to go back home with my sister - to Virginia.

One of the leaders, Sherry, in her early thirties with short, reddish blond hair, was small of stature but provided safe haven for my mother who was sitting behind her, hoping in, and banking on her every word. On and on she went about how we would be dissecting all kinds of passages with commentaries and concordances.

She was a "deprogrammer," a self-proclaimed expert in exposing every mind-control master-mind from Jim Jones (who murdered many hundreds of his followers including hundreds of children and babies with cyanide laced Kool-Aid) to Billy Graham. As such, she was ready to deprogram me.

"We can't do all that tonight! When are we going to do all this?" I asked her. "We're going back home tomorrow morning."

She and my mother exchanged a look that told me I was not going to the airport in the morning. Sherry cocked her head and offered me a condescending smile as she explained what would happen if I tried to leave. Spare me the drama; it was rather obvious with the Triton lying across the bedroom doorway, what would happen if I tried to leave. The giant man with a knife would be my guard all through the night hours, making sure that I did not try to leave or shut my bedroom door for privacy. A normal sized man would have sufficed in keeping a 115 pound girl in her room. After several nights, he would sleep in the room with me. My second story windows were locked and boarded. I was accompanied to and from the bathroom.

What had my mother plotted against us in order to carry out a personal vendetta against the faith of her mother and father? Her unreasonable obsession with losing her daughters to Christianity made her vulnerable to a deception that would prove very costly for her girls.

At that time many will turn away from the faith and will betray and hate each other and many false prophets will appear and deceive many people. Matthew 24:10-11

Deprogrammer is a title that may suggest an intellectual mastery of psychology, brain function, family therapy, mental health, counseling – something! I would come to find out that the motley assembly presiding over my sister's and my every move was nothing more than a group of embittered and deeply troubled social deviants, at least one suicidal and at least another a convicted felon. Neither intellect nor education were represented by this group of kidnappers. Soon I would be left alone with my guard, Larry Ironmoccasin, an enormous half American-Indian, half African-American covered with tattoos and convicted of statutory rape, he was pulled from a auto-mechanics garage in downtown Minneapolis for the gig.

When I first realized that my sister and I were not going to be allowed to leave, Sherry patronizingly explained that if God did not want me to be there, that he would not have allowed it.

I disagreed and explained, "He obviously does want me here. It is a trial for me. I will pass this test and he will get me out." She graced me with a sweet, haughty smile and left with my mother. I never saw my mother again during my deprogramming.

On that first night, I heard my sister screaming in the basement. My first instinct was to run down two flights of stairs and help her. I felt enraged and completely helpless that we were being forcibly contained in rooms by a band of thugs, wanna-be professionals, and by our mother.

I had never even thought to try and imagine, how I would feel in such a situation. If I had tried, I don't think I would have imagined that the worst part of the whole thing for me was that no one knew where we were or what was happening to us. We found out later that my step father, Bob, not to be confused with Bob the deprogrammer, made calls explaining that we would be on an extended ski vacation up north. A competent, rags-to-riches, self-made multi-millionaire, Bob's persuasive lies could convince anyone. Nevertheless, people at home started to become suspicious after we did not show up on our return date and did not call.

After examining my situation and seeing how well orchestrated this operation was, I understood that trying to escape would not only be vain, but worse, would give them the satisfaction of gloating about their accurate predictions of our cultish behaviors. Maybe I'd throw them a bone and "speak in tongues."

I was angry inside, then frantic, a prisoner who did no crime with no idea of how long my sentence would be. Even though I wanted to scream and destroy the room, I surrendered to my predicament as I sank onto the bed to soberly plot with God a scheme to escape. Thank Him he was there.

I started talking to my giant, Larry, talking and talking. I asked questions.

All he muttered was. "I'm not allowed to talk to you."
Then I said, "Boy, would my dad ever be mad about this!"
Nothing.
I pushed a little more. "He's a lawyer and he is rich."
He was listening.
And so I said, "If he knew about this, he would pay a lot of money to get us out of here."

My dad and I didn't have the best relationship in the world so suddenly I found myself wondering about how much he would pay for my sister and me.

It was quiet, but then I heard a throaty whisper, "How much?"

I quickly calculated. "Five thousand dollars, just for the address."

I knew to Larry that would be a fortune. We couldn't let anyone else hear us talking. He let it all out. He was angry with my mother because his agreement to do this job was based upon guarding and an additional $500 snatch fee, a fee from which he was cheated. The original plan to snatch us off the street and force us into the back of a van was aborted. My mother and Bob had decided is was unnecessary as they could lure us into the house.

Most cult followers have bad to non-existent relationships with their parents, hence the necessary trauma of snatching them from a sidewalk. My sister and I were mature in our relationship with our mother and stepfather, as we lived our lives, and let them live theirs. The fact that this principle was not reciprocated was no indictment of our peacemaking efforts. Going in peace, we were greeted with knives, literally.

So Larry turned on the clan of kidnappers. I was very careful to explain the notes I gave him, unsure of his level of literacy. The guards would switch around; he would be with Whitney soon, so I said, "First, give this to my sister" I had written, 'Don't worry, we're getting out.'

I did not know that he would promise to get her out if she had sex with him. She did not do it.

Looking back, I should have simplified the instructions, he messed them up so badly. It turned out not to matter because of the careful oversight of the Person who was really in charge of this subterfuge.

"Call my father at this number and tell him we are being held at this address." I knew the address by heart since it was my mother and Bob's former house, a house they kept for this purpose. "And call this number and tell them to contact my father." It was the phone number of my boyfriend's family.

The days that followed were filled from beginning to end with emotional and psychological harassment. The relentless attacks on our "belief system" were mean spirited and demeaning. I was accused of mind control techniques as the spiritual leader of the apartment, depriving my two followers (Whitney and our roommate friend, Carolyn) of food --feeding them only donuts to dull their minds, and of sleep to create disorientation and increase their susceptibility to whatever I was brainwashing them with.

Larry could not leave the house to use a phone. Whole days would go by and no progress was made in his ransom dealings. He was scared of getting caught. I was increasingly frustrated and completely cut off from what was happening. He spent a lot of time in the basement with my sister. Another deprogrammer flew in from Texas.

The purpose of their constant barrage was to "break" us. Larry told me that my mother was not going to stop until we broke. She was staunch and resolute. I knew that was right. Bob and my mom would not care how much money it would cost for them to hear us deny our faith. Larry had been with people as long as six weeks before they broke. He assured me that it would eventually happen.

He warned that the deprogrammers would slowly begin to infringe on our personal space, sleeping inside the room, going into the bathroom with us; these were not female guards. Larry told me they would start to put stuff in our food. After breaking us, they would send us to some kind of re-introduction camp in Minnesota. He strongly suggested that I yield. He said to just say what they wanted to hear, to fake it. Just pretend to 'break.'

Hell no.

Whoever acknowledges me before men, I will also acknowledge him before my Father in heaven. But whoever disowns me before men, I will disown him before my Father in heaven. Matthew 10:33

Another regret I have is that after a while, the deprogrammers spent less time with me and more time, a lot more time with my sister. She was acting out in her anger and frustration at their merciless provocations, a caged animal, stuffed in a dark, corner basement room, seriously considering being raped by Larry so she could have a hope of escape. The deprogrammers were happy with her rages and tears; she was weakening.

They finally abandoned me because I disengaged from the verbally abusive conflicts. I think it was also because I inadvertently insulted Bob the deprogrammer. Pudgy and pasty white, he was in my room flaunting his ignorance about healing and demanding answers on which he would then spit and trample. His deprogramming credentials were based on having been a Moonie, having belonged to several other cults, having attempted to hang himself, and his apparent untreated eating disorder.

Instead of responding to his persistent badgering, I told him that I would no longer "cast my pearls before swine." Speaking Bible was to them the most tell tale sign of my cult membership. He lunged his face toward mine. You could not have squeezed a New Testament between our noses.

"Are you calling me a pig?!" I did not affirm that, but remember thinking it would have been fitting because he did look like one. From then on, the deprogrammers stayed away. Unfortunately, they haunted my sister instead.

Well into the week, in carefully measured, barely audible phrases, Larry told me he still had not given the address to my dad. I was so discouraged.

This is what was happening --unbeknownst to me: When he finally got to a phone, Larry called my boyfriend's house to make a ransom demand. He was not going to give any information until his sister in Minneapolis received the money.

But he called the wrong number! He was supposed to call my father. This was in 1983 before cell phones or even the popularization of answering machines. It could be days before he got to a phone again.

My boyfriend's mother, Barbara was home alone and about to leave for the grocery store. She said she came back inside the house very disturbed about something. She sat on a step in the kitchen, praying and trying to figure out what was holding her up. Then the phone rang. She said she could hardly make out the words of the deep raspy voice on the line, but she heard "sisters" and "$5,000" and "send the money if you want the girls." She was terrified but had the presence of mind to write down the parts she understood and call my father immediately, whose business card just happened to be on the microwave next to the phone.

The FBI tapped Barbara's phone, my father's phone, every phone they thought might receive a call. They ended up sending agents with the money to Larry's sister's house in Minneapolis, thinking we were being held there.

At the time I did not realize that there were plans to move us to a more discreet location. Two black limousines drove around the circular driveway one day making my step-father Bob nervous. This prompted the plans to move. Larry told me he would not be told the address and we would be blindfolded. There would be no way to let anyone know where we were.

There was not time to make the kind of mistakes Larry was making, or be so lax about getting out to call. He would wait for his sister to secure the money before releasing the address and he was paranoid about the others' catching him. But we were moving! He would have to tell my father soon and then tell him to hurry! I begged him to quickly call my dad. He seemed cavalier and uninterested.

I have never been successful in praying with timetables. Telling the Lord I have to have $200 by Tuesday doesn't usually go over too well for me. But, Larry came to tell me that the move was set, that they were moving us in the morning. He hurried away. He was so elusive, and someone else was guarding me. It was New Year's Eve. There was nothing else I could do. I didn't know if Larry had called, what was said, or if any one had even answered. I did not know my father's house was teaming with FBI agents. I knew nothing except that my dad, who was several states away, may not have the address. If he did, maybe he would not take it seriously. Larry didn't really seem to care, my sister was being hammered and we were moving to some dark hole in the morning. I put on my flannel night gown, laid in my bed with my face to the ceiling and waited.

I prayed, "This is it Lord. You have to rescue us tonight. You have to do it tonight."

Not two minutes later, I heard a rapping on the huge oak front door, then loud banging. I froze. After a pause of silence, I heard frantic shuffling and loud panicked whispering. Then it sounded like a bomb exploded, followed by yelling. Someone was there! I was not going to let them get away. I stood up, threw my fists to my side and screamed as loud as I could. Suddenly I saw the silhouette of an FBI agent poised with a gun in the upstairs hall outside my door. He hurried me downstairs and made me lie on my stomach in the foyer. The Chief of Police had kicked in the whole front door. A half eaten ice cream bar was on the floor next to Bob the deprogrammer. who was lying face down with a rifle pressed into his back. They made everyone lie on their stomachs all over the house because they had to sort out who was who. It took only a moment for them to see that I was one of the girls they were looking for.

"Where's the other one ?!" an agent shouted.
"She's in the basement!" I was so anxious for them to get Whitney.

After they sorted and restrained everyone, they let me go down to see her in her corner back room, I thought she would run and hug me. Instead, she stayed curled up in a ball at the foot of the bed clenching her knees to her chest with her arms and staring. Her hands were wide open, and with her fingers interlaced she was rapidly jerking them together. I was so proud of her for never giving in to those people. When she got up and I hugged her, she was like a piece of wood. Our relationship was never the same again. My sister's experience was worse than mine. She didn't break for them, but she was broken. I regret that so much.

We emerged from the basement to find every deprogrammer and guard sitting against the walls with their hands cuffed behind their backs. My sister and I were free to move around and they were not. Sherry and I caught each other's eyes. She had scoffed when I told her that God would get me out, because she was arrogant and she had never been caught, until now. I could have cast a sweet and haughty smile her way. She deserved it. But. . . Jesus saved me, and they would all have to admit it.

They will fight against you but will not overcome you, for I am with you and will rescue you," declares the Lord. Jeremiah 1:19

Hatred for God, betrayal of loved ones, these are facts of life. It is also a fact that forgiveness absolves the pain inflicted by these human vices, regardless of whether the perpetrator is sorry.. I have never believed the pop dogma that time heals everything., I gave it a try anyway. More than 25 years later, I can personally testify that time definitely does not heal. Only forgiveness.

Part Three

Thorny Lies That Make You Sick

Chapter 19
No More Child Organ Donors

Sometimes Christian television makes me want to bang somebody's head on a wall.

Often, you hear people surrender to belligerent illnesses and disabilities, or acquiesce to child death by confessing these tragedies as special purposes or thorns. Christian talk shows often have guests with heart wrenching stories of the loss of children to cancer. One mom testified to being thankful that her daughter was chosen to give life to other kids with her little girl's organs. We have to find a more effective and honest way to minister comfort. This does not help parents who are struggling to believe for healing.

According to the many champions of these blemished Christian values, the unfortunate purpose sent from on high, or thorn, is harm that God endorses for whatever grandiosity they charge him with. So --why bother too much in trying to get rid of it? By the way then, if it is their very special thorn, should they be trying to get rid of it medically?

Paul's thorn is the most predictable disruption to anyone's healing journey. Someone is always ready with it, an alert needle poised at the bobbing belly of a freshly inflated balloon. It tugs into the sky, begging and pulling, "Let me go!" Just one little mention, one tiny touch with the sharp point to the proud rubber body, and it erupts into a withered shred on a curley ribbon.

You work so hard to build up your faith in Jesus and his word. Just when you're set to launch your balloon, here comes a bearer of the good news, "Don't forget about Paul's thorn!" and BAM!

--Unless there is education, understanding and knowledge.

I love those people but I don't dare let them near my balloons.

Remember his people perish for lack of knowledge? (Hosea 4:6) If we do not have it, we need to get it. What do we know about Paul's thorn, as opposed to what has been manufactured about it? If you have not heard about Paul's thorn and are trying to believe for healing, don't worry, you will. Many Christians teach that the thorn Paul received from the Lord was sickness. We will prove otherwise. Now to expose this saboteur.

The Apostle Paul never took exception to God's acts of power. In no way did he ever limit God's miraculous power exerted through humans. It was thematic to Paul's life mission. His 'thorn' provides no exception to this, as many would have it. He summarized his whole ministry as being a display of God's unfailing power.

My message and my preaching were not with wise and persuasive words, but with a demonstration of the Spirit's power, so that your faith might not rest on men's wisdom, but on God's power.
1 Corinthians 2:4,5

The demonstration or the Spirit's power was Paul's self-professed ministry credential. The acts through Paul which showcased God's invisible power were Paul's own seal of authenticity.

His street smarts and privileged education were not even listed on his apostolic resumé. Neither was any ability to come up with explanations as to how God's power could manifest in contentment with being sick.

When Paul said that when he was weak, he was really strong, did he mean that in the final analysis he was weak or strong? Strong. He meant delivered, rescued, above and not beneath, the head and not the tail, a winner not a loser, strong not weak. It is always a trade up with God. We give ashes; he gives back beauty. He takes the sadness and gives joy. He bestows,

A crown of beauty instead of ashes, the oil of gladness instead of mourning, and a garment of praise instead of a spirit of despair. Isaiah 61:3

We need a basic understanding of God's consistent character -- how he operates. Paul always ended strong: spirit, soul and body. Sick is not strong.

Did God show his strength by making Paul strong about weakness? No. It takes a lot of manipulating scripture and juggling to conclude that Paul's strength in weakness was ultimately staying weak but feeling good about it --so as to be construed as strength. Convoluted and confusing. Not God.

The miracle is that we show off the saving mightiness of God in our frail human flesh and misery.

When you cannot take another step, he invigorates you to take three, and then to run. When you hate your sister, he surprises you with an unexpected package of forgiveness and good will toward her. When you are scared, he sets you on a high and open place beating your chest. When you are diagnosed with bacterial meningitis, he is health to your whole body.

Pay attention to what I say; listen closely to my words. Do not let them out of your sight, keep them within your heart; for they are life to those who find them and health to a man's whole body. Proverbs 4:20-22

The words God has given us, so many words on healing, are actual medicine to our body. They are *How-To* get from weak to strong. In verse 22, the Hebrew word for health also means healing and cure. The person's whole body, or flesh, in other translations, is the isolated target of the health or cure. The verse cannot be reassigned to mean that the words of God are health to a person's mind or spirit only. Although that is also true; this verse focuses on physical health — of which our minds are a part. We accommodate physical health through our spiritual access to God.

We are commanded to pay attention to the words that cure, to listen closely to the words that heal, to not allow them out of our sight, to keep the words that cure within our heart, because they are life --only to we who find them. The words that bring health and the words that cure are medicine to all our flesh. It is by our obeying the directions and words of God that brings his power into our weakness.

His strength does not look like maladies of every kind, listless children in hospital beds, men in wheelchairs and women enslaved to pain. His strength in our weakness looks like loving each other, escaping the tyrannical dictators of poverty, infection, depression, addiction, infertility, greed, idolatry and crippling pain. His strength in our weakness makes us strong, it does not leave us the same. It does not leave us still weak but with a good attitude, still weak but having learned a good lesson. His strength changes us. Let the weak say I am strong!

Paul's ministry credentials consisted of only one item, the demonstration of God's power. But he did have a sub-list of qualifications which detailed the sufferings through which God's power showed itself, sufferings about which he so famously boasted. Did he boast because they were the worst anyone ever had or because he endured them so patiently as have millions of other people regardless of religious affiliation? No, he boasted in them because they demonstrated God's power to deliver, and the strength that God showed in and through him. His boasting was not in his great endurance, but in God's great power --the hallmark of his ministry, the *"demonstration of the Spirit's power, so that your faith might not rest on men's wisdom, but on God's power." 1 Corinthians 2:5*

There may be many reasons why Paul listed in such detail these troubles, but especially noteworthy is the conspicuous absence of disease, sickness or accidental injuries. All his troubles were sent directly or indirectly by the hands of purposeful persecutors, inspired by at least one demon (the thorn) that we know of. They are found in *2 Corinthians 11:23-28*

1) I have worked much harder,
2) been in prison more frequently,
3) been flogged more severely, and
4) been exposed to death again and again.
5) Five times I received from the Jews the forty lashes minus one.
6) Three times I was beaten with rods,
7) once I was stoned,
8) three times I was shipwrecked,
9) I spent a night and a day in the open sea,
10) I have been constantly on the move.
11) I have been in danger from rivers,
12) in danger from bandits,
13) in danger from my own countrymen,
14) in danger from Gentiles;
15) in danger in the city, in danger in the country,
16) in danger at sea; and
17) in danger from false brothers.
18) I have labored and toiled and have often gone without sleep;
19)I have known hunger and thirst and have often gone without food;
20) I have been cold and naked.
21) Besides everything else, I face daily the pressure of my concern for all the churches.

Not a single disease nor any allusion of any kind to one is found in this list of specifics --no sniffles, nor virus, not even an Oriental eye disease.

Why these trials? …is the important question.

The answer is good works in Christ, not random assaults on his health or freak accidents. We are not to fear accidents because we think they might possibly be a vehicle through which God wants us to suffer. An accident is defined as anything that happens by chance or without an apparent cause.

None of Paul's physical sufferings came without a cause. They were all persecutions. They were all suffering for bearing the name of Jesus and for doing good on his behalf, something for which the world community has vituperative disdain. As mentioned earlier in Psalm 91, God promised that we who make the Most High our dwelling will have no harm befall us, and no disaster will come near our tents (homes/temples/bodies).

In the same psalm, we are required to obey the command to not fear the terror of night, nor the pestilence, nor the plague, nor an abbreviated lifespan --regardless of the thousands around us who may be thus affected.

The very same psalm promises the posting of angels by our sides and our ability to trample and tread on all kinds of evil.

Paul had the benefit of all these promises of health and protection evident in his life. Paul's beatings, hardships, attacks and eventual beheading were not random incidences of violence, sickness, car crashes, plane crashes, drownings, burns, school yard shootings, holiday shopper tramplings, bridge collapses or miscarriages. Paul's list was exclusively about persecutions, a list to which later he referenced when he said of his troubles that the Lord delivered him from them all.

Martyrdom is the only Biblically sanctioned premature death. Unless you choose, as the martyred saints described in Hebrews 11, the better resurrection, you are assured that you can believe to be satisfied with a long life. It is God's desire that you fall asleep in your old age when you are finished with your race.

What if a twelve year old has had a full life span?

That is either a silly question of a legalistic antagonist to healing, or the desperate question of a broken hearted mother trying to make sense of the premature death of her child. How does a twelve year old die? Of old age?

No, it would have to be by disease or injury, both of which are covered by the wounds and blood of Jesus. I want my life's work to honor the mother who did not experience this earthly deliverance, whose baby is with Jesus. How could there be greater pain than this?

A voice is heard in Ramah, weeping and great mourning, Rachel weeping for her children and refusing to be comforted, because they are no more. Matthew 2:18

I do not want it to happen ever again to any parent. I do not want to hear another Christian testimony about how the cancer death of an eleven year old was to save the lives of five children who received her organ donations. It is amazing that she was so compassionate and unselfish, and that good came from this tragedy, but to say that her purpose was complete at eleven and that she was born for such a time as this? to donate her organs? No.

This kind of emotional religion does nothing but shred the hope and faith of parents of terminal kids. They do not want their kids to be organ donors, and neither does God.

It is easy to slip into a thinking whereby our weaknesses become a badge of piety. Look how much we suffer for Jesus! Look how much we endure at his hand! See what great martyrs we are!

The real damage comes when we impose that load of garbage on families who really need someone to stand with them against Satan's attacks on their children. Sometimes we need intolerant warriors, not consoling encouragers.

Chapter 20

Emo-Faith & Child Sacrifice

"Be sure you put your feet in the right place, then stand firm."
-Abraham Lincoln

Being a fitness instructor was great because whether I felt like it or not, I had to exercise, lest there be a studio full of cardio dancers all standing around wondering what to do next. Among them would be Ellen.

Recently, she asked me to pray for her twelve year old nephew who was in the final stages of cancer. A malignant tumor on his brainstem was destroying his precious little body. Still, he was sure that Jesus would heal him. We prayed. A few days later he went into a coma, and a few days after that, he went to be with Jesus forever.

No doubt that now he would not even want to come back. What do we say to comfort such a devastating loss? How do we explain it? We have forged many answers based on our feelings, instincts and emotions. It's our emo-faith.

We teach that God allowed the tragedy to effect something greater for others, that he had a mysterious purpose which we will someday comprehend, that he wanted another little angel in heaven. What is wrong with these well-meaning, albeit corrupt sayings?

First of all. there is no disputing that God can make great things of tragedy. He can redeem any forlorn situation for our good. That does not mean that he desired it or initiated the tragedy. God is no peddler of misfortune.

The firstborn children in Egypt were in danger of the death angel because of disobedience. It was an act of judgment, not something God initially wanted. The Lord passed over the houses whose doors were stained with blood and he did not allow the destroyer to enter. In the same way, we have access to the blood of Jesus, the only protection from judgment.

When the Lord goes through the land to strike down the Egyptians, he will see the blood on the top and sides of the doorframe and will pass over that doorway, and he will not permit the destroyer to enter your houses and strike you down. Exodus 12:23

If there has been a breach, and the destroyer has entered your house for any reason, do not say, "Oh he is here for some good reason." Get him out!

But wait, if tragedy has come to your home, didn't God allow it?

If my daughter disobeys me by playing in the street at night when I think she is sleeping, and gets hit by a car, did I allow it? I would never allow or permit my child to get hit by a car.

When that demoniac psycho mom drowned her five children in the bathtub, did God allow or permit it? Would you allow your husband or wife to do that? Of course not. We have free wills and God has never claimed that he would usurp our authority over our own decisions and destinies.

In the case of the Israelites, God did not allow the destroyer to enter the houses because they obeyed his instructions. In the case of the Egyptians, they allowed the destroyer access by their disobedience. They could have applied the blood too.

This does not mean whenever tragedy comes, someone sinned or disobeyed. It may just be because we live in a fallen world that is still bound by the laws of sin and death. It means that

Satan, who is the god of this world, still has control until we exert our authority over him.

Satan, who is the god of this world, has blinded the minds of those who don't believe. 2 Corinthians 4:4 NLT

And often, by the way, even believers don't believe.

Unless we counter him, he, as the ruler of this dark world, has control. Our struggle is not against people.

Our struggle is not against flesh and blood, but against the rulers, against the authorities, against the powers of this dark world and against the spiritual forces of evil in the heavenly realms. Ephesians 6:12

If we are passive and choose not to struggle, we allow him to maintain control. Until Jesus comes back, this fallen world is our spiritual domain to the degree we are willing to take it. Apathy is surrender.

I have given you authority to trample on serpents and scorpions and to overcome all the power of the enemy, nothing will harm you. Luke 10:19

It is we who have been given authority over the devil to undo and destroy his works. We need to exercise this authority instead of accumulating more dumb excuses like "maybe God needed another angel in heaven."

Does God ever need another angel in heaven?

This is a wretched attempt at consoling the grief stricken, at best. Furthermore, for those who propose that God allows terminal illness in children because he wants them to be with him in heaven, are in no position to discuss God's intentions, as they do not know him very well. Everything he stands for, everything about his character, everything he gives us and charges us to do, opposes this theory.

In his earthly ministry, we have no record of Jesus ever meeting a child he did not heal. When Jairus' daughter was dead, he did not say, "Good, she can be with her heavenly Father now, and I'll get to see her up there in a couple years too." He brought her back to her daddy. How silly we can be, because when children are on this earth, they are already with Jesus. They certainly do not need to go to heaven to be with him.

Indeed, all the many children who have crossed into the next life could not be happier, so why is this an issue? What is wrong with teaching that God wants another little angel in heaven, or that he just wants your baby? It is wrong because it is not true; Jesus does not want our children to die any more than we do. How easily our emotional musings lead us from truth.

We resort to other unbiblical explanations for premature death that contribute to the Christian community's doubt and unbelief. Unbelief restricts our ability to believe for miracles. It is disguised as noble Christian suffering or sacrifice.

A celebrated Christian author recently shared in a television interview that he was approached by a man who asked why his loved one had died so young. The grieving man revealed that several people had been saved at the funeral.

The author answered him, "That's why."

Someone other than Jesus had to die in order to save those people? My father also died suddenly at 47. I would like to find this Christian author and ask him why my father died, because no one got saved at his funeral.

Of course God can redeem a tragic death and people can get saved. Salvation for others is absolutely not the reason his loved one died, as the author impetuously deduced by his own warped justice. There is no scriptural basis for such a conclusion. There is only one person who had to die for the salvation of the people at that funeral, Jesus Christ. He needs no other human sacrifice in order to save. You do not have to sacrifice your life or the lives of your children through accidental death or disease so that others can be saved.

At 15, Courtney was rocked by the news about her friend Britanny. She had been in a car with her boyfriend when they were pulled over for a traffic violation. The boyfriend, who was scared of the police because of another offense, pulled out a gun, shot Brittany in the head and then shot himself. She looked like a tiny blonde princess in her casket of flowers. Several kids came up to receive Jesus as Lord at her funeral. I guess if Britanny's mother asked that Christian celebrity author why her daughter died, he would point to those at the altar and say, "That's why." Easy for him to be flippant. How irresponsible to handle the word of God so sloppily.

I am sure that this particular Christian celeb loves God and people, and that his heart is sincere and full of compassion, but that is no excuse. If we are in positions of leadership, then it is incumbent upon us to be disciples of God's word. We have no right to council based on our personal impressions, rationale or understanding. It is the word of God, and not our great intellectual musings or experience that has been given to teach, correct, rebuke and instruct.

God saved the kids at Brittany's funeral because he is a redeemer. He can take what was meant for harm and make it turn to something good. But he did not cause or desire the evil so he could do the good. Jesus does not need Satan. Let's not use God's good nature against him.

The dangerous thing about these false doctrines is not just the fact that they are cheap, offensive and insulting comfort for unfathomable loss. They are bad seeds yielding brittle, dead branches of doubt and unbelief. How conveniently the devil places this faith escape at the back door of our minds as we pray and believe for a terminal child. These sweet sounding sympathy card doctrines pollute our minds with lies that cripple our ability to fight for the lives of the sick children who rely on our spiritual fortitude in battle to bring them out of danger.

We can never really be sure, never really be convinced in our prayers because of the murky area of doubt we create by emotionally contrived healing theology. Our minds torment us, "God might have other plans... We don't always understand God's mysterious ways... He might want this baby in heaven with him..." Lies.

We cannot have faith with these trite sayings infiltrating our minds. Remember the Hebrew 11:1 definition of faith. It is the assurance of what you hope for. Faith is the evidence of what is not yet seen. It is knowing, without a shadow of a doubt.

Now faith is confidence in what we hope for and assurance about what we do not see. Hebrew 11:1

God's being mysterious is even a bogus charge. He is only mysterious to those who wish him to be so. He gave us a library of 66 books, hundreds of pages worth of mystery revealed. Virtually every mention of the mystery of God in the New Testament is a celebration of the mystery revealed. The mystery is Christ. There is nothing hidden. We have everything we need. You may want to seek God's will about what job to pursue, what class to take, what to buy for your friend's birthday, where to move, or who to marry. But, you do not need to seek God's will on things about which he has so irrefutably spoken and commanded --our salvation, healing, peace, joy and our eternal home. We should not be free to use his mysteriousness as a cop out for healing --since he himself is not mysterious about it.

Does that mean we know everything? Of course not. But the areas about which we claim, "mysterious," he is not. Even about his will for us which was mysterious until Christ, he clarifies,

No eye has seen, no ear has heard, no mind has conceived what God has prepared for those who love him.

Sounds like we'll never know!

Should we wait around to see what happens? No. because in the very next sentence we find that these matters about which no eye has seen, nor ear heard, nor mind conceived, has indeed been revealed by his Spirit!

...But God has revealed it to us by his Spirit. 2 Corinthians 2:9,10

Loving him is the stipulation to unlocking all the secrets for me. How do I love him again --especially if I don't feel like it? Jesus said, *"If you love me, you will obey my commands." John 14:15*

The whole thing is so simple and not mysterious that a child can understand it. He tells us exactly how it works and what he expects from us.

I believe that dangerous theology evolves from the delusive comfort we offer. Emotion motivated sympathy has seeded the Church with pop-doctrines about healing which undermine those who still need to resist the devil and disrupt his claims on their babies. Even in consoling those who have been deprived of their children, it is important to be true to God's word. It is safer for everyone and of more comfort. Express your sympathy with compassion through actions, prayers and tears.

Mourners need a friend more than an explanation. It is neither time to explain nor correct.

And the next time you pull something devil, there's gonna be hell to pay. I recount the story of Ellen's little nephew who lost the battle to cancer because I do not believe we can come to terms with the mechanics of this teaching if I present exclusively victorious healing testimonies. Unfortunately, for now, miraculous healing results do not represent most of our experiences. We have to make a strong resolve not to base our doctrines on our experiences, and not to let our experiences form our doctrines. We want the word of God to form our healing protocols, and for our experiences to line up to them.

It is important to examine wreckage to find out what went wrong, so it can be avoided the next time. The sheriff's department engaged in a meticulous examination of the wreckage of Chris' helicopter to diagnose the cause of the crash. This investigation by professionals offers valuable information that can help to avoid future tragedies. If a disaster occurs, we need to know all the details so we can figure out why it happened and how. There is nothing wrong with that. We may create speculative scenarios if we neglect such an inspection. If we ignore the evidence and fail to fix the problem, more sheriffs could lose their lives. We can learn by our mistakes --or not.

Usually, prayers for healing are not answered –or so it seems. Actually, every prayer for healing is answered and always has been. Should we accept no for an answer sometimes? No. The answer is never no and we should never take no for an answer. No is not a Biblical answer for a promise so foundational as healing. The answer was, is and always will be yes. In fact all the promises are yes.

No matter how many promises God has made, they are yes in Christ. 2 Corinthians 1:20

Healing was accomplished on the cross; it is a historical fact that cannot be reversed. *By his wounds you have been healed. 1 Peter 2:24* The incident took place. The consequences are for us to experience.

So how do we account for all those who are not healed? How do we account for all the testimonies about how loved ones were not cured?

This discrepancy between promise and experience is the reason we end up shaking our fists at God. We did not get what we asked for. We change the rules to make us or God look good. Did God really say, *"I am the Lord your healer"*? Did he really say, *"By his wounds you have been healed"*? The apparent discrepancy is that God promised and he did not deliver, so there must be a good reason.

The accurate assessment is that God delivered. It is I who skipped a step. I must not have signed for the package. Therein should be my point of focus, my part. The clog in the machinery is on my end, not his.

I never cease to be amazed at how offended Christians are at the prospect that it may be they who are culpable when healing is not manifested. Isn't it we who are journeying to be more like Jesus? When we fall in any area, isn't it we who need to get up? When we fall short, isn't it we who need to conform, reform and transform? Do these rules change for some reason when it comes to healing?

Healing failure should be no different from any other kind of failure. Let us learn from our mistakes, get up when we fall down, start it up when we stall out, and rebuild when we are in ruins --instead of resigning, surrendering and giving up.

A first string pro-quarterback fails to complete a touchdown pass that causes the team to lose the game. Should he learn from his mistake by studying the replays, working with his coach and showing up early for practice, or should he say that God must have wanted him to lose the game? He will lose his job if he says that.

An Olympic ice skater contends for the gold in her final round. She approaches the decisive moment of her performance, the feat on which all her hopes and dreams hinge. Like a snow bird, she lifts into the air and morphs into a furious glittering blizzard of spins. She lands into a statuesque glide to the eruptions of her parents and the world. She did it.

How many times did her little body come crashing down onto the rock hard ice? How many failures to land the trick? Hundreds? Thousands? And yet she did not relinquish her aspirations to a false doctrine dictating that in light of her many failures, she should submit to the possibility that it may not be God's will for her to succeed as a skater. Neither did she give up on her goals because she believed God was trying to teach her some kind of lesson in patience or love.

Indeed, her falls were lessons. She had hundreds of painful little teachings. But they were not God's attempt at teaching her some unrelated thing. They were thousands of examples of what not to do, how not to do them, and why not to do them. Ouchy. Yes, God wants us to learn lessons from our failures in receiving healing. He did not want her to fall. He wanted her to land.

He wants us to learn what not to do, what to do differently, to study the rules book, examine our form, consult our coaches. He wants us to know the mission at hand, healing, not some other unrelated issue.

He is not using sickness to teach a lesson about something else, like being on time for work or resisting a big sale. He obviously wants us to get this healing machinery working, or he would not have dedicated such a preponderance of scripture and modeling to it. No more cop outs or excuses, just buckling down for practice. We can make it work when we understand the importance of dedicating ourselves to the word of God, even in failure. In failure we are to be comforted, corrected and disciplined by God's word. We are not to be comforted by long sermons of benevolent thoughts and gentle pats. They provide no power and no wisdom to help anyone in any future attack.

Neither accidents nor sicknesses from which Paul was healed and protected, were the source of Paul's hardships. His troubles were not caused by anything other than persecution for his faith in Christ. They were humbling because of the strength of God that was given to him, strength that Paul could not have himself mustered given the severity of his troubles. It made Paul realize his own inadequacies, and more so, the incredible honor God gave him by showing up in his weakness. Humility brings honor, and honor is humbling.

Paul was not conceited despite the *"surpassingly great revelations"* that God gave him. Paul's persecutions revealed his insufficiency. He had no illusions of self-sufficiency.

To keep me from becoming conceited because of these surpassingly great revelations, there was given me a thorn in my flesh, a messenger of Satan, to torment me. Three times I pleaded with the Lord to take it away from me. But he said to me, "My grace is sufficient for you, for my power is made perfect in weakness." 2 Corinthians 12:7-9

Paul, just a few sentences earlier, boasted in a long list of persecutions. Now, he boasts all the more about his weaknesses, realizing it makes his endurance of extreme persecution even more obviously God's strength in him. He does not make a case that he is still weak. He boasts of human weakness because by all outward appearance he is divinely strong.

Therefore I will boast all the more gladly about my weaknesses, so that Christ's power may rest on me. That is why, for Christ's sake, I delight in weaknesses, in insults, in hardships, in persecutions, in difficulties. For when I am weak, then I am strong. 2 Corinthians 12:9-10

Here he sums up his thoughts, reiterating that his struggles make him strong. Before, after and while discussing his thorn, he speaks of strength in weakness. He frames the discussion of the thorn with lists of persecutions, the detailed list before and a summary after:

That is why, for Christ's sake, I delight in weaknesses, in insults, in hardships, in persecutions, in difficulties. 2 Corinthians 12:10

Paul identified his thorn, a demon, that continually attacked him in the listed persecutions. Unlike sickness, God does not promise to keep from us the things in Paul's lists. In other words, Paul's testimony is "I asked three times and God said, 'My grace is enough to take care of this,' and yes sir, I was delivered." It is not "I asked three times to remove it and God said, 'No.'"

It is a fallacious assumption we have that Paul asked three times for his thorn to be removed and God refused the request. No, he said, *"My grace is sufficient."* We erroneously assume it means God said no. His grace was indeed sufficient to deal with the thorn, because Paul was ultimately delivered from all the trouble the demon caused. Referring to all the persecutions and sufferings Paul endured, Paul concludes,

The Lord rescued me from all of them. 2 Timothy 3:11

Paul leaves no room for a case to be made that God refused delivering him from anything.

He has delivered us from such a deadly peril, and he will deliver us. 2 Corinthians 10:10

And again, *"But the Lord stood at my side and gave me strength, so that through me the message might be fully proclaimed and all the Gentiles might hear it. And I was delivered from the lion's mouth. The Lord will rescue me from every evil attack and will bring me safely to his heavenly kingdom." 2 Timothy 4:17-18*

Paul's thorn, the messenger from Satan that acted out in persecution after persecution, dealing blow after blow, was himself also being dealt blow after blow. Although we are assured the attacks of persecution by menacing demons and people hostile to the message of the gospel, we are also assured the delivering rescuing power that God's grace bestows on us without measure. The thorn was the tormenting messenger bringing so many attacks against Paul, as opposed to the disease that many insist.

Paul's intimate relationship with the Lord would prohibit his asking God to take a sickness or disease away. Why? Because Paul knew that is not how it works. His encounters with disease were like his Master's. Healing sickness was something you did, not a question or favor to be asked. Paul had many experiences with healing. His healing 'prayers' sounded like Jesus'. They were not questions or pleas.

"Get up!"
"Be opened."
"Be clean."
"Be healed."

It was not Paul's style or nature to ask if God would take away a disease or sickness. He understood the authority he had in Jesus' name. Even if he had deviated from his character this way, God reminded that his grace was sufficient to accomplish whatever Paul was asking. Jesus was all done. He was finished. He gave all the tools necessary.

Persecutions are a different kind of suffering, the kind we are meant to deal with. We are not meant to put up with sickness in the same way. We are to abolish sickness and ideally, are not to even get sick. That is the goal. It is not a good goal to never be persecuted.

Not being sick and confronting sickness was the motis operendi for Jesus and all the disciples. They did not ask and wait for answers. They commanded disease, fully confident in their contracts with heaven. It is a very pro-active format for healing that Jesus left for us to follow. He went up into heaven and sat down. Our turn.

Chapter 21

Do-It-Yourself Healing

If Jesus were to sum up Biblical healing theology in a phrase, I believe it would be, 'Do-It-Yourself.' How many times and in how many ways does he have to tell us what he expects for us to do regarding healing before we stop praying and begging for him to do it for us?

By his words and by his deeds, he trained us for action. What did he demonstrate for us on a regular basis --aside from teaching and preaching --aside from talking?

What was so routine for him that it is impossible to number the incidents in the gospels?

Because we want our daily lives to be reflections of his, we begin by looking at an overall summary of Jesus' daily life. A synopsis of Jesus' ministry is recorded by Matthew.

Jesus went throughout Galilee, teaching in their synagogues, preaching the good news of the kingdom, and healing every disease and sickness among the people. Matthew 4:23

Teaching, preaching and healing is what Jesus did. If he had an overall job description, that would be it. Since we are Christ's body on earth and imitators of his, then we too, are to go around teaching in their churches, preaching the good news of the kingdom, and healing...every 'spiritual and emotional' disease and sickness among the people? No, *every* disease and sickness among the people.

That is not spiritual, that is too physical! I can't heal every disease and sickness among the people; only Jesus can do that! Yes, and that is why he sent the Holy Spirit to do it through us.

He both showed us how to heal, and then on several occasions, commanded us to do so. We are not to just pray for it, we are to do it.

Paul and Barnabus, who were not Jesus himself, but the embodiment of some dang good preachers, showed us how it is done. A normal visit for them would be like this one to Iconium.

Paul and Barnabus spent considerable time there, speaking boldly for the Lord, who confirmed the message of his grace, by enabling them to do miraculous signs and wonders. Acts 14:3

It was Jesus' power, but by their hands. The believers in the brand new Church understood this, hence the prayer:

Enable your servants to speak your word with great boldness. Stretch out your hand to heal and perform miraculous signs and wonders through the name of your holy servant Jesus. Acts 4:29.30

They understood that healings, signs and wonders were their job, to be implemented through the name of Jesus on their lips and by the hands of Jesus in theirs. They did not spend their prayer time and effort asking God to do it; they spent their prayer time and effort asking God to do it through them. They remembered the gist of Jesus' teachings, 'Do-It-Yourself.'

'Do-It-Yourself' Verses:

1) *He called his Twelve disciples to him and gave them authority to drive out evil spirits and to heal every disease and sickness. Matthew 10:1*

2) *As you go, preach this message: "The kingdom of heaven is near." Heal the sick, raise the dead, cleanse those who have leprosy, drive out demons. Matthew 10:7,8*

3) *Go and make disciples of all nations, baptizing them in the name of the Father and of the Son and of the Holy Spirit, and teaching them to obey everything I have commanded you. Matthew 28:19,20*

4) And these signs will accompany those who believe: In my name they will drive out demons; they will speak in new tongues; they will pick up snakes with their hands; and when they drink deadly poison, it will not hurt them at all; they will place their hands on sick people, and they will get well. Mark 16:17,18

5) Then the disciples went out and preached everywhere, and the Lord worked with them and confirmed his word by the signs that accompanied it. Mark 16:20

6) When you enter a town and are welcomed, eat what is set before you. Heal the sick who are there and tell them, "The kingdom of God is near you." Luke 10:8,9

7) I have given you authority to trample on snakes and scorpions and to overcome all the power of the enemy; nothing will harm you. Luke 10:19

8) Anyone who has faith in me will do what I have been doing. John 14:12

9) Your enemy the devil prowls around like a roaring lion looking for someone to devour. Resist him. 1 Peter 5:8,9

The ball is in your court. We often think we are waiting on God, but he is waiting on us. It is as we build up our faith in Jesus through his word that we are able to implement these commissions. The best time to start is now.

As far as healing is concerned, his grace is sufficient. He says it is all done. He says, "I gave you everything you need; stop looking for more. Go into all the world --preach, heal and deliver. I'm sitting right up here to work with you to confirm my words by miracles wrought by my power through your hands."

Chapter 22

❧⚜☙

Will He Do Wonders Without You? Hail No

When the Israelites were slaves in Egypt, they needed a deliverer. At 40, Moses, having failed a rescue attempt for the Hebrews, found himself living his next 40 years leading sheep not armies, living in tents not palaces and married to a shepherdess not a princess. But once again, the Lord allured him with talk of a land of milk and honey. God said,

I have indeed seen the misery of my people in Egypt. I have heard them crying out because of their slave drivers, and I am concerned about their suffering. So I have come down to rescue them from the hand of the Egyptians and to bring them up out of that land into a good and spacious land, a land flowing with milk and honey Exodus 3:7-8

Surely Moses was happy about that. It was about time after all that God did something about his people!

"So now, go." The Lord continued.

"What?!" Moses must have looked frantically behind him. "What the heck?!"

"I am sending you to Pharaoh to bring my people the Israelites out of Egypt." Exodus 3:10

So who would go? God or Moses?

Both.

So I will stretch out my hand and strike the Egyptians with all the wonders that I (the Lord) will perform among them. After that, he will let you go.   Exodus 3:20

The Lord would perform wonders.

But take this staff in your hand so you (Moses) can perform miraculous signs with it. Exodus 4:17

Moses would perform wonders. What a good example of the Lord's supernatural working relationship with us.

Perform before Pharaoh all the wonders I have given you the power to do. Exodus 4:21

We are to perform the wonders with the power God gave us. We are the conduit. Power without a conduit is useless. God expects us to activate our faith with his power.

Even in their time of deliverance, the Israelites could not rely on Moses to do it all for them. They had to exercise their faith for salvation. They had to do something as an expression of their faith in order to avoid judgment, condemnation and death. They had until the tenth plague to get their theology straight. Until then they could spectate.

The first nine plaques were called down on the Egyptians by the faith and actions of Moses and Aaron.

1) BLOOD -All the water turned to rotting dead blood
2) FROGS -Frogs infested the houses, kitchens and beds
3) GNATS -Biting gnats gnawed the people and animals
4) FLIES -Dense clouds of flies filled their houses and land
5) LIVESTOCK PLAGUE -Disease killed the farm animals
6) BOILS -Festering boils on the people and animals
7) HAIL -Killer hail and lightening terrorized the nation

8) LOCUSTS -The land blanketed with swarming locusts that stripped every green thing

9) DARKNESS –Gross darkness haunted for three days

The Israelites were protected from all these nine plagues through no effort of there own. Not so with the tenth plague, the one that ignited their deliverance.

10) DEATH OF FIRST BORN

Escaping this one required something of them, It was not enough to say, "I am a Hebrew," anymore than it is enough to say, "I am a Christian." Labels mean nothing, only obedience.

Unlike the previous nine plagues, the people had to participate in their escape of this last plague, the one through which their deliverance would come. Escaping this plaque would be the first step to their deliverance and new life. They had to smear the doorframes of their houses with the blood of lambs or goats to set this plan of action in motion.

When the Lord goes through the land to strike down the Egyptians, he will see the blood on the top of the doorframe and will pass over that doorway, and he will not permit the destroyer to enter your houses and strike you down. Exodus 12:23

If we want Biblical blessing, favor, healing and deliverance, it is incumbent on us to obey --not just say.

Chapter 23

Be Aggressive & Possessive

It was about 3400 years ago, 1400 years before Christ, that the Israelites were living in the desert. After about a year from their exodus from Egypt, living in tents with their families, they were ready for a change. It was exciting at first, but they were definitely ready for their permanent homes.

Even though freedom was better than the bondage from which they came, they still complained all the time and wanted to go back to Egypt. Instead, they should have been looking forward to the Promised Land. This Promised Land represents for us all the promises that we are expected to claim and the enemies we should conquer. Yes, it requires effort on our parts.

The nomadic life was not a novelty any more; they were ready to go into the Promised Land. They needed a new start. They needed a new beginning. They needed a New Year's resolution.

We continue to make New Year's resolutions even though we know they do not work. Hope springs eternal. Everyone needs a fresh start sometimes. Remember when you were little and you went shopping with your mom for school supplies? You were all excited for school because you were going to do good and get all A's. Then, after a couple weeks everything fizzled.

For a fresh start, you assess your life and decide to change what is not working or start something better. That is the way the Israelites were feeling.

They had come out of Egypt, gotten the Ten Commandments,

reconnected with God, and moved into a ready position outside the Promised Land. Moses sent twelve men to scout out the land where only their distant forefathers had ever been. Moses wanted them to find out what it was like: the people, the soil, the vegetation, the cities, the fortresses...

Forty days they waited for this report.

We went into the land into which you sent us and it does flow with milk and honey. Here is its fruit. Numbers 13:27

This sounded great! They were used to dry dirt, sand and rocks. They had the fruit to verify the reports. A single cluster of grapes was so big that it hung on a pole between two of the men. They brought pomegranates and figs, heavenly for them to see that kind of abundance.

Then the twelve spies added,

But, the people who live there are powerful and the cities are fortified. We even saw the descendants of Anak (giants) there. Numbers 13:28

The spies all agreed about the goodness of the land and the dangers of the land.

The people were fine about everything, even the fortified cities, But when they mentioned the descendants of Anak, the people lost it, and this is where the twelve spies parted ways. About the conditions they agreed, on strategy they did not.

Caleb silenced the people before Moses and said, "We should go and take possession of the land for certainly we can do it." Numbers 13:30

Ten spies represented the sentiments of the people saying, "It's really beautiful, it's great but the descendants of Anak are there. There are fortified cities and we can't do it. We are scared." Only two of the spies, Caleb and Joshua said, "We can do this."

The other ten that had gone with them said. "We can't attack those people; they are stronger than we are." And they spread among the Israelites a bad report. "The land we explored devours those living in it. All the people we saw there were of great size. We saw the Nephilim there (the descendants of Anak come from the Nephilim)." Numbers 13:31-33

The bad report was not that there were giants! It was true; there were giants. The bad report was "We can't do it." It is not your circumstances, but how you react to them that is good or bad. The bad report to God isn't really even the cancer; it is the "We can't beat this."

The Nephilim, forefathers of the Anakites, were magnificently huge.

We seemed like grasshoppers in our eyes and we looked like grasshoppers to them. Numbers 13:33

The Nephilim were conservatively eight to nine feet tall. Like the tribal Pygmies in Africa, there are people groups of all sizes. The Nephilim were not an anomaly or victims of the condition giantitus, but were a race that have since died off. They populated much of the Promised Land. The King of Bashan, Og, was one of them. His iron bed was thirteen feet long.

Remember David and Goliath? Goliath was one of the descendants of the Nephilim. He was not the only giant, but by his time their numbers were depleted because Joshua and Caleb had killed most of them --along with the other enemies in the land.

Maybe Caleb and Joshua looked like grasshoppers to the giants but they were not grasshoppers in their own eyes. They were not intimidated.

We do NOT want to be among those who say:

"We saw the Promised Land, but Nephilim are there, and they are too powerful for us."

"I saw the promises of healing, but the spinal cord is completely severed, and it is too far gone."

"I saw the promises of healing, but it's stage four cancer,"

"I saw the promises of healing, but it's an incurable STD."

The same goes for provision.

"I see the promises for provision but the economy is bad, I have no job, I foreclosed on my house, there is no power, no food, no gas for the car . . . never mind, no car."

Caleb and Joshua separated themselves from the consensus, "We saw the Promised Land and we should take it. Yeah there are giants, yeah there are fortresses, but we want it. God promised it and we're gonna do it --with his direction, power and might."

The difference between Caleb and Joshua and the others was the confidence they had that God was going to go with them. They were willing to take the risk and do something scary. We can stay safe in the desert and go no where, or battle against the big scary stuff, and really get places.

Chapter 24

"Feed My Baby to a Crocodile"

Too cowardly to advance on their enemies and claim their land, the Israelites opted instead to stay put and dream about the good ol' days.

And retire in their own ash heaps.

The Israelites said to them, "If only we had died by the Lord's hand in Egypt! There we sat around pots of meat and ate all the food we wanted, but you have brought us out into this desert to starve this entire assembly to death." Exodus 16:3

Only a little more than a year before, they were backed up to the Red Sea by Pharaoh's army, probably the mightiest military force in the whole world at that time. The entire army and its officers charged the families at the water's edge, but God completely wiped them out. Every chariot, horse and soldier was destroyed in the Red Sea. Yet now the Israelites were saying, "Why is the Lord bringing us up here only to fall by the sword?" How quickly they forgot what God did for them as they obediently fled Egypt (with great wealth) and advanced into the Red Sea. . . for starters.

Our wives and our children will be taken as plunder. It would be better for us to go back to Egypt. Numbers 14:3

Better in Egypt? How quickly we forget. Let me give you just one example of what it was like for them as slaves in Egypt. In Florida, our alligators get to be Godzilla sized, but they do not compare to those in Egypt. Egypt is home to the most terrifying, Nile Crocodiles, second only to the Saltwater Crocodile, which is only negligibly larger.

The largest alligator that has ever been measured in Florida came out of Lake Monroe at 14 feet 6 inches with the sprawling girth of a hippo. A terrifying spectacle. It is against the law for us to feed alligators so they don't consider humans to be food sources. A Nile Crocodile can reach up to 21 feet and hold a hippo in its stomach. . . and it has a taste for human flesh.

While the Hebrews were slaves, Pharaoh, who was threatened by their growth in numbers and strength, commanded his officers to take their newborn boys and throw them into the Nile River, the feeding grounds of these crocodiles.

A mother could not keep her own baby. Soldiers took cartloads of screaming babies reaching for their moms, to throw them to these beasts. The Israelites would rather have gone back to that kind of oppression than trust God to inherit a beautiful and dangerous land. He had proven by so many miraculous events that he was fighting for them --parting the sea, drowning their enemies --water from a rock, food from the sky. . . He kept hundreds of thousands of families alive in a fruitless wasteland.

Joshua and Caleb were distraught. This alluring land beckoned them. They addressed the entire Israelite assembly.

The land we passed through and explored is exceedingly good. If the Lord is pleased with us, he will lead us into that land the land flowing with milk and honey and will give it to us. Numbers 14:7,8

The reason God was not pleased was because they were saying "We don't want go. We're scared! We don't believe you God! You're not really going protect us. You're not going to do what you promised!" They deemed him a liar by their refusal to follow him. The Bible says that God is not a man that he can lie. It goes on to ask, does he make promises and not keep them?

God is not a man, that he should lie, nor a son of man, that he should change his mind. Does he speak and then not act? Does he promise and not fulfill? Numbers 23:19

No. He is not a man that he can lie, yet they were calling him a liar. So Joshua pleaded with them.

Do not rebel against the Lord and do not be afraid of the people of the land. We will swallow them up. Their protection is gone. The Lord is with us. Do not be afraid of them. Numbers 14:9

Joshua was not afraid because he knew the Lord was with him. Because Joshua was not afraid, God was with him. Because he was not afraid, his enemies' protection was gone. No matter how big those giants were, their protection was gone. History tell us, Biblical and otherwise, that Joshua and Caleb with their families, and no one else, did get to go to the Promised Land. Why?

...Because my servant Caleb has a different spirit and follows me wholeheartedly. Numbers 14:24

God let him in. Because Joshua had a different spirit and followed wholeheartedly, he also got in. The ten spies who chickened out were stricken with a plague and died in the desert. Pali, Gahdi, Nahbi are some of the names that died with them. No one remembers them. The names Joshua and Caleb live on in thousands of boys. Who names their kid Pali?

The Lord told the rest of the congregation that they would have to stay in the desert 40 more years, one year for every day that was spent spying out the land --until all of the adults were dead. The children they confessed would be plunder for their enemies --they were going to enjoy the land after their parents' generation all died out.

Joshua replaced Moses to lead the people into the land. After the 40 years was complete, it was time once again for them to go in. God assured Joshua,

Every place where you set your foot will be yours. Deuteronomy 11:24

Joshua would have a lot of work to do. Every place, every promise where you set your foot, God is going to give it to you. That means you are to move. You cannot just sit there. Go. Does that mean everything we do, every where we go, God will give it to us? God will bless us? He will give us success? Yes, provided we are in the promised places. We have to be laboring, treading and working among promises of God.

At the beginning of the Book of Joshua it says,

No one will be able to stand up against you all the days of your life. As I as with Moses so I will be with you. I will never leave you nor forsake you. Joshua 1:5

That is a promise. Again in the New Testament it says,

I will never leave you, I will never forsake you. Hebrews 13:5

That's a promise. You can count on it. God is not a man that he can lie. To Joshua he said,

Be strong and very courageous. Be careful to obey all the law my servant Moses gave you; do not turn from it to the right or to the left, that you may be successful wherever you go. Do not let this Book of the Law depart from your mouth; meditate on it day and night, so that you may be careful to ...

To what? To keep it in your mouth? To say it? To think about it? No, that you may be careful to... DO IT!

...to do everything written in it. Then you will be prosperous and successful. Joshua 1:7,8

If you believe it, you will do it. Do God's word. Don't be confused. Jesus is the word. You can get all your instruction in him. Connect with him through the written word, prayer and listening. You know what? If you do, you will be prosperous and successful.

Do you know that if a famous person writes a book about how to be prosperous or successful he will almost surely be on the New York Times Bestseller list? There are books and books on how to be prosperous and successful, but the secret is all right here:

Do not let this book depart from your mouth, meditate on it day and night so that you may be careful to do everything written in it. Then you'll be prosperous and successful. Have I not commanded you? Be strong and courageous. Do not be terrified, do not be scared. Joshua 1:8-9

If you take action and fearlessly go after the promises, they will be yours. If you are sick and you go after the healing promises, they will be yours. The Bible is over a thousand pages of promises and guidance for our lives. It speaks of dreamy ground to possess. He has given it to you. It belongs to you, as long as you do not stay in the desert. You have to go get it -- you have to cross the river, face all the giants and conquer.

If you are sick, trust him and go after the healing promises. You will be healed if you do not give up.

If you look back, give up or lose heart, you are a slave. If you stay and do nothing, you die in the desert.

Trudge forward, learn his great plan for you, and do it --giants or no giants. It takes more than a resolution, more than a statement of intent. Do your homework, get your supplies ready, do your weapons testing. Practice with your sword of the Spirit, the word of God.

Take the helmet of salvation and the sword of the Spirit, which is the word of God. Ephesians 6:17

I don't know what you need, but you will know. That is between you and God. He will tell you what you need. The enemies of the Old Testament are a foreshadowing of our enemies now. Who are they? They are probably not physical giants.

The Bible says our enemies are principalities, evil spirits in the world, demons. Sickness is our enemy. Poverty is an enemy. Depression is an enemy. Alcoholism is an enemy. Fear is an enemy. How many times does God say not to be afraid?

Make an assessment of your life progress, where you are now and where you want to be. No one wants their life to be wasted. This can be a new beginning, but you need help, supplies and a strategy.

I pray the Holy Spirit will tell you what he wants for you. He said he would never leave you or forsake you. There have been friends and even family members that have forsaken and hurt you, but not Jesus. He is closer than a brother. There is no one that can be closer to you than Jesus. He is in your room at night.

I pray that you would discover one thing that he puts his finger on and says, "I want this from you. I'm asking you to believe me and trust me to fight for this. I will be with you. I will help you. I will not leave you alone."

Over and over in the gospels, Jesus said to fishermen, "Follow me," and to a tax collector, "Follow me."

When he told one guy, "Follow me," he said that he wanted to go bury his father first. Jesus told him,

Let the dead bury the dead, you come and follow me. Matthew 8:22

He told several other people, "Follow me." That is all he wants from us –is to follow him as a priority above all else.

Like watching a horror movie on a comfy couch with a loved one, it feels safe around giants with Jesus around.

Chapter 25

※

Mega Pastor Mega Death

One afternoon, I had a meeting with the pastor of a mega-church in town to discuss my healing seminars. He preached and believed in healing but had some issues from my website that he wanted to address. From behind the closed doors of his spacious, eclectic office, he started down his list of concerns. The items centered around:

> 1) my statement that churches would have standing room only if the people were moving in supernatural power, and

> 2) my dogmatic approach to healing.

I was open to correction from this man who was far more educated than I, and who also had increasing numbers of available seats in his church. But first, as a mega-church pastor, did you not read *Boundaries*? Even if not, is it not common Christian sense you should not have a woman alone in your office with the door shut?

As soon as I perceived that I would have to subscribe to his watered down healing doctrine --that God does not always choose to heal, and that we would all probably have to die by some cursed illness, I knew I would not be doing any workshops at his church.

I cringed as he leaned forward in his chair, pointing to the world outside, "What are you gonna do, clear out the entire wing at the hospital!?"

"Uhh…no?"

I felt like I was in the principle's office.

"Next gig," I thought to myself.

Then he dropped the real bomb. His wife had breast cancer and they both prayed and believed, the whole church prayed and believed, even a blockbuster healing evangelist prayed and believed --and nothing.

He demanded an answer from me. "My wife still has breast cancer and she is not healed. If she were standing here right now, what would you say to her!?"

Sheepishly I answered, "I...I would never say she is not healed."

Trying to be extra respectful I was not going to push my point, but since he required my scriptural back up for saying that, I let him have it.

He was pierced for our transgressions, crushed for our sins, the punishment for our peace was upon him and by his wounds we are healed. Isaiah 53:5

(We are healed)

And --

By his wounds you have been healed. I Peter 2:24

(You have been healed)

This is exalted above all other facts and truths. This pastor was conflicted because he knew this word was true, but he remained unwilling to change his stance because of his experience. He was not fully convinced that his wife had been healed. This was no time to give up or give in. It was time to persevere in the truth, to be steadfast. She has been healed.

Until our bodies line up with that truth, we should press on to grow in faith, no matter who prayed and believed.

Renew a steadfast spirit within me. Psalm 51:12

This common belief among Christians is really unbelief and stems from a misunderstanding of what healing really is. We need to clarify it so we do not give up when our flesh is unresponsive to the word of God.

Q: If it is God's will for everyone to be healed, then why are not all healed?

A: Healing is
1) Universally provided (by his sacrifice/wounds)
2) Individually appropriated (by our faith)

While it is true that we are all universally healed by Jesus' wounds, it is only by faith that the healing is transmitted into our bodies. Faith is what we need. Faith is what is needed to make the physical change and, to a person, we all need more.

The same answer applies to the question:

Q: If it is God's will for everyone to be saved, then why are not all saved?

A: Salvation is
1) Universally provided (by his sacrifice/blood)
2) Individually appropriated (by our faith)

We are universally saved by Jesus' blood, but we can only experience this salvation if we believe. Everyone who is now in hell was saved, but did not experience it. We have to implement our salvation by faith.

The father of an epileptic boy approached Jesus, asking him if he could drive a demon from his son because the disciples could not.

The dad pleaded, *"If you can do anything, take pity on us and help us."* Mark 9:22

As pitiful as it was, this boy convulsing on the ground, flailing and foaming at the mouth --pity was not the transducer for healing power. Jesus corrected the father's prayer.' It was bad enough that the boy's father questioned Jesus' ability by saying "if," but that was not even what alarmed Jesus about his petition. It was the "take pity on us and do something" part that Jesus addressed. God's pity does not bring his power. What an obnoxious pity party we should all have if that were the case. Those never work. An aggressive expression of faith is what brings God's power.

Jesus threw it back in his face, reproving the dad's perspective, *"'If you can?' everything is possible to him who believes."* Mark 9:23

It was not a matter of Jesus' ability to perform but the man's ability to believe. Jesus placed the responsibility for change back on the father. It should be clear to us that we are to receive by faith the things which Jesus has already provided for us.

If something is not happening, it is not because he could not or would not, it is because we did not. He wants everyone to be sozo'd (saved and healed) but he also wants us to learn how to obtain those benefits. This was not about what Jesus could do but what the boy's father could do.

God not willing that any should perish, but that all should come to repentance. 2 Peter 3:9

Even though God's will is clearly universal salvation, man does not have to comply with it.

If anyone's name was not found written in the book of life, he was thrown into the lake of fire. Revelation 20:15
It is not enough that God is unwilling for any to perish, His desire for everyone to be saved does not ensure their salvation. They have to want it and go after it. That is why Paul said:

It is by grace you have been saved (universal) through faith (individual)" Ephesians 2:8

Everyone has been saved by grace, but it is only through faith that it is realized in a person's life. Jesus saved everyone; everyone does not benefit. Jesus healed everyone; everyone does not benefit. "I prayed and the answer was no." This is a common misconception.

Therefore I tell you, whatever you ask for in prayer, believe that you have received it, and it will be yours. Mark 11:24

1) Pray, 2) Believe 3) Receive

We are so quick to give up because we think praying is a one step thing we throw up to God. It is really a two way conversation, the communication necessary for a rewarding relationship. As in any healthy relationship, the communication is a process to which we must dedicate ourselves. It requires tenacity, perseverance and discipline on our part. When we are trusting God for anything, it requires more than just repeating a request. Mark 11:24 emphasizes the believing part after prayer in order to receive what we are asking for.

Matthew says 'if.'

> *If you believe, you will receive whatever you ask for in prayer.*
> Matthew 21:22

I like Matthew's way of saying it because it gives 'believing' the preeminence. Believing is the key to getting what you ask for. It is the condition. Asking is not the key to receiving, no matter how many times you ask, and no matter how many people you get to ask for you.

Making an effort to believe more will get us the results that God wants us to have. He is always agreeable to his word. We need to be also.

When the father of the boy with seizures complained that the famous disciples could not heal his boy, Jesus said, *"Bring him to me."* It was not over.

Just because the mega-church pastor had a world renowned healing evangelist pray for his wife to no avail, did not mean his faith journey was over.

We are healed by our *faith* in his *wounds*.

It takes faith and wounds.

Chapter 26

No Matter How Grim

Hope does not disappoint --if you hope in God's promise and if you persevere --no matter how grim the circumstances.

Daddy's Girl is a true story of a respected and wealthy man, a member of the religious elite in an institution that was intimidated and threatened by Jesus' power. Eventually, they would kill Jesus because of it. But this man, one of them, would find himself parting their company, in desperation.

He woke up, still kneeling by her bed, still holding her hand and hoping for a moment that this was just a terrible nightmare. Instead, his belly churned as his eyes focused on his wife holding a spoonful of broth to his little girl's lips, "Please baby."

Their only daughter was sick. She had stopped eating days before. Her face was hollow. Her once plump pink cheeks had become flat and grey…Daddy's girl… her arms were so skinny. He would have rather awoken in hell.

He had exhausted every doctor and every medicine. Every scripture, every ritual and every prayer only marked her further decline. All the powers of his religion were idle. Was there anything left he could do, anything he could give? His mind tormented him, demanding a solution, but neither his life nor his death could do anything to help his princess.

As a religious leader in the community, people always came to him for answers and spiritual guidance. For his own child, he had no answers and no guidance. He felt forsaken, lonely and forgotten.

Her tummy was sunken, her once dancing brown eyes were dull and unresponsive. Her breaths were shallow. He would give everything he owned, his very life if she would just take one tiny sip. His girl was so sick, listless. She was.... she was....he couldn't think it.

He remembered something. It was something that he would never have considered until he saw the cravings of death on his baby girl's face. His esteemed position in society, his spiritual authority, his good name, meant nothing to him anymore. His wife knew what he was thinking as he stood to his feet.

He whispered into his daughter's ear. He would never leave her, he would never forsake her --and yet leaving now would be the hardest thing he had ever done. But he walked away from his daughter's deathbed, for a hope.

Through tears everything was a blur as he ran out of the house. He shouldn't leave her now of all times; she was fading fast. This was when she needed her daddy the most. What if she was scared? What was he doing? He was confused, running. Did he abandon her? What if she was calling for him? What if she thought he abandoned her? What if he wasn't there when she...he could not think of that.

The ground escaped under his feet, everything was confused -- even the reports and rumors swirling in his head --about a healer. He and his colleagues had laughed and mocked about him, but everything was different now. He cared nothing about his associates, his position, reputation or career. He ran faster.

He stopped at a crowd waiting by the edge of the lake. He pushed through until he got to the water's edge. Immediately he knew which one he was. He ran and fell down at his feet, no longer an esteemed and competent religious ruler, but a frantic, broken man. He <u>surrendered everything to this hope</u>, this man of miracles.

For this hope he risked living the rest of his life being taunted with the thought of forsaking his daughter as she exhaled her last breath He risked the agony of imagining her panicking eyes searching for him as she departed the safe world he had provided her. Jairus believed. He could not have exercised more faith than this.

Yes, he 'threw himself to the ground' as the Greek language describes it, as in devotion and reverence; he fell prostrate as one would before a high ranking person or divine being, as one approaches with a petition.

Seeing Jesus, the synagogue ruler fell at his feet and pleaded earnestly with him, his face to the dirt, "My little daughter is dying. Please come and put your hands on her so that she will be healed and live."

What would be the response? So many needy people were pressing toward him with so many demands, and there was no time for all of that. Jairus was stunned when he realized the teacher agreed to come.

So Jesus went with him. Jairus wanted to grab his hand and run ahead of the crowd; it felt like they were moving in a cumbersome fog. All he could see was his little girl's face. Faster, faster his mind screamed at him.

Instead of going faster, the teacher stopped and asked who touched him. One of his followers reminded him that all the people were pressing against him, but he kept looking around to see who had done it, and kept insisting that no, someone touched him, because he felt power going out from him.

The girl's father pressed his hands to his forehead "My baby, my baby we're coming -- hold on, wait for us, wait for us, baby please."

Who was this woman detaining them, crying and trembling on the ground like an old begger? She was going on and on -- would it ever end? He hoped it was finally over because he heard the teacher say that her faith healed her and to go in peace.

He could hardly refrain from pulling Jesus' sleeves and running. Could he endure this delay? Everything in him was driving him to his baby's side and to abandon this dulling hope. He chose to keep trusting.

But then, while Jesus was still speaking, a dreadful sight for Jairus, some men from his house approached with ashen faces.

"Your daughter is dead," they said. "Don't bother the teacher anymore."

This was a bad report. The messengers were not malicious, but well-intentioned and broken-hearted. Jairus was paralyzed at their words and the instructions of death, "Don't bother the teacher anymore. It's too late."

The teacher overheard the report. Ignoring what they said, Jesus told the synagogue ruler, "Don't be afraid; just believe and she will be healed."

Jairus chose the Carpenter's instruction –do not be afraid of this report and believe. He chose hope because of the person who was promising. The teacher parted with the crowd, allowing only his three friends to follow, Peter, James and John.

Earlier when Jairus had left the house, it had been still and quiet. Now distant sounds of wailing called him. There was commotion, loud moaning and crying. His once commanding presence gone, Jairus could not have functioned without the teacher's controlling the crowds the way he did.

When they came to the house, Jesus went in and said to them, "Why all this commotion and wailing? The child is not dead but asleep."

But they laughed at him, knowing that she was dead. The sight of the dead child stunned her father. She was gone. Her spirit had departed.

Before she got sick, Jairus never imagined there would be a time he would cling to every word, every directive, every glance of this wandering preacher.

Everyone was made to leave the room except Jairus, the girl's mother, Jesus, Peter, James and John. The mourners loved her but had no vision for this. <u>The unbelief had to leave the room –</u> and the stillness was dreadful.

The teacher took her by the hand and said to her, "Little girl, I say to you, get up!"

Her spirit returned. Her black lashes fluttered and color rushed into the skin. Her anxious chocolate eyes found her daddy and immediately the girl stood up and walked around. Her parents were astonished.

The teacher told them to give her something to eat. His command was sweeter than honey.

Jairus' daughter came back from the dead, and the days that followed were the happiest days of his life ––preparing meals and snacks for a little girl with a ravenous appetite.

From Mark 5 and Luke 8

Chapter 27

Sitting In An Open Prison Cell

Lies and error keep us in bondage. We waste away in dungeons, the doors of which, unbeknownst to us, have been unlocked.

A poor man who is unaware of a large trust fund in his name will stay poor. He is really a rich man living in squalor because someone has successfully withheld valuable information from him, like an account number. He will also stay in poverty if he gets the information but lacks the perseverance to get to the bank.

Most people, myself included, have subscribed to lies and erroneous teachings, like those regarding Paul's thorn. Because we have read books and heard sermons but never really looked at it for ourselves, some of the most popular and I believe, Biblically unfaithful and damaging teachings on Paul's thorn are:

3 LIES about Paul's thorn that steal faith for healing:

1. Paul's thorn was a disease of some sort, an eye disease, perhaps a wasting Oriental eye disease

2. Paul asked three times for the thorn to be taken away but the Lord would not.

3. Your disease or disability may be your thorn that God will not remove.

Even though I believe there is no credible evidence that Paul was sick in this instance, such a condition would not be the insidious thing about these fallacies. In fact, Paul's being sick would be as normal as if he had sinned --which I'm sure he did from time to time. But in the case of his thorn being a sickness, it provides the necessary condition for an attempt to prove that

    A) God did not heal him and

    B) God similarly, may not heal us.

With facts as evidence, I argue that he was not sick in the first place and was not even asking to be healed from a disease.

The purveyors of this teaching are in a lose-lose situation because even if Paul were sick here, God healed him. This is indicated in three separate testimonies:

1) *You, however, know all about my teaching, my way of life, my purpose, faith, patience, love, endurance, persecutions, sufferings – what kinds of things happened to me in Antioch, Iconium and Lystra, the persecutions I endured. Yet the Lord rescued me from all of them. 2 Timothy 3:10-11*

The Lord rescued Paul from ALL his sufferings. Thorns too?

2) *The Lord will rescue me from every evil attack and will bring me safely to his heavenly kingdom. 2 Timothy 4:18*

The Lord rescued Paul from EVERY evil attack. Even thorns?

3) *He has delivered us from such a deadly peril, and he will deliver us. On him we have set our hope that he will continue to deliver us. 2 Corinthians 1:10*

As always with Paul, the focus of his suffering is persecution. It is not just suffering for being miserable's sake. There is a reason and a purpose for Christian suffering.

You do not have to be a Christian to suffer cancer or epilepsy.

You do have to be a Christian to suffer the persecution Paul and Jesus warned of.

In fact, everyone who wants to live a godly life in Christ Jesus will be persecuted. 2 Timothy 3:12

Again, if Paul's thorn were a sickness, he would engage all the resources that he did for everyone else's sicknesses, not ask God to do something. At no time in the gospels or in the Book of Acts did healings come because Jesus and the disciples asked God to take away the sicknesses. They knew their authority over disease and demons, and they used it.

Paul claimed these promises over many people and would certainly have done the same for himself, were he faced with a disease.

The reason Paul did not handle his thorn in this manner is because he was *not* sick or demon-possessed, but was under the battering of demon-inspired harassment and intense persecutions, something that won't ever totally cease --till heaven.

Chapter 28

Surrender Your Wheelchairs!

The ramifications of teaching that Paul had a sickness from which he was not healed are devastating for the successful operation of the Modern Church.

It defuses her from destroying the devil's work.

It excuses her timidity in the face of raging fevers and deadly diseases that Jesus told her unequivocally to heal.

It provides that one neat little escape for us when believing God for healing. Just like a little hole in a dam, all the water rushes to that one spot and soon bursts the mighty wall.

If the great Apostle Paul had a horrible disease that God would not heal, then who do we think we are? Obviously, if the lauded Apostle Paul could not get victory over a disease, then should we expect to be delivered from our own tormenting thorn-diseases? If Paul had to be denied, shouldn't we expect the same? After all, I tell my kids, "Sometimes you just have to take no for an answer."

Does that mean if I had the power to heal my son of a deadly staph infection, I might not, because it might not be my will to do so? Hmm. . . I imagine I would think, "I don't know --a nasty, flesh eating bacteria might teach him a lesson or two, good idea." That sounds a little like Satan.

God is no less willing to heal us than we are our own children.

The truth is that Paul was not denied healing and we are not either. The fallacy that God says no sends us down all kinds of dead ends. What is the motivation for the false teachings that bring us to false conclusions about Paul's thorn? For some it is ignorance and others laziness, but for many it is religious, Pharisaical pride.

They would never admit their thoughts aloud, "If I, a great theologian, priest, pastor, seminary professor cannot heal my cancer, crippling arthritis, degenerative multiple sclerosis, not even a head ache --then it is my thorn. Yes because I the Great, am on the level of Apostle Paul."

It is so tempting to linger here telling story after story of church elders who tell people they cannot be healed because of sin or God's grander scheme --anything to take the pressure off their inability to do it. The religious spirit is not motivated to inspire for healing or trouble-shoot for a sick person's cure, but only to preserve the holy image. If a religion-bound man has a sickness, he can boast that it is his thorn, and be equivalent to Paul.

How offensive it was that they who were at the pinnacle of prestige both for their education and religious piety, were out-shined and overshadowed by the powerful supernatural feats of dirty, uneducated fishermen, tax collectors, waiters and even a carpenter.

This is the religious pride that exists today. How can a long-haired tattooed kid with piercings and no formal religious training preach a dynamic sermon, heal a broken wrist, become a pastor, be known for miracles, and have the reverence of the masses? How can he be greater than I, an executive presbyter, professor of theology who spent twelve years in seminary, obtaining multiple impressive doctorates in divinity?

It is hard for some religious people to realize that true greatness will only come from their smallness. A Baptist was best known for that. Jesus said of him,

Among those born of women there has not risen anyone greater than John the Baptist." Matthew 11:11

That may be because John did not have such an opinion of himself. He thought of his life mission in terms of smallness.

He must increase, but I must decrease. John 3:30

And so John was great.

Paul's thorn controversy is more an indictment on the religious of our day than it is a bona-fide theological dilemma. The quandary for the academic religious is that their one little holdout for dismissing healing, Paul's thorn, cannot withstand conflicting scripture or the life of Christ.

If they can dissuade followers from believing that healing is God's adamant will, and that it is an essential part of the atoning work of Christ, then they do not have to explain their lack of fruit in the signs and wonders department. Pride.

They spend so much time and energy picking through scriptures to amend them to fit their personal extra-Biblical agendas. If they would spend as much time taking Jesus at his word as they do complicating it, their followers might have some testimonies to share on Sunday morning.

Perhaps they would have church members canceling surgeries and surrendering wheelchairs to the altar.

Chapter 29

Satan Pain in the Neck

There was given me a thorn in my flesh, a messenger of Satan, to torment me. 2 Corinthians 12:7

In the Bible, 'thorn' is used exclusively as either a piece of wood, a literal thorn, or as slang for a depraved personality or group, the way we refer to someone as a pain in the neck or thorn in our side. In Ezekiel, Judges and Numbers, thorns are Israel's bad neighbors.

No longer will the people of Israel have malicious neighbors who are painful briers and sharp thorns. Ezekiel 28:24

Micah speaks of a wicked people group as a thorn hedge.

The best of them is like a brier, the most upright worse than a thorn hedge. Micah 7:4

The scripture's equating those with bad character to thorns offers a clue to Paul's use of the term to describe the evil spirit that tormented him. Paul's mastery of the Old Testament explains his proclivity to use OT lingo.

So, thorn to Paul was either an actual piece of wood that was sent to be stuck in his side, or an evil personality. If he were impaled with wood, I am sure Paul would have removed it. It is reasonable to assume it was the wicked personality, especially since he said it was. Paul was explicit; the thorn was a messenger.

Messenger is translated from the Greek 'aggelos.' Really, it was this messenger or aggelos that Paul was asking to be removed. Aggelos is translated 179 times in the New Testament as angel, and 7 times as messenger. Every time aggelos is used, it is for the personality of either an angelic envoy or a human. It is never used metaphorically, allegorically or symbolically for anything like a sickness. Paul even describes the mission of the aggelos.

And to keep me from being puffed up and too much elated by the exceeding greatness of these revelations, there was given me a thorn in the flesh, a messenger of Satan, to rack and buffet and harass me, to keep me from being excessively exalted. 2 Corinthians 12:7-8

Paul used the known phrase thorn in the flesh to describe the menacing nature of the messenger (angel of Satan) who was causing his predicaments. This should have prevented any confusion. Paul was concise and on task when he described the culprit of his persecutions. He was not suddenly being metaphorical about disease after a long passage about specific persecutions. If it were an eye disease he would have said so. Apostle Paul was a straight talker.

As to the job this evil deviant was sent to perform? Once again, no need for conjecture, Paul tells us plainly.

There was given me a thorn in my flesh, a messenger of Satan, to torment me. 2 Corinthians 12:7

Clearly this tormenter was sent to persecute Paul, and if you need specifics, I refer you again to his comprehensive list of torments in 2 Corinthians 11:23-28 (pages 206-207). As hard as you might look, you will not find a disease.

The Greek word that is used for 'torment,' or 'buffet' as King James translates is 'kolaphizō.' It is used four other times in the New Testament. All five usages of kolaphizō translated torment, buffet, even harass, are in the context of persecution, not of disease or demon possession. The original language has to be manipulated and nuanced in several places in this text in order to concoct the notion that Paul was incurably sick from something.

A straight, contextual read will not lead to such a conclusion. But, if you hear that teaching enough, you will believe it.

Most teachers pass along this popularized theory about Paul's thorn's being a sickness without researching. It's conjecture at best or pride at the worst. Throughout history, man has assumed many things to be true because of effective marketing, propaganda, false assumptions, charismatic leaders and even just plain old repetition. Repetition of a lie will cause it to ingratiate itself to our core values if we are not careful. We can be thoroughly convinced, convicted and hence passionate -- about a lie.

If you tell a big enough lie and tell it frequently enough, it will be believed. -Adolf Hitler

Some U.S. politicians have gained rock star status by repeating attractive phrases which appeal to the human quest for meaning and purpose. Rather than substantive solutions based on the facts and the spirit and letter of the Founding Documents, their followers are content with emotional bumper sticker promises. These sound bites provide cover for the real agenda, one which ultimately costs their freedom. Whatever policies these political geniuses harbor will be enacted once they have climbed to power. Vacuous mantras have been the catalyst to the rise to power of many leaders whose intentions are to be served, not to serve, to control, not to be controlled.

What keeps us safe from being swept up with the masses in inspirational, feel good hogwash?

The truth, Jesus. He is the truth. The slogans and speeches are charged with passion, but what is the truth? Always hold everything up to the word of God, the only reliable standard for truth. Obedience to that word is the only thing that will bring blessing and freedom. Be on the alert for teachings that are promoted and accepted just because they are familiar --like Paul's thorn teaching.

Such deceptions are usually promulgated by people who may have perfectly good motives but they themselves have been duped by the repetition either coming down through the generations, academia or even pop culture.

Think of how heartily children believe in non-existent things like Santa Claus and Easter Bunny just because everyone tells them they exist, talking about them year after year, over and over. They believe it with all their hearts because of the influence of parents, television, stores, schools and even church. Whether you like Santa or not; is total sensory brainwash. Hogwash.

Hitler was right about lying, and although most politicians never reach his level of depravity, repetition can create an assumption of truth. It is a psychological phenomenon that kings, dictators and even presidents exploit maliciously to their benefit.

Whether the motive is malevolent, innocent or ignorant, the result of believing lies can prove deadly.

God gave no one cancer for their thorn.

Why an Eye Disease?

Many theologians hypothesize that Paul's thorn was not a demon as he said, but instead an eye disease, the Oriental one I mentioned. These are the two verses they use to form their opinion:

1) You welcomed me as if I were an angel of God,.....if you could have done so, you would have torn out your eyes and given them to me. Galatians 4:14-15

2) See what large letters I use as I write to you with my own hand! Galatians 6:11

The context of the first verse requires that Paul did have a problem. He describes it in the previous verse.

As you know, it was because of an illness that I first preached the gospel to you. Even though my illness was a trial to you, you did not treat me with contempt or scorn. Instead, you welcomed me as if I were an angel of God, as if I were Christ Jesus himself...if you could have done so, you would have torn out your eyes and given them to me. Galatians 4:13-15 (from the NIV 1984, the version from which I usually quote)

The Greek word for 'illness' here is 'astheneia' It means want of strength, weakness or infirmity. The word appears 24 times in the Bible. In the gospels and Acts it is often used for sickness or disease. Of the 24 biblical appearances, Paul used it most, 16 times (assuming he wrote Hebrews).

Once, Paul used 'astheneia' for Timothy's weak stomach to advise Timothy to take a little wine (as opposed to a lot of wine). Once, he used the word to describe his thorn trials that we are currently diagnosing and the rest of the 14 times he used it to describe a general weakness of the flesh inherent in the human condition, not sickness or disease. In the context of Paul's use of language, it makes the most sense that he used the word 'astheneia' as he normally did, and not to describe illness, but weakness.

'Atheneia' is translated into English language Bibles as either illness or weakness. Because of the historical context, The New International Version 1984 incorrectly translates the word to be illness, as does the New Living Translation and the New American Standard.

Astheneia is accurately translated 'weakness of the flesh,' 'infirmity of the flesh,' 'physical infirmity' or 'bodily ailment' in The King James Version, The New King James Version, The Amplified Bible, The English Standard Version, The Revised Standard Version, The American Standard Version, The Robert Young Literal Translation, The Darby Translation, The Noah Webster Version and The Hebrew Names Version. We know their translation is correct because A) it is Paul's normal use of the word and B) because the Bible reveals why Paul had messed up eyes, and it was not from a disease.

Here are some examples of more accurate translations of *Galatians 4:13,14* depicting Paul's condition.

Ye know how through <u>infirmity of the flesh</u> I preached the gospel unto you at the first. And my temptation which was in my flesh ye despised not, nor rejected; but received me as an angel of God, even as Christ Jesus. (King James Version)

You know it was because of a <u>bodily ailment</u> that I preached the gospel to you at first, and though my condition was a trial to you, you did not scorn or despise me, but received me as an angel of God, as Christ Jesus (Revised Standard Version)

270

You know that it was on account of a <u>bodily ailment</u> that [I remained and] preached the gospel to you the first time. And [yet] although my physical condition was [such] a trial to you, you did not regard it with contempt, or scorn and loathe and reject me; but you received me as an angel of God, [even] as Christ Jesus [Himself]! (Amplified)

How would we understand the Bible without the Greek to run to? Original languages are a lot of fun and great for arguing points but, as with most scripture, we do not really need access to the original language to understand this passage. Some people use their knowledge of Greek and Hebrew to flex their spiritual muscles. We can determine that the proper meaning for astheneia in Galatians 4:13 is weakness or infirmity as is reflected by most translations because we have context.

We do not need the Greek to figure out what was wrong with Paul's eyes that day! It was certainly no disease, but something for which he needed some tender loving care.

First, we saw Paul's lengthy and specific descriptions of his trials and torments, none of which included sickness or disease. If an illness had been listed, it would also have been included in the clump of sufferings from which Paul said he was rescued --confounding those who contend that God refused his healing.

Second, we have historical record of a treacherous incident that occurred during Paul's First Missionary Journey. He was stoned to probably death! Those friends that gathered around him, probably had to raise him from the dead.

They stoned Paul and dragged him outside the city, thinking he was dead. But after the disciples had gathered around him, he got up... Acts 14:19,20

It was after this, on this same missionary journey that Paul first preached to the Galatians, where he felt such love that if they could, they would have given him their eyes.

If he was not speaking analogously as we do when we say things like "he would give his right arm for me, I'd jump in front of a truck for her" or "I'd give my eye teeth for that," then I imagine he was referring to the fact that his eyes probably looked like a Halloween Horror Nights creature for several days.

My teenage boys came home after getting in a fight. Joey's face was bloated, nose smashed and eyes lost somewhere in all that swollen flesh. I am *sure* he was the innocent one but anyway, gross.

Yet, for how scary he looked, he was not as bad as Paul, stoned to what was thought to be death, and dragged outside the city to be left as what was thought to be a corpse. I am sure at the time Paul would have gladly traded for some annoying Asian eye problem.

Paul's bodily ailment among the Galatians was the result of one of the stonings in his persecution list. This was not *the* one and only of his buffetings, but was one from which he was delivered.

Neither bad eyes nor any other sickness are included in Paul's carefully enumerated list of afflictions.

Does it even matter whether his problem in Galatia was an illness or attempted murder? Yes, it does matter. Jesus makes a clear distinction between suffering disease and suffering persecution. God would not go against his word and send sickness to buffet Paul. God does not keep us from getting conceited by making us sick.

We are commissioned to defeat sickness but to expect persecution. Persecution perpetuates the gospel. Cruelty to believers by those who are hostile to God are the sufferings of Jesus we are expected to share in. We are not to share in his sicknesses. Jesus was never sick! Neither are we to share in his sins. Jesus never sinned.

Sin and sickness are the things he suffered for us. This was a substitutionary suffering, meaning he did it instead of us, so we would not have to. The power of all sin and sickness was destroyed in our lives on the cross.

By sharing in his persecution sufferings, we advance the kingdom. By "sharing" in sickness, we thwart the progress of the kingdom as we are less effective.

We need to leave sin and disease in hell where they belong. Freedom from sin and disease are benefits of the cross.

Bless the Lord O my soul and forget not all his benefits, who forgives all your sins and heals all your diseases. Psalm 103:2,3

So, yes it matters that we do not get confused about suffering. There is a right way and a wrong way. We need to know if we are suffering the wrong way so that we can be rid it! We need to be aware of unbiblical suffering so we can remove it! So many are suffering needlessly, thinking it is a duty or honor.

The Bible qualifies the kind of suffering you are to participate in: suffering as a Christian, suffering according to God's will. This is a specific kind of suffering, different from the normal trials of life we all have to face. Sickness, sin and curses are not the "Christian suffering" God expects. God wants us to have no part with them, except to heal and deliver people from them.

Our example Jesus, never in sin and never sick, was often persecuted. His message was, repent, heal the sick and as you go, you will suffer persecution. It is of critical importance that we understand that our role as believers is to suffer persecution, but to relieve the suffering of the sick and disabled. Of course this begins with us.

My healing theology would not be the least bit threatened if Paul were to have this eye disease or any other disease. It would simply have been included in the batch of things from which he was delivered. It would not merit the status of some unhealed condition sent by God.

Jesus was not indecisive, inconsistent, unpredictable, shifting or unreliable about healing. He was one way with sickness, its enemy and terminator. Paul was the same way in his ministry to the sick. For someone to say that God would not take away Paul's thorn or sickness contradicts many Biblical passages and has no others that can back it up.

The second place we are taken by proponents of Paul's eye disease is later in the letter to the Galatians.

See what large letters I use as I write to you with my own hand! Galatians 6:11

They assume he said that because he could not see well. How out in left field that would be in light of the context in which Paul said it. Although we glean important truth from it, Paul's letter to the Galatians was not intended to be a collection of good advise and wise council for the general Christian population. The letter had one specific goal, to protect and defend Paul's life work, his calling, his entire mission.

As the Apostle to the Gentiles, Paul felt he was in danger of losing his converts to the Judaizers (legalists/religionists) who would have them go back into the slavery of rote laws. This letter was his impassioned plea to them not to abandon the freedom they had in the person Jesus. It has universal application for us in that once we have been saved by grace, we do not go back into the world or back into our own strength or man-made rules to save ourselves.

So earnest was he about this that, at the climax of his letter, he used impassioned language like, "*As for those agitators I wish they would go the whole way and emasculate themselves!*" *(cut off their privy parts – Thayer's Lexicon) Galatians 5:12*

How silly to think he would preface his most urgent warning with a quick diversionary reference to a toothache or eye irritant or something. It is an insult to Paul's legacy to imply he would be so scatterbrained and petty. For all the beatings with rods and whips he endured, he never looked for sympathy, much less in the midst of making such a heart wrenching plea.

Saying, "*See what large letters I use as I write to you with my own hand!*" was intended as an emphasis of he was about to say. It would have been in all caps and bold on his computer. John Hancock pledged his life, fortune and sacred honor by signing his name in oversized script on a document. "See what large letters I use as I sign with my own hand," he may have said. Were the large letters because he was so zealous for the Declaration of Independence, enough so that he was willing to part with life, fortune and honor, or was it just because he could not see a darn thing!?

We would then have to conclude then that kids who banish pesky siblings from their rooms by hanging signs on their doors bearing gigantic letters KEEP OUT, must have bad eyesight.

No, it would not offend my healing doctrine at all were Paul to have such a disease, just as it would not offend my salvation doctrine to discover Paul sinned. God rescued Paul from all his trials and persecutions; including any unmentioned sickness he may have had. It is not so scandalous that the promoters of Paul's disease/thorn are worried he was sick; that would be legitimate.

What is so insidious about the teaching is that it is a made-up disease and, contrary to Paul's own confession about his deliverance from all his sufferings, that God would not remove it.

Even though many persist in error, insisting the thorn was an eye disease, it was not anything except what Paul said it was. I do not take anyone's word for anything anymore without checking God's.

Think of all the wild and wacky teachings we could come up with if we were to extrapolate this way on everything we read in the Bible, a book which was meant for a child to understand.

I have hidden these things from the wise and intelligent and revealed them to babes. Matthew 11:25

Do we think we can out-smart the Holy Spirit? "Ah ha! Lord you didn't say it was an Oriental eye disease, but we figured it out!"

It is dangerous to infer unknown facts from known facts just to fortify a personal agenda.

There is enough in the word that we do not need to venture outside of its pages.

Chapter 30

Poverty & Misery: Your Prerogative!

My favorite thing about the 80's was George Michael's t-shirt, **CHOOSE LIFE** --even though I don't think he did.

The Book of Job is one of the most misunderstood and misquoted in the Bible. Job is often categorized as a book of suffering. Job is memorialized as the icon of human suffering. Suffering is indeed part of Job's story but is a bad synopsis of his life.

Job is a story of redemption. It is a story of healing and restoration.

The Lord will sustain him on his sickbed <u>and restore him from his bed of illness</u>. Psalm 41:3

Job is another rendition of the recurring Old Testament theme, that of God rescuing his people from the curses of rebellion. This theme takes on new meaning in the New Testament as we experience such redemption through Christ, a redemption that is by our choice as much today as it was in the Old Testament. You could title an Old Testament Survey class "Choices."

Here they are:

1) Life/Blessings
2) Death/Curses

I have set before you life and death, blessings and curses. Now choose life, so that you and your children may live. Deuteronomy 30:19

Job's story is the same as the one told over and over as the Israelites did not learn from their own history. They continually defaulted to choosing death by choosing rebellion and sin against God. The predictable consequences would follow. After being overtaken by their enemies, oppressed and abused, they would repent and cry out to God, who would forgive and restore them –only until they forgot about the source of their blessing and rebelled again. So the cycle continued.

Rebellion>Bondage>Repentance>Restoration>REPEAT

The lesson they apparently did not learn?

Restrain yourself or be restrained.

In Job we have another version of this, but did Job sin? Of course he did. Everyone has sinned. I hate to give away the ending, but Bible teachers usually ignore the ending of Job. . . where he repented.

Job needed redemption from the curse of the law just like we do. Without God's saving power, we are among the cursed. We naturally default to the curse.

Christ redeemed us from the curse of the law by becoming a curse for us, for it is written: "Cursed is everyone who is hung on a tree." Galatians 3:13

What exactly are we saved from? What does it mean to be under the curse?

The curses can be summarized as sickness, poverty, pre-mature death and disaster. If you are experiencing any of these things, you need to get out from under them. You can find an exhaustive list of the curses in Deuteronomy 28. If you are looking for your diagnosis under the curse and cannot find it, note *"every kind of sickness."*

It is easy to diagnose Job's problems, as all his symptoms can also be found in the Deuteronomy 28 curses. He had the disadvantage of living before the enlightenment of even the law and the prophets. He had to wade through all kinds of speculation and bad theology to realize his deliverance. These are the things he suffered, all found in the curses of Deuteronomy 28.

Symptoms of Job:

Poverty
Overcome by enemies
Painful sores from soles of his feet to top of head
Pain in bones
Fever
Skin broken, scabs, black and peeling
Emaciated, dark circles, red face from crying, moaning
Public disgrace, humiliation

The lesson we need to take from Job is not how well he endured, as much as how completely God rescued him.

Neither Job, nor any other Biblical player is meant to be an example to us. Job is not our leader any more than David is. We learn about God through their experiences.

Chapter 31

Careful How You Quote The Old Testament!

The child of David's adultery died even though he prayed and fasted for healing. People use this to justify doctrine that God does not always heal. They confuse God's judgment (the curse) with God's will (blessing).

Judgment, or curse, is not his will but the unavoidable result of rebellion. David's disobedience resulted in judgment. The difference now is that Jesus took all our judgment on the cross. He became a curse for us. That is why when we repent from sin we have every right to expect that we will not suffer from the curse or the judgment of God. Our babies do not have to die for our sin. Jesus did that for them.

The judge of the Old Testament is the same judge of the New Testament. It is 'the judged' that is different. In the Old Testament it was the people. Now it is Jesus. Jesus took all the judgment that was meant for us. If you are in him then your judgment is complete. It is over. Judgment of the OT is N/A. In Christ there is no condemnation, no judgment –as long as we repent.

There is now no condemnation for those who are in Christ Jesus. Romans 8:1

The perpetual gravitation of our bodies to sin and death is broken in Christ.

Who will rescue me from this body of death? Romans 7:24

We learn truths, morals and principles from Old Testament events and from God's dealings with his people. We are never directed to model our lives after anyone in the Bible except the Lord God, Jesus Christ. As great as these O.T. heroes were, we are not Mosesians, Davidians or Elijains. We are Christians.

Peter said to Jesus, "Lord, it is good for us to be here. If you wish, I will put up three shelters — one for you, one for Moses and one for Elijah."
While he was still speaking, a bright cloud enveloped them, and a voice from the cloud said, "This is my Son, whom I love; with him I am well pleased. Listen to him!" Matthew 17:4-5

Listen to <u>Jesus</u>. As close as we get to a directive to follow a man is by Paul. Still, he carefully qualified his statement,

Follow my example as I follow the example of Christ. 1 Corinthians 11:1

We could justify any behavior or doctrine as Biblically sanctioned if we were to model our lives after OT figures. Many of their behaviors were examples of what not to do. Noah got drunk. Abraham lied. Samson slept with a prostitute. They were never really charged with wrong doing in these cases, so are we allowed to behave thus? No.

The Old Testament must be read in the larger context of the then believer's limited knowledge and limited access to God's power. We know from the whole council of God's word that drunkenness, lying and whore-mongering are wrong. Job is equally a part of the OT journey to discover the Savior, to whom we now have all access --NT

Chapter 32

When Bad Theology Happens To Good People

Job's sayings demand context. The book of Job is replete with examples of bad doctrine. This is evidenced not only by God's rebuke to Job's friends for their bad theological advise but by Job's repentance in the end for all the dumb things he said about God. We should not cavalierly quote from Job as it is a spectacle of bad theology. Paul could say of Job as he did of his fellow Israelites,

For I can testify about them that they are zealous for God, but their zeal is not based on knowledge. Romans 10:2

Although he was of exemplary character and a godly man, Job admitted in the final analysis,

Surely I spoke of things I did not understand...therefore I despise myself and repent in dust and ashes. Job 42:3...6

Job is not a book of neat little proverbs by which we can guide our children. I can't think of a worse book to open randomly for good quotes, than Job.

The emphasis in this book needs to shift from Job to God. In the Book of Job, we miss the lesson from the Lord by lauding every word that comes from Job's mouth. The theme of the book, revealed through the perseverance of this suffering man, is not his perseverance, but God's redemptive work.

Maybe we over exalt Job because we misunderstand God's praise of Job's righteousness and perfection. If he were so righteous and perfect, does that mean everything he said and did was perfect too? Of course not. Only God is perfect.

Job's perfection must be regarded in light of his oft babbling untrue statements and false accusations against God. Job was commended for his patience and perseverance, not for his faith, as was Abraham or his wisdom like Solomon.

Q. If Job were so perfect, why did he have to repent?
A. For anyone, repentance is the key to perfection.

Because of his humility and propensity to repent, Job had consummate human integrity and virtue. Job's repentance is the first clue as to why God said he was perfect. It is our repentance that makes us perfect to God. When he sees us, he sees Jesus, his perfect Son. That does not mean we are complete or without fault.

My sixteen month old grand baby Hazel is perfect, but if she were still wearing diapers and nursing at sixteen years old, there would be a problem. Some people already think it's weird she still nurses (go extended nursing!). Job, although "perfect," had a lot to learn, a lot of growing. We too are expected to be perfect. . . but to continue to grow.

Be perfect even as your heavenly father is perfect. Matthew 5:48

We are perfect when we are in Christ, even though he is not finished with us yet. For insight into Job's secret to perfection, let's jump to the end of the Book. The Lord confronts him, he confesses, he repents.

The Lord said to Job, "Will the one who <u>contends with the Almighty</u> correct him? Let him who <u>accuses God</u> answer him!"

Then Job answered the Lord, "I am unworthy – how can I reply to you? I put my hand over my mouth. I spoke once, but I have no answer — twice, but I will say no more."

Then the LORD spoke to Job out of the storm, "Brace yourself like a man; I will question you, and you shall answer me. Would you <u>discredit my justice</u>? Would you <u>condemn me</u> to justify yourself? Job 40:1-8

Job answered God, "You asked, 'Who is this muddying the water, ignorantly confusing the issue, second-guessing my purposes?' (You asked, 'Who is this that <u>obscures my counsel</u> without knowledge?') I admit it. I was the one. I babbled on about things far beyond me, made small talk about wonders way over my head. You told me, 'Listen, and let me do the talking. Let me ask the questions. You give the answers.' I admit I once lived by rumors of you; now I have it all firsthand — from my own eyes and ears! I'm sorry — forgive me. I'll never do that again, I promise! I'll never again live on crusts of hearsay, crumbs of rumor." Job 42:1-6 Message (NIV 1984)

It is ironic that we now use Job as a doctrinal resource. It has become a go-to book for rumors and here-say about healing. If, like Job, we would determine to get all our information from the Lord, "firsthand," we would not stumble like he admitted to doing. His biggest problem was thinking he knew how God worked, based on rumor and here-say. When we are quick to use Job to back up 'suffering for Jesus' doctrine, let's remember these sins from which Job finally repented:

1) Contending with the Almighty (challenging his word and his will, correcting and rebuking through ignorance or pride)
2) Accusing God (assigning false attributes and actions to him)
3) Discrediting God (dismissing God's righteousness based on man's standard of right and wrong)
4) Condemning God to justify self
5) Hiding or obscuring God's counsel without knowledge (clouding God's counsel with man's, blabbing advice with a lack of understanding, forming hasty conclusions without divine wisdom and spreading it around)

If Job had bad theology, we should not use it for song lyrics:

The LORD gave, and the LORD has taken away; Blessed be the name of the LORD. Job 1:21

Job was a righteous man who wrongly thought that God did to him what we know was Satan. But God allowed it you say. He permitted it. Yes, but Job as we have just noted, perfect and righteous as he was, had some vulnerabilities: ignorance and lack of knowledge and understanding of God's ways.

So, was it God who allowed/permitted it, or was it Job? hmm...

My people (even Job) are destroyed for lack of knowledge. Hosea 4:6

We might not always know the reason --or even be directly responsible for the reason, but there always is a reason and we should find out what it is --for ourselves and our posterity. You may or may not have sinned. You may have ancestral curses which need to be broken. You may be surrounded by doubters who constantly undermine your faith. You may need to find someone who will agree, stand and fight with you in the Spirit. You may need to eat more vegetables and drink less beer. You may have a demon. You may need to study. You may need to learn some promises. You may need to fast.

Like a fluttering sparrow or a darting swallow, an undeserved curse does not come to rest. Proverbs 26:2 NIV 1984

As the bird by wandering, as the swallow by flying, so the curse causeless shall not come. Proverbs 26:2 KJV

The curse cannot land without a reason. It has to be legal. In the Old Testament, when God's people made themselves vulnerable to judgment for any reason, even through the sin of another, it was by the curse that judgment came. It transferred legally into their lives through disobedience. God reverses the curse, as he did for Job.

So --when Job says the Lord gives and the Lord takes away, his understanding is wrong. It is reflective of the apathetic, passive way Christians today yield to the curse as 'just the way God works.' Quoting Job's ill-informed *"The Lord gives and the Lord takes away,"* they relent, give in and surrender --not to God but to the curse. Oh well!

This learn-to-live-with-it verse is a perfect example of contending with the Almighty, accusing God, obscuring God's counsel without knowledge and speaking of things without understanding. Many of us need to repent of these things too. Job made bad requests; he did not pray healing prayers. . .

Oh, that I might have my request, that God would grant what I hope for, that God would be willing to crush me, to let loose his hand and cut me off! Job 6:8-9

Job blamed God for assigning evil for him. We remember Job as being consigned to a life of misery when, as scholars agree, his trouble was months, not years.

So I have been allotted months of futility, and nights of misery have been assigned to me. Job 7:3

Job grossly misunderstood God's character as does the modern Western Church.

Why have you made me your target? Why do you not pardon my offenses and forgive my sins? Job 7:20-21

Blaming God for making us or 'allowing' us to be sick is accusing him. Whether we accept it graciously or not. It is a false accusation no matter how good or thankful we are to him. That is not how he rolls.

Some Christians think they have been targeted for sickness as their 'cross to bear' or as their 'thorn in the flesh' for no reason other than 'God is sovereign.' There is no Biblical precedent for God's imposing sickness on someone just because he can, just because he is all powerful and in charge, just because he is sovereign. There is always a reason and you can be sure as a NT believer that God didn't do it. Again, Job flaunts his ignorance in this matter.

He would crush me with a storm and multiply my wounds for no reason. Job 9:17

First of all, he would not do that. Second, it wouldn't be for no reason. Why are we so eager to quote Job in backing up our healing theology when he says so many off the Biblical wall things?

When a scourge brings sudden death, God mocks the despair of the innocent. Job 9:23

Really? God mocks innocent people? No, this is what Satan does. We have to be more disciplined in our study.
The big lesson from Job is what not to say.

Job continues to attribute characteristics of Satan to God. This is especially dangerous in that we should be able to recognize the enemy, and to distinguish good guys from bad.

This is not the God we serve:

Does it please you to oppress me, to spurn the work of your hands, you smile on the schemes of the wicked? Job 10:3

You bring new witnesses against me and increase your anger toward me; your forces come against me wave upon wave. Job 10:17

One of the most self-destructive things we do when we desperately need God, is to shake our fists at him and impugn him for our disaster, when it is really Satan who deserves the spurning. Ascribing his misery to God was one of the things about which Job was ignorant, whether he was angry about it or not, whether he had a good attitude or bad.

Turn away from me so I can have a moment's joy. Job 10:20

Is it a sin to accuse God, even as a faithful believer like Job? As we see by the end of this book, it is considered to be sin --but remember that sin means missing the mark. Does it make God mad when we do that? I do not believe he is mad at us but, it is bad because it is counter productive. As with all sin, we only hurt ourselves; we postpone our deliverance. We miss an opportunity to reach out to a rescuer who is called to action by our faith.

God responds to faith in a much bigger way than he responds to anger, frustration and other emotional ventings. We need to move from begging and feeling sorry for ourselves mode to search and destroy every remnant of the curse mode.

Job provides a great example of making up doctrines based on negative experience and human reason. He concluded that God must reward unrighteous idolaters who provoke God because, he, a righteous man, was made to suffer.

Those who provoke God are secure – those who carry their god in their hands. Job 12:6

This is exactly opposite of truth. Those who trust in and rely on created gods: self, earth, body, music, sex, drugs, celebrities, obsessions, beauty, religion, intellectualism, materialism... and who provoke God --they are not secure! The fact that we can indeed be devoted people of integrity and exemplary character, while simultaneously be shackled by harmful beliefs, is well modeled by the account of Job. There is so much ridiculous conversation between righteous Job and his friends, from both sides.

Right after I got saved in college, I was staying with some Ivy League educated family friends who were sharing thoughts on their last night of Bible study. I was listening (eaves dropping) at the top of the stairs outside the living room.

"What have we learned from this study?"

"Uhhh." Someone contributed.

Then silence.

"So, I guess we haven't really concluded anything. What we have learned is that there really are no absolute answers."

They formed their beliefs from their opinions. Their opinions were formed from their intellects, not God's word.

What separated Job from his friends was his affinity for quickly changing his beliefs and repenting when he heard God's word. Job's honorable trait of perseverance and patience was grounded in his devotion to God. He persevered in trusting God regardless of circumstance. When this kind of patience or perseverance is *combined* with truth (which Job was soon to discover) then the promise can be realized. If you persevere in truth you will obtain blessings; if you persevere in lies, you will obtain curses.

This was a good man, snared by bad theology. We can comfortably quote Job's sayings about his unswerving commitment to his God. Job understood his commitment to God more than he did God's commitment to him. Like many Christians today, he was convinced that after all the hell, he would be safe. Where was he wrong? He didn't have to wait.

Though he slay me, yet will I hope in him; I will surely defend my ways to his face. Indeed, this will turn out for my deliverance, Job 13:15

I know that my Redeemer lives, and that in the end he will stand upon the earth. And after my skin has been destroyed, yet in my flesh I will see God. Job 19:25

Job needed to find out that God was committed to his healing and deliverance. He also needed to find out that he had a part to play in that. He needed to first know it, and then believe and receive it.

Another lesson we can learn from Job is not to listen to believers (which Job's friends were) who do not speak according to God's word. For example, Elihu postulated that God may have been disciplining Job. This lie is still so rampant in the body of Christ that I cannot believe it, especially considering the unanimous consensus in the Church that Job's friends had terrible advice. Constantly I hear that someone is not healed because he has sin or because God is teaching him something. God's chastening or teaching something sounds less judgmental but is just as bad. Spare me. Such was the teaching of foolish Elihu:

A man may be chastened on a bed of pain with constant distress in his bones, so that his very being finds food repulsive and his soul loathes the choicest meal. His flesh wastes away to nothing, and his bones, once hidden, now stick out. Job 33:19-21

This ascribing sickness to discipline is flippantly parroted all the time in the Church. It is never our duty to judge why someone does not receive healing. It is our duty to persevere with them in the trial by either helping them to trouble-shoot some areas as to why they have not yet received, or by encouraging, enabling and praying for them to receive.

A believer's washing his hands of someone's curse and walking away with a judgment of failure does not coincide with the healing mission Jesus assigned to us all.

After Job repented and prayed for his friends, The Lord made him prosperous again and gave him twice as much as he had before. The Lord blessed the latter part of Job's life more than the first. After this, Job lived a hundred and forty years; he saw his children and their children to the fourth generation. And so he died, old and full of years. Job 42:10,12,16-17

The fact that Job was perfectly healed to live another 140 years seems to escape the popular narrative of Job's life. Job the righteous got attacked by Satan, learned how to obtain the good promises of God during the process and emerged healthy and prosperous to live a long life... according to God's will.

With long life will I satisfy him and show him my salvation. Psalm 91:16

We stay out of trouble in understanding this book if we just concentrate on the greatness of God and not the greatness of Job.

When bad things happen to good people, there are Biblical recourses. There are solutions. Instead of validating the bad, let's concentrate on getting rid of the bad, and keeping the good.

Chapter 33

Patient No More

"Never give in. Never, never, never." -Winston Churchill

The end result of perseverance, or patience, is the obtaining of the hope; it is the goal realized. At this end there is no lacking any of the good promises of God. Victory awaits you.

Consider it pure joy, my brothers, whenever you face trials of many kinds, because you know that the testing of your faith develops perseverance (patience). Perseverance (patience) must finish its work so that you may be mature and complete, not lacking anything. James 2:2-4

Again, we know this because the end of the book of James concludes, as did the end of Job, that healing is the final result of patience. James even uses Job to drive his point. The process, (patience or perseverance) is for obtaining something.

Patience is not just for testing to see if you can hang on for dear life, for your whole life…without denying God. James clues us in as to how to have patience. How can we persevere through it all in our faith?

If any of you lacks wisdom, he should ask God, who gives generously to all without finding fault, and it will be given to him. But when he asks, he must believe and not doubt, because he who doubts is like a wave of the sea, blown and tossed by the wind. That man should not think he will receive anything from the Lord; he is a double-minded man, unstable in all he does. James 1:5-8

This is where troubleshooting comes in. God will download the specifics we need so we can proceed without the doubt which disables. I focus a lot on healing but it works with any of the promises, and with any trial. If there is confusion or misunderstanding, do not consult your powers of reason or what you have heard, or what is the consensus of this depraved society. Do not consult compromised church doctrine. Ask God, don't doubt him, and then go for it --not stopping till you get your promise.

Blessed is the man who perseveres under trial, because when he has stood the test, he will receive the crown of life that God has promised to those who love him. James 1:12

Why are we so quick to forget the purpose of our test? It is to pass. There is always a reward for passing a test. God does not give us evil things. He gives us power to overcome evil things, like diseases. They may come as the result of sin, over medicating, vaccines, bad nutrition, ignorance, accidents, this dark world, evil spirits, family curses, idolatry or witchcraft, unwitting or not. This is something we have to stop mixing up.

Don't be deceived, my dear brothers. Every good and perfect gift is from above, coming down from the Father of the heavenly lights, who does not change like shifting shadows. James 1:16-17

Being deceived about God's nature is not something to take lightly. Satan is the deceiver and once you are operating in his realm then he is operating in yours.

As you know, we consider blessed those who have persevered. You have heard of Job's perseverance and have seen what the Lord finally brought about. James 5:11

At some point, if you do not give up, there will be a point at which you no longer have to be patient. You will be a patient no more!

Chapter 34

Don't Pray About Healing

"Try not. Do or do not, there is no try." –Yoda

Anybody got trouble? Anybody sick? James makes a clear distinction between trouble and sickness. Two different problems with two different solutions. Once again, we will find sickness in its own special category with sin, in the 'don't entertain these' category. Trouble? Might have to hang with him a little.

Is any one of you in trouble? He should pray. James 15:13

The Greek word 'kakopatheo' James uses for trouble means affliction, to suffer or endure evil or hardships. Aha! sickness is evil, hardship and trouble so and if someone is sick he should pray about it and who knows the outcome! Praying about being sick is never suggested by Jesus or any of the Early Church leaders.

James takes exception to the claims of those who contend that sickness is an affliction or trouble that should be prayed about. He segregates sickness from trouble.

Is any one of you sick? (as opposed to being troubled/afflicted) If that is the case,

He should call the elders of the church to pray over him and anoint him with oil in the name of the Lord. And the prayer offered in faith will make the sick person well; the Lord will raise him up. James 5:14 -15

James leaves no alternative for the outcome of the prayer of faith. The prayer offered in faith is not to divine the desired outcome. We already know what is desired --healing. The prayer of faith is to produce the desired outcome, a well person, a person who gets up.

There is no need to pray about healing.

Sickness is among the problems whose solutions are known to us. We do not pray about them; we pray for the strength or faith to follow through to resolution, to persevere in obtaining what is hoped for.

A man is invited by co-workers to meet after work at a 'gentlemen's club' where the only women to be found are on stage or the table. "Lord, is it your will for me to go home after work or go to the ....restaurant?" He does not need to pray about that.

Was Jesus Patient With Sickness and Disability?

If an intruder were to break into your house in the middle of the night, if a strange man reached out of a van to snatch your child from the front yard, if a baby fell into the pool --would you need to pray and seek God's will about what to do? Would you endure these things with patience? Or would you take immediate and aggressive action to defend and protect what belongs to you?

Of course, in any of these situations we would be fierce and unstoppable. Should we react any differently when struck by sickness or disease? There are some things for which waiting around patience is not a virtue. God did not leave us powerless in the face of such enemies.

A friend has been diagnosed with breast cancer. Do not pray

about that, instructs James. Go to the elders of the church. The prayer of faith will make the sick person well and the Lord will raise her up. Note that James says go to the elders of the church. Does that mean the old guys in suits and pew ushers? Not exclusively!

The Greek word for elder means one who presides over, or is in charge of the assemblies (or churches). The churches are groups of people not necessarily assembled in cathedrals, sanctuaries or rented public school auditoriums. They may meet in houses, coffee shops or dark basements. Their presbyters or elders may be wearing robes, jeans, dresses or surfer shorts. They may be in their eighties or teens. Accepted church tradition can dull our understanding and so handicap our ability to receive all God has for us. It can limit our access to otherwise accessible promises.

Brenda suffered a debilitating stroke. She called for the elders of her church and they came to anoint her with oil and pray. When their prayer of faith didn't work, they said it was because of sin in her life. Perhaps if she were not such a nice person, she would have read them the sentence immediately after the one about the prayer of faith they had just prayed that did not work... *"If he has sinned, he will be forgiven."* James 5:15

She was more than happy to confess anything she could think of. It says "if" the person had sinned, which she had not. Other believers, like those with Job, would accuse God of smiting her for some soaring reason or valuable lesson. Both are wrong.

Note also that James says the prayer of faith would raise her up. Some of you go to churches where the elders don't have a lick of faith for healing, but you do! Here is how they can get it:

So then faith comes by hearing, and hearing by the word of God. Romans 10:17

Go to the word and then go to the elders…..or find another church.

The anointing of oil may be accompanied by your prayer of faith. It is not the prayer of the elders that will make the sick person well, but the prayer of faith, out of whoever's mouth. It is the Lord who will raise up.

As a caution against ritualizing healing, be aware that calling for the elders and anointing with oil is one among many dozens of methods of healing in the Bible. Actually, healing was rarely effected the same way twice. Lord knows we are creatures of ritual and habit. We love to make traditions and rely on format instead of Jesus --hence all the liturgy and bang your head on a cement wall rote prayers in so much of the Church. My friend Kirsten brags that she can make her whole grocery list while reciting the Apostle's Creed.

The Holy Spirit makes it impossible for us in good conscious to cleave to one healing method. He describes healing by repeated dunking in water, falling on top of a dead person, touching clothes, touching a hand, grabbing a hand, touching eyes with mud, touching a boy's coffin while telling his mom not to cry, yelling at people across a field, falling under a shadow, touching a handkerchief, touching an apron, ordering demons from afar, commanding disease, anointing with oil….

The message is obvious. It is not the method; it is the faith expressed in the name of Jesus. However we express that faith is a point of contact for our faith.

One night my friend called to pray about her baby who for 20 hours was unable to hold down any food or liquid. We agreed that because of the wounds of Jesus her baby boy (and this was the point of contact for our faith) would go to sleep that very night, very shortly with a beverage in his tummy, maybe some crackers, and Mommy would have a worry free night.

I called her the next morning and asked "How's the baby?"

"He's healed," she chirped. "He went down with a bottle and woke up to wreck up his sister's toys again."

Skeptics would say he would have been better anyway. Fine. If raising kids without trusting God to heal their little stuff works --they can go for it. I like being able to trust God to banish everything that attacks Lucy from the earaches he has healed to the fevers to the pink eye. Yeah it's just little stuff, and we're gonna keep it that way.

Would it have been easier in each of those cases to just give her antibiotics? Probably. Would I rather get in bed with her and battle my enemies with the word of God – sometimes for hours.? Yes I would. Lucy knows that Jesus heals her and not just because I told her so.

If God is against something, then he does not like or want it. It is against his desire or will; it is not his will. The James prescription for suffering sickness is to end it by the prayer of faith, not to endure it without end. . . because God is against sickness.

We are to eradicate suffering that is not God's will.

As is so often the case, Peter suffered persecution for alleviating human suffering. If you suffer for relieving sufferers, you are suffering right!

Of the 69 times that suffer (or suffering) appears in the King James Version of the New Testament, it is never used to connote suffering disease or disability. The word is used as we would use 'allow" like when Jesus said,

Suffer (allow) the little children to come unto me, and forbid them not: for of such is the kingdom of God. Mark 10:14

It is predominantly used in speaking of the religious and governmental persecutions of Christ and his followers. It is common in such phrases as suffer loss, suffer need, suffer for the Name's sake. In the popular New International Version 1984, of the over 80 times suffer or suffering appears, only eleven times is it used in the context of sickness or disability. And, in each of the eleven appearances of the word suffering where a disease or sickness exists, so also does Jesus --to promptly heal it.

There are no examples of suffering sickness to support an alternate view, that there were some sick whose suffering was not relieved. Here are examples of such suffering that were all healed.

1) *News about him spread all over Syria, and people brought to him all who were ill with various diseases, those <u>suffering severe pain</u>, the demon-possessed, those having seizures, and the paralyzed, and he healed them. Matthew 4:24*

2) *"Lord," he said, "my servant lies at home paralyzed and in <u>terrible suffering</u>." Matthew 8:6*

3) *My daughter is <u>suffering terribly</u> from demon-possession. Matthew 15:22*

4) *He has seizures and is <u>suffering greatly</u>. He often falls into the fire or into the water. Matthew 17:15*

5) *She had <u>suffered (bleeding)</u> a great deal under the care of many doctors and had spent all she had, yet instead of getting better she*

grew worse. Mark 5:26

6) *Now Simon's mother-in-law was <u>suffering from a high fever</u>, and they asked Jesus to help her. Luke 4:38*

7) *There in front of him was a man <u>suffering from dropsy</u>. Luke 14:2*
8) *But Paul shook the snake off into the fire and <u>suffered no ill effects</u>. Acts 28:5*

9) *His father was sick in bed, <u>suffering from fever and dysentery.</u> Acts 28:8*

In every account of suffering physical impairment, there was healing.

Pain, demon-possession, seizures, paralysis, dropsy, fever and dysentery were said to be suffered by those who were healed after an encounter with Jesus. There are no accounts of sufferers of disease or disability who were abandoned to their sufferings.

The original languages do not even require the use of the word suffer to portray each condition. You can get the point across without saying suffering. For example: The man suffering from dropsy is 'dropsical' in the original language. He has a condition of dropsy. So, today instead of some saying, "You are suffering for Jesus," they could say more accurately, "You are dropsical for Jesus." How dumb.

Or, regarding the woman who touched Jesus clothes, instead of saying that she was suffering for Jesus, she could say, "I'm chronically bleeding for Jesus" --for his glory. Dumb.

Why does it matter the word suffering could be removed or replaced by experiencing or enduring? Because we have re-tooled the word suffering. We have made it to mean being sick.

In Greek, suffering is not equivalent in meaning to being sick. Sicknesses are nouns. They are something you have, and need to get rid of. Suffering is not something you have. It is a verb. You do it. So what is it we are suppose to be suffering? Persecution for the Name of Jesus? Yes. Domestic abuse? No. Hunger? No. Addiction? No. Sore muscles from Cardio Dance Class? Yes. Sickness? No. Demonic possession? No. We need to be much more exacting about consigning loved ones to 'suffering for Jesus' when they are not being persecuted, but are sick or demon-possessed.

In the Bible, suffering for Jesus has nothing to do with demon-possession. We do not have to guess or assume and especially we do not have to throw everything a human could suffer for any reason into one big cesspool and stick a yard sign in front of it --Suffering for Jesus.

We have been given a big black book with hundreds and hundreds of pages in it so we don't guess and assume. God has revealed too much detail about what he wants for us to squander his word with such sluggish theology.

SUMMARY: Biblical Indications 'Suffering For Jesus' Was Never Intended to Include Sickness

Suffering sickness always ended in healing.

• Suffering from demonic possession, dropsy, leprosy, dysentery, blindness, severe pain, paralysis, and every other disease and disability always yielded healing.

• Suffering for Jesus or as a Christian is persecution that is propagated by the hands of pagans, heathens or otherwise nice seeming people that do not like Jesus was taught to be expected.

We also know that suffering disease is not God's will, because of Jesus' personal example.

• He was never sinful or sick, disabled, in pain, or having accidents.
• He did not get sick for us anymore that he sinned for us.

• He was punished for our sin and sickness.

• He suffered punishment by persecution; he did not suffer sickness or the bondage of sin.

• *He was pierced for our transgressions… and by his wounds we are healed. Isaiah 53:5*

Sickness is not to be included in our sufferings because in Jesus' sacrifice, God specifically addresses its proper place with sin, removed.

• *He was pierced for our transgressions… and by his wounds we are healed. Isaiah 53:5*

Sickness was not included in our sufferings because the driving force of Jesus' life and ministry was to save.
• His will is to save their souls and even more glaringly their bodies –relieving physical suffering, and then turning them out into the world to continue the work.

• *As you sent me into the world, I have sent them into the world. John 17:18*

The world is sick and miserable enough. We don't need more of that junk in the kingdom of heaven. Did you know the kingdom is here --that it is among us? and that sickness is not in that kingdom?

Repent, for the kingdom of heaven is near. Matthew 4:17

The kingdom of God is within you. Luke 17:21

Whenever the subject of sickness came up, Jesus was not there to comfort, console, strengthen, teach, chastise or encourage the sick. He was there to heal the sick, in every case. It was not according to whether he was willing to do it or whether the timing was right, but according to the sick person's willingness to believe.

His will is never called into question in the Bible.

He said he couldn't do many miracles in his hometown because of the unbelief of the people. Remember that his disciples could not heal the epileptic boy because of their unbelief. Jesus repeatedly pointed to the unbelief of his disciples, the very faith giants who stormed this world with the original revolution. We should not feel the least bit insulted for the Lord to tell us we have unbelief, when we consider the company it puts us in!

When it comes to God's timing regarding healing, it is now. It is God who is waiting for our timing --to receive.

Jesus shows us incident report after incident report to illustrate his dealings with the suffering that comes from disease, disability, accidents, mental disorders and birth defects. In every presentation of pain, sickness, paralysis, disability or deformity, Jesus deals the immediate death blow. He fulfills in each case his stated mission,

The reason the Son of God appeared was to destroy the devil's work. 1 John 3:8

We are not provided in scripture any alternate reaction by Jesus. Jesus was always swift and deliberate in dealing with this kind of suffering.

If we are like him, then we should be able to say, "Stand up on your feet heart...Lungs be clean...Leukemia cease raging." If we accept that the Church should emulate Jesus' ministry of relieving physical suffering then how do we get there?

Let's start by changing our emasculated prayers.

Chapter 35

Achsah: True Story

Achsah is the poster child for the Emergent Church. She flies in the face of Big Religion. She is brazen and forward and unrestrained about her mission. She is not a man, a priest, a pastor or a college graduate. She has everything that the Church needs to have in order to get out of its pious, faux-reverent rut.

Achsah was excited about growing up in God, moving forward, building and not stagnating in the desert. She was born in the wilderness and loved it as the home where she was happy and well-nurtured by her parents and by their God. It was normal for her to depend on him on a daily basis. Every morning she and her mom would gather manna for the day, and in evening, she helped her mom cook quail for dinner. She had several brothers, but was the only daughter of a well respected man. Of him the Lord said, *"He has a different spirit and follows me wholeheartedly." Numbers 14:24*

Because Achsah was secure in her relationship with her family and the Lord, she grew up to be submissive and respectful, necessary qualities for successful leadership. She had no cultural, social or religious influence beyond the Mosaic law. She was untainted by the negative Egyptian influences that afflicted her elders, or the idolatry of other cultures. She had the added protection of a father whose courage, bravery and godliness set him with only a couple others above the whole assembly of this nation parading in the desert.

Although women differed in function socially, spiritually they were equals. Miriam, one of the original triumverate, along with Moses and Aaron, was one of the spiritual and social leaders Achsah emulated growing up.

When it was finally time to go into the Promised Land, Achsah's father asked the new leader, his longtime friend Joshua, for the hill country where giants lived.

In accordance with the Lord's command to him, Joshua gave to Caleb son of Jephunneh a portion in Judah — Kiriath Arba, that is, Hebron. (Arba was the forefather of Anak.) Joshua 15:13

It did not faze Achasah that her father wanted the land of the giants. He had been waiting 40 years to get at them. She knew by heart the story about the ten cowards that went with her father and Joshua to spy out the Promised Land long before she was born. Was she ever glad her dad was not one of those who was struck down by the plague! She could hardly wait for him to fulfill his life long dream. How exciting that would be for her family. She would cheer as he slayed those abnormally large men.

From Hebron, Caleb drove out the three Anakites — Sheshai, Ahiman and Talmai — descendants of Anak. From there he marched against the people living in Debir (formerly called Kiriath Sepher). And Caleb said, "I will give my daughter Acsah in marriage to the man who attacks and captures Kiriath Sepher." Joshua 15:14-16

Achsah had her daddy wrapped around her little finger. Caleb would be sure that her husband would be the bravest and most courageous warrior, one who would gladly risk his life for his daughter. Achsah was desirable, a worthy prize to motivate the Hebrew boys to face down the giant men in hopes of winning her. Achsah was happy about the deal; she was assured of having a strong and mighty husband just like her father. Maybe she prayed for the Lord's favor on the boy she loved.

Othniel son of Kenaz, Caleb's brother, took it; so Caleb gave his daughter Achsah to him in marriage. Joshua 15:17

Caleb's nephew, Othniel, fought his heart out to win Achsah.

Caleb gave them land in the Negev, a portion of Southern Israel. It seemed an uninhabitable, dry, forbidding, rugged, wasteland. Achsah did not mope that her family would not be living in the lush colorful northern regions of the Promised Land. Her father wanted the land to the east of the Dead Sea, dry and desolate. Well why not? She had thrived in those kinds of conditions. She loved her childhood stomping grounds. Only now, it would be her own territory with her own responsibilities. She would be sure to secure everything she needed to accomplish the mission her father gave her, and possess her land well.

One day when Achsah came to Othniel and urged him (incited, allured, instigated, enticed, persuaded) to ask her father for a field. He said for her to do it. She hurried to see her father. When she got off her donkey, Caleb asked her, "What can I do for you?"

Arguably a Hebrew princess, she more than any of the other girls, deserved to live in the lovely and breathtaking land to the north. Achsah did not complain about her inheritance; that was not the stock from which she came. Caleb probably wondered whether she had heard enough scary stories growing up about complaining relatives or, if her contentedness was just that he and his daughter were cut from the same rock.

She loved her portion of dirt. It was beautiful. She had been spoiled by her doting father alright, not a spoiled brat -but she needed something else. What she had was not enough for the job she was determined to do. She knew she could do anything with her father's help and she was going to get it. Caleb did not ask her what she wanted. He asked her what he could do for her. He was ready for action. He anticipated giving to her. It was his predisposition.

Achsah did not lift her voice meekly at the end of her request. She called the portion of the Negev given to Othniel and her, "my land." She did not say, "give us" or with manipulative humility, "if it be your will" or "if you should be so gracious." Neither did she entreat with the cowering timidity of a beggar that is so religiously virtuous. Instead, with the confidence and zeal of a five year old scrambling into his lap and smashing his cheeks, *"Give me the springs."*

Caleb had done his part raising her and done it well. Now, she was about her father's business by approaching him and saying, "Give me the rest of what I need daddy! I can't wait to make my home just the way I like it and have you over for dinner! I get to decorate my own living room, have my own children and pick out all the colors.

She replied, "Do me a special favor Since you have given me land in the Negev, give me also springs of water." Joshua 15:19
("Give me a blessing. Give me a present," --according to other translations)

She and Othniel were in agreement, but it was her vision and excitement about making a new home that drove her. She was a bride now and wanted to get her own food, feed her own goats, find her own water, make her own bread, provide for her children. Her father took care of her as a child, now he would give her the resources by which she would be able to take care of others. She still needed him, but one day there would be many who would need her.

So Caleb gave her the upper and lower springs. Joshua 15:19

As time passed, Achsah's elders died. In the picturesque regions of the north, on every high hill, *"they forsook the Lord, and served Baal and the Ashtoreths." Judges 2:13*

So they were oppressed by other nations, but when they cried out to the Lord, he raised up for them a deliverer, Othniel, husband of Achsah, who saved them. *"The Spirit of the Lord came upon him, so that he became Israel's judge and went to war." Judges 3:10*

And the land had rest. Yes, all the land of Israel needed her.

The Church needs Achsah

Q. How did Achsah pray? How did she ask her father for what she needed?

A. With confidence based on an established and intimate relationship with her father. Not...

"Daddy, please can I have the springs?"
"Will you give them to me?"
"Father in heaven, will you heal me? Please?!"
"Lord God, Jesus, Heavenly Father will you forgive me?"

These questions presume the thing desired has not already been granted or that there is doubt about the thing being requested. It is insulting to the spirit of grace. Can you, will you forgive me God? Reverent sounding maybe, but immature.

It is the earnest desire of every parent for a child to cry out for help when in trouble or need. This is the way we need to pray from now on. No question.

"Give us this day our daily bread."
"Forgive us our debts."
"Do not lead us into temptation."
"Deliver us from evil."
"Forgive us."
"Extend your hand to heal and perform miracles."

All the promises are yes. They are not "ask and wait to see what I say." He already promised it. He already answered.
First know what you need. What are your springs? Maybe you need to do some research.

Whatever God gives you is useless by itself. It needs your input. Without you it is not a complete kit. Activate it. God is waiting for you to ask for what you need to complete the task he has given you. It proves you want to work with him and do his will; it is an act of faith. He is not going to do it all; he is providing the power to ignite your dreams.

The Negev would have been like a curse to anyone else, but Achsah, having grown up in the desert, loved it. To her it was a great opportunity.

She boldly took the initiative to achieve her own dreams She was not waiting around for her husband or dad to do it. We should not wait around for anyone either, not even God.

When I called, you answered me; You made me bold and stouthearted. Psalm 138 3

The righteous are as bold as a lion. Proverbs 28:1

Open wide your mouth and I will fill it. Psalm 81:10

Get ready. Open your mouth wide.

Biblical healing prayers don't sound remotely like most we hear on Sunday morning. Jesus never told us to pray for the sick. He said to heal the sick. Praying is something we should do before we heal the sick. It is something we need to do a lot if we want to be able to heal the sick. If we wait till we are presented with cancer to start praying, it's too late. This is what 'praying for the sick' sounded like in the Bible:

"Be clean." (to a leper)
"Be opened." (to a deaf man)
"Get up." (to a lame man)
"Go. It will be done just as you believed." (to a centurion)
"Get up." (to a dead girl)
"Go wash." (to a blind man)
"Come out." (to a dead man in a tomb)
"Walk." (to a man who never walked)
"Stand up." (to a man lame for a eight years)
"Stretch out your hand." (to the man with a shriveled hand)
"According to your faith will it be done to you." (to blind men)

'Prayers' for the sick were touches and shadows, rebukes and commands. Jesus simply held hands with Peter's mother-in-law and the fever left. He drove out spirits with a word, rebuked demons, and touched eyes. Peter's shadow and Paul's handkerchiefs healed people. These 'prayers for the sick' were points of contact for faith in Christ, demands that frail flesh line up with the truth of God's word. A little less wordy a little more confident.

And when you pray, do not keep on babbling like pagans, for they think they will be heard because of their many words. Matthew 6:7

It is not our smooth or many words that compel God to move. It is our faith in the moves he already made.

Chapter 36

Be Prepared Be Preprayed

The praying we so desperately need is to connect with God's power and wisdom. It is to draw from our heavenly strength, to spend quality and large quantities of time listening, reading and talking with him. This is where we muster the supernatural fortitude to see his works accomplished in the sick and needy.

The prayer work has to be done before you can heal the sick. If you start praying at the hospital bed, it's too late and you will wear people out. It was after Jesus' long nights of solitary prayer that he would wow the crowds with spectacular miracles. Yes, that is one of the things we want, to wow the crowds with Jesus.

He went up on a mountainside by himself to pray. When evening came, he was there alone. Matthew 14:23

Very early in the morning, while it was still dark, Jesus got up, left the house and went off to a solitary place, where he prayed. Mark 1:35

This pattern of prayer was Jesus' lifestyle. His ministry sessions were proceeded by extensive prayer.

Jesus went out to a mountainside to pray and spent the night praying to God. Luke 6:12

It was after this night that Jesus chose the Twelve Apostles. Later that day, he healed all those who came to hear him from diseases and demons. It was a productive day.

Those troubled by evil spirits were cured, and the people all tried to touch him, because power was coming from him and healing them all. Luke 6: 18,19

Jesus' ministry success can be yours if you follow his example. "Be healed" are not magic words. They are the release point for faith that resides where there is an abiding communication between God and you. Over and over you see this in the disciples. Paul did not 'pray for the sick.' Even where prayer is mentioned, he prayed first in preparation until he was ready. Then he laid hands on the sick.

[Publius'] father was sick in bed, suffering from fever and dysentery. Paul went in to see him and, after prayer, placed his hands on him and healed him. Acts 28:8

Lots of praying in solitude as opposed to lots of praying for the sick is best. We know this from the incident of the father who could not get the disciples to heal his epileptic son.

After assessing the situation, Jesus commanded the demon to leave the boy, "*I command you, come out of him and never enter him again." Mark 9:25* and it obeyed.

That is all Jesus said. And yet, when the disciples asked why they couldn't drive it out, he answered, *"because you have so little faith." Matthew 17:20* Along with his diagnosis also came a prescription. *"This kind can come out only by prayer." Mark 9:29*

"But we did pray!" They must have thought. They prayed more than Jesus' twelve word prayer for that demon to get out. Jesus' "I command you" was an act of healing, not a prayer. The disciples needed to spend more energy in prep prayer if they wanted to see more of God's energy in action.

The disciples showed the kind of great character that clues us in as to why Jesus chose them when they asked, "*Why could not we cast him out?*" *Mark 9:28*

How many leaders, teachers and pastors make excuses or adjust healing doctrine to accommodate prayer failures, instead of just trying to understand where they went wrong?

"Why couldn't I do it?" is a better question to ask God than "Why didn't *you* do it?"

The answer is almost always that we were not properly prepared.

Prepare by prepraying.

Chapter 37

New Testament Commandment Raise Your Dead!

Shocking New Testament commands to all Jesus' disciples, extending down through the generations to us--

Heal the sick, raise the dead, cleanse those who have leprosy, drive out demons. Freely you have received, freely give. Matthew 10:8

Heal the sick who are there and tell them, "The kingdom of God is near you." Luke 10:9

And these signs will accompany those who believe: In my name they will drive out demons; they will speak in new tongues; they will pick up snakes with their hands; and when they drink deadly poison, it will not hurt them at all; they will place their hands on sick people, and they will get well. Mark 16:17-18

Go and make disciples of all nations, baptizing them in the name of the Father and of the Son and of the Holy Spirit, and teaching them to obey everything I have commanded you. Matthew 28:19-20

"*Everything*" he commanded them to do? Clearly healing is one of those commands. It was not enough for Jesus that his disciples were healing the sick already, he wanted them to teach everyone else to do it too.

Healing is essential. It is at the core of the gospels. It is in the foundation of the Church, but has been treated as a peripheral element, a side note, a matter of denominational and personal taste --like sprinkling or immersion, cross or crucifix, wine or grape juice.

So why does it matter so much? It matters because people are not getting saved in droves.

A great crowd of people followed him <u>because they saw the miraculous signs</u> he performed on the sick. John 6:2

When the crowds heard Philip and <u>saw the miraculous signs he did</u> they paid close attention to what he said. With shrieks evil spirits came out of many and many paralytics and cripples were healed. Acts 8:6-8

You will get no converts teaching people about all the reasons God doesn't heal. It is our responsibility to obey, not to wait for someone else to do it, for some spiritual big shot to come and heal. We should not be special event or Christian celebrity dependent.

Tell me there is not relief for a terminal patient to find out the ball is in his court, that he is not subject to some kind of divine whim, some randomly scattered grace. Healing is not according to God's grace, God's love, God's forgiveness or God's power. If it were, none of us would ever be sick. Healing is according to our faith. It is not according to God's mood that day.

This is good news to a person who has been given a death sentence by a doctor. He has something to fight for. God will not stop him. He doesn't have to stay sick. He has control over his destiny. He has abiding promises to go after. Remember, the Bible does not say about our lives, "God is in control." God is in control only as far as we are willing to allow him to be. We get to choose who is in control of our lives.

When you see that it is God's best and highest for you to be healed, you will find strength in persevering because you will not be worried about fighting against his will.

But Raise Dead People? Really?

Heal the sick, raise the dead, cleanse those who have leprosy, drive out demons. Freely you have received, freely give. Matthew 10:8

Yes they scoff and mock, call you radical and fanatical when you believe such things... until they are desperate, then they come looking for you.

Somebody died. So,

When the disciples heard that Peter was in Lydda, they sent two men to him and urged him, "Please come at once!" Acts 9:38

Their beloved Tabitha was dead, and the wailers were going at it, so they sent for Peter.....

I was in Washington DC, heavy with my first child, real heavy. My father 'just so happened' to be staying in Washington on business supposedly, at the Marriott where I normally took up a couch in the lobby before my morning art class. He had recently moved from DC to Palm Beach with his Hollywood diva wife, Mary Costa, an opera legend whose first gig was the voice of Walt Disney's *Sleeping Beauty*.

My dad had called me the night before to tell me he would be there, and to ask if he could be in the delivery room when Courtney was born a couple months later. The call was so strange and flattering because he never called me for anything. But no, he could not be in the room at her birth.

Hogging my usual lobby couch, I decided I would go up to his room and see if he wanted to get some breakfast. I knocked on the big wooden hotel door and stood there with my big stomach sticking out almost touching it. And stood. It was awkward because my dad is easily irritated and I didn't want to bug him so early, so I went back down to read some more of my Bible.

Again, I went back up the elevator and knocked on his door. Nothing, so I went back down to read some more of my Bible.

Every few minutes I did this.

Finally, I called his room. He answered the phone. "Dad? -- Dad?" He didn't say anything. I called several more times, each time he answered but said nothing. I went back up to his room, knocked on the door and called him, "Dad? Dad!"

Nothing, and then faintly I heard from off to the left of the room in what I thought was the bathroom a muffled, "Betsy."

I called on the phone again and he answered with silence. I called again and it was busy. It stayed off the receiver after that. Still not wanting to bother him but worried, I got a maintenance worker to let me in the room next door and get on the balcony where I could peek in. The drapes were closed.

I went back and kept banging on the door. Finally, I got the maintenance guy to open it and break the chain. Timidly, I opened the door. "Dad?"

It was deathly silent.

The bed was to my left where I thought the bathroom was. My father was on his stomach, face down in the mattress. I crept up to him, and poked his arm with my finger.

"Dad?" It was not warm. I picked up an empty prescription bottle from the nightstand where the phone receiver was lying. I didn't see the note. I knew he was dead. Still, I ran to the room next door and frantically called 911, begging them to hurry. If I had known Peter was in the next town, I would have called him instead.

What did Jesus really mean when he said for us to raise the dead? Did he mean people who are spiritually dead but need the life of Christ? Did he mean getting teenagers out of bed? Or when he said to raise the dead, did he actually mean for us to raise dead people?

Yes, that is what he really meant. He did it, the disciples did it, and he told us to do it.

Jesus raised Jairus' little girl from the dead. Some people try to make a case that she was not really dead because Jesus said she was sleeping. He said Lazarus was sleeping too, so when the disciples thought that Lazarus would wake up, Jesus had to clarify that he was really dead. Jesus called Lazarus out of his tomb. We know that Jairus' girl was dead also, because when Jesus told her to get up her spirit was gone. It came back at his command.

Her spirit returned, and at once she stood up. Luke 8:55

Jesus raised a widow's only son during his funeral procession. That is to be expected because he is Jesus, of course. But he didn't just tell us to believe in it; he showed us how it is done! He said for you to do it! When he referred to raising the dead, he was referring to bringing actual dead people back to life.

Peter, raiser of Tabitha, was just a fisherman with no credentials, no formal training, no college, no seminary and not a respected businessman in the community. He raised Tabitha from the dead. He had to spend a little time praying first and had to kick out the howlers, but he did it.

Paul, highly educated but with a violent past, raised Euticus, the kid who fell asleep during his sermon and tumbled to the ground from a third story window.

Peter and Paul took Jesus seriously. Of the countless miracles and healings that were performed by the hands of these two men, these are the only detailed accounts of their raising dead people. It may not be something we all do, or do very much.

"Heal the sick" and "cast out demons" is hard enough take in our modern, materialistic, digital driven, medicine worshipping culture. We are down the road a long way once we hear the "raise the dead" mandate. It seems so outrageous and causes the credibility and relevance of the scriptures in our daily lives to be called into question. The difficulty in reconciling raising the dead with our HD, wi-fi, iPhone, iLives gives more credence to such platitudes as 'miracles aren't for today.' I am not proposing walking up to a casket during a solemn ceremony and tugging on the corpse. How awkward, but I want to be like Jesus --I do I do I do. Here is what I'm saying, and this may not seem reasonable to some; it should be though to believers.

Let's say you go to someone's house and you find a baby at the bottom of the pool. You bring her up and, although someone begins CPR and calls 911, it has obviously been too long for rescue breathing or a paramedic to do any good. It only takes a few minutes for lack of oxygen to cause severe and irreversible brain damage. Drowning is too common a form of death for small children, especially here in Florida. Do you conclude, "Oh well, too late." Isn't your first instinct to save? Deep in our spirits we know it is still not too late.

If the Spirit of him who raised Jesus from the dead is living in you, he who raised Christ from the dead will also give life to your mortal bodies through his Spirit, who lives in you. Romans 8:11

It is the resurrection power and life of God from which you derive your authority to demand, "Baby, you will live and not die. In the name of Jesus, life and breath return!" Use his name. Use your authority! He gave it to you to use, not to keep it in your sock drawer. Speak life into that little body as Christ charged you. Do not submit to the enemy who comes only to steal, kill and destroy. Jesus came that we might have life; he came to destroy the works of the enemy.

Heal the sick, cleanse the lepers, raise the dead, freely you have received, freely give. It is your duty, your solemn charge. We could only justify not doing it by long complicated arguments that only a really smart theology professor could understand -- not no fisherman let me tell you.

It's okay to start with baby steps, and be nervous at even the thought of raising the dead. That is most of us. It is better to make this the goal. If someone dies a pre-mature death as a result of disease or accident, I don't care how old they are, we do not say that it must have been their time to go, or that God called them home. Even if they did go home, there is no way to make a Biblical case for those suppositions.

If we are unwilling or not ready to walk this out, let's at least stay out of the other ditch by making up random reasons why God wanted them to die. These concocted dogmas only sabotage faith, seeding more sickness and death as believers passively allow the enemy to wreak havoc in their families.

I wish I would have called my dad's spirit back, gone such a short time from his body, having just escaped while I was going up and down the elevator. That would have been easier to believe for than four days stinky from a tomb.

Chapter 38

7 Miracle Power Tools to USE!

Open your tool box and he will fill it..

Tool #1 God's Word

As we have seen, time in the word --studying, meditating, memorizing, discussing, hearing the spoken word --nothing is more important for building faith than the word (promises/message) of God. If you are sick, and have no energy to read, study and memorize, then listen to healing verses, or watch! I can hook you up. Got dvds, cds, books, music-videos, coaching, live events and video devotionals at BetsyB.tv (email me@betsyb.tv)

By whatever means ....

Faith comes by hearing and hearing by the word of God. Romans 10:17

Of course, by saturating yourself in the word of God, you will find all kinds of other, more specific tools to use for battling curses, tearing down walls and building up other things, including people. Every person is unique and has a different road map. Find your personalized strategy for health, wealth and happiness in this life.

What else can you do when praying and reading your Bible doesn't seem to be enough? Here are six more highly effective tools for your tool box.

Tool #2 Thankfulness

It is so easy to forget about being thankful. It is key to receiving from God because we thank him before we actually have whatever we are trusting for. Music is one of the best vehicles to create a Holy Spirit charged atmosphere of thanksgiving in your life. Find worship music that you like, not hymns if you like heavy metal, not big band if you like country and not opera if you like hip hop. There is praise music for every taste.

Being thankful for your blessings shows appreciation; being thankful during storms while clinging to the hope of promise shows faith. God can do a lot with a grateful, faithful you.

Tool #3 Forgiveness

Forgiveness is maybe the hardest to engage, but nothing will unclog your promise receptors like it. Unforgiveness clogs our heavenly plumbing so we are unable to receive through the blockage!

People have often asked me how I could forgive my mother for the kidnapping shenanigan. I could parrot a scripture verse.

If you forgive other people when they sin against you, your heavenly Father will also forgive you. But if you do not forgive others their sins, your Father will not forgive your sins. Matthew 6:14-15

If I forgive someone when they sin against me, my heavenly Father will also forgive me. But if I do not forgive someone his sins, my Father will not forgive my sins. If it has to be an obedient compliance with that truth --though the feelings are absent, so be it. Sometimes we just have to grit our teeth and do it.

But --I am cured of obliged forgiveness, or the holier-than-thou attitude that can accompany forgiving our debtors, when I consider my own former wretchedness. Forgiveness for my mom comes generously as I shun to recall my own sin.

Once, when I was a single mother, irresponsibly obsessing over my now husband, I left my kids home alone late at night to go to a friends in the neighborhood, neglecting to lock the door. The boys were eleven and twelve and my beautiful blonde daughter was fourteen. They heard someone in the house and saw the boots of a man walking past their bedroom doors. He left.

No one can convince me that I do not deserve all the punishments and penalties of all the powers of hell. I will spend all of eternity praising God's merciful, merciful, holy name. If the only thing he ever did for me was to protect those children that night --eternity on my face before him would be the least I could do, and not nearly good enough. How can I thank him? There is no way. My kids are my great treasures, the loves of my life. I fear greatly to hold anything against anyone after what Jesus has done to forgive me and protect me from myself.

One night, I was lying in my bed feeling unforgiveness and anger toward my mother for offenses she had committed against me.

In your anger do not sin; when you are on your beds, search your hearts and be silent. Psalm 4:44

Searching my heart I knew I should pray for my mom. I was silent, but the Lord was not. My eyes adored my five year old daughter who was fast asleep in the bed next to me, my love for that little girl stronger than death. The voice of conviction brought me back to my mother, "She is not your mother, she is Herman's little girl." My grandpa adored her this way when she was five.

I owe my life to my grandpa. He would expect for me now to keep praying for my mom and to never give up, the way he used to do for all of us. That would be the least I could do for him.

Forgiveness is the central consideration for any area of growth or blessing we desire from God. God forgives us so we can forgive others. He heals us, so we can heal others. If we harbor unforgiveness, we cannot effectively walk as Jesus did, we cannot begin to accomplish the works for which he has commissioned us.

Our most effective ministry will be showcased before the lost and swarming crowds when we are first enjoying the gifts of forgiveness and health, and second, sharing the gifts of forgiveness and health.

Our experience with forgiveness has to be turned outward toward others. What at first is so fulfilling will become stale if it is not shared.

There is nothing so delicious as the fat cheeks of little babies. How our arms yearn for them. How gingerly first time moms slave for their happy bundles. There is no love story like the one between a mother and her cub, except for maybe the one between a daddy and his little girl. And yet, as much as we crave and cherish our one year olds, we would never choose to stifle our children's growth. Healthy things grow, healthy kids grow, and healthy Christians grow. Forgiveness has to grow. But how and into what?

We grow by giving and sharing the love of God which takes the form of forgiveness and healing. The mission and the message is the same for every follower of Christ. Go... look at the Great Commission in the gospels. Go...although the Messianic orders are the same, they will be manifested in millions of different ways. Each person's unique plan will accomplish the same end, making disciples and ultimately populating heaven. Go and grow.

Imagine being rescued from sleeping in a city dumpster, and being put up in a five star hotel suite. You luxuriate in a bubbling jacuzzi with bouncy white towels piled at the edge of the marble tub. Can the excitement of our first experience with Jesus be kept alive? How can we maintain the exuberation of going from freezing in septic dumpster sludge to bundled in a thick warm robe eating shrimp and chocolate dipped strawberries?

We should stay fresh and saved by refusing to step back into holding grudges, stealing, gossiping, lying, murdering, getting drunk and fornicating. Staying clean and fresh is our new default as Christians. So, where does the newness and excitement come from anymore? The Plaza was thrilling -- lavish and exhilarating at first. It felt great for a long time actually. But as with everything, we grow accustomed to the treatment and need something more. It becomes not as special. We may still be clean, but we are bored. This makes us vulnerable to the danger of looking for illicit thrill. What could ever match the excitement of moving from a metal bin of decayed garbage to arranging giant pillows for a queen's breakfast in a king-sized bed?

There is only one thing that can surpass that fun, only one way to satisfy your soul. It is by retrieving the ones you love from greasy rodent filth and checking them into the suites down the hall.

When I look at the offense committed against me and my sister, and the stumbling it caused, I also see the repercussions for the offender. I want her to have the accommodations that I have.

But whoever causes one of these little ones who believe in and acknowledge and cleave to Me to stumble and sin [that is, who entices him or hinders him in right conduct or thought], it would be better (more expedient and profitable or advantageous) for him to have a great millstone fastened around his neck and to be sunk in the depth of the sea. Matthew 18:6 Amplified

Sunk to death would be better for such a person than to cause a little one to stumble. The consequences are unimaginable and I do not want anyone to undergo torments of the grave, especially not my own mother. She is no more deserving of that than I. Hell, eternal fire, worms that do not die.... is the reason I am committed to this saving gospel. Jesus is the only escape, he is the only way out. It is incumbent upon me to preach Christ. Because of this, Jude bluntly exhorts Christians.

Snatch others from the fire and save them. Jude 20

Tool #4 Fasting

This disciplined practice brings breakthrough and desperately needed insight for particularly stubborn situations and people. Fasting is not fun, but so worth it.

We do not fast to move God. We fast to move ourselves --out of the way.

We do not fast so he can hear us better. We fast so we can hear him better.

We do not fast to more effectively provoke God. Biblical fasting is abstinence from food for a time. Physical hunger is the power of fasting. Fasting media, sugar, caffeine or certain people may be good discipline, but this is not fasting which produces physical hunger, the necessary component. I know a lot of people who go on liquid fasts for seven days and say they fasted for a week. I have gone on seven day liquid fasts. Oh please, that is not a fast. That is a liquid diet. You can drink thousands of calories a day on a liquid fast and never be hungry once. Hunger humbles and sharpens. It opens us for revelation and enlightenment. It clears the foggy fog.

Fasting alone without a lively relationship with God is not very fruitful either. I once spent a month in New Mexico's Gila Wilderness on a survival trip before I was a Christian. We had to spend three days and nights alone in the woods with a tarp, a knife and a bottle of water. Every one said it would be so enlightening and spiritually deep. All I thought about the whole time was m&ms and hamburgers.

When I have a healing crisis and am not getting a breakthrough, I fast. I am not a good faster. If I go more than a day, I throw up. For me for now, 24 hours works. I eat at night, say at 7:00 pm and then not until the next night after 7:00 pm. I pray during the day a little, but most importantly, I pray that last hour before I eat when I am the hungriest. This has never disappointed.

For example, when Lucy was about two, she had a cold that would not go away. After lingering for so long, my husband started worrying. Her grandparents were concerned every time we saw them, which was almost every day. I was frustrated that I, a teacher of healing principles and application could not beat this stupid little cold for what was going on six weeks. If this doesn't work for me at home, then I have no business teaching it. I prayed. I confessed. I did everything I knew to do and I then I beat myself up.

I refuse to give in to sickness, even though it is sometimes easier to give in and give up. There is always a reason for the curse; I was going to find out what it was, this obstacle to my breakthrough.

James says, if any of us lacks wisdom, ask of God. I would ask. Also, Jesus said to his disciples that this one comes out by prayer and fasting. I would fast. This much trouble just for a little cold?

Sure enough, in my Bible study time after missing three meals, I stumbled upon Peter as he entered the room of the dead woman Tabitha. That was it. Peter cleared all the women out of the room. Their mourning was compassionate and sincere, the expression of broken hearts, but it was not conducive to faith. Mourning the dead is not conducive to raising the dead.

Peter had to preserve or create an atmosphere of faith and, although their intentions were good, he banished the doubters from the room. When you are believing for healing or anything else, sometimes you have to separate yourself from well-meaning, compassionate souls who do not share your understanding of Biblical healing. There are times you will have to isolate with believers who are spiritually like-minded. Stop sharing the things you are believing for with people that are not in full agreement with you, even Christians...especially Christians. They can be the worst.

No one loved my little toddler Lucy more than one particular family member —-who would gladly have thrown himself in front of a truck for her. His motives were love, but every time she coughed he declared, "Oh you poor dear, that cough sounds terrible! You are gong to get pneumonia! . . .She could have walking pneumonia!" Fear gripped me when I heard these things; I was blind-sided every time I went to his house.

As soon as I read the account of Peter and Tabitha, I knew that I would have to keep Lucy from his house. A few days is all it took. After fighting this harassing thing for six weeks, I heeded the wisdom imparted to me during my fast, and it worked. God's wisdom always works.

At other times, we might turn to fasting right off the bat. A couple years ago, my daughter Courtney who was 23, called me. "Mom, the doctor called me about my test results. He wants me to come in."

We both knew this was not good. I went with her to the doctor and cried the whole way home. She was so stoic and emotionless. I didn't know she had spent the night before in tears. She thought I was only worried about what treatment she might choose to undergo.

"Courtney no! I don't want to have this fight at all. You do not have to go there! Can we believe that when you go back in ten days that there will be no cervical cancer?"

"Yes." She answered and we agreed in Jesus' name that she would be healed by the next appointment.

I prayed and I believed and I was devastated. It is so easy to believe for someone else's kid. Why?

With someone else's kid there is no fear. I did not have the assurance of what I hoped for, I did not have the evidence of things not seen, my baby's healthy cervix. I cried the rest of the day.

The next morning I woke up to a nightmare, realizing that through all my life's trials, I never had one that woke me up to this sickening a feeling. To say my daughter and cancer in the same sentence... I found myself clinging to God so desperately that I couldn't even make my own schedule. I wiped everything off my agenda. "Oh my God! What do I do?! I can't even make it through the next five minutes?!"

He gave me a plan:

Fast the rest of the day (Tuesday). Fast all day Thursday. Spend the night with Courtney Thursday night. Lay hands on her stomach and pray in tongues through the night. Separate yourself from unbelief.

I watched nothing, listened to nothing, read nothing except God's word. I turned my face away from the RIP memorials on the back windshields of people's cars. I spent one day at the Holy Land Experience. I asked my husband to turn off his secular music station when I rode in his truck. I gave Courtney a verse to put up in her room and say every morning and every night.

No harm shall befall me, no disaster will come near my tent. Psalm 91:10

At one point after about six days of this, Lucy and Courtney were laughing at me jumping around and singing like a crazy person in her bedroom. I was happy. I realized I'd had a breakthrough. I had the assurance of what I hoped for, the evidence of what was unseen, Courtney's healing.

Four days later, I sat in the waiting room while the doctor was scraping her cervix so he could determine his course of action. When she came out, I couldn't read her blank face. She pulled me out into the hall.

Through the first tears I had seen since this happened, she said, "He kept making noises like hmph and then he finally said, 'For the life of me, I cannot find a thing.'"

The lab results came back a week later –not a thing. Fasting can give you the bunker busters you need when the big one comes.

Tool #5 Deliverance From Demons

Sometimes you really can just blame it on a demon.

Sometimes when things hit inexplicably hard and often, or if a child has uncharacteristic behavior, it might simply be an evil spirit.

We struggle and pray and fight and study and medicate and still --no relief. Are you demon-possessed, oppressed, or harassed? It doesn't matter how those hellions are affecting you; you just don't want them around, and you have the authority in the name of Jesus to make it so.

It seems far-fetched to think our kids may be affected by demons. Some people would think you were insane to cast a demon out of a kid. Oh please, there are so many demon-possessed kids.

I prayed for a desperately broken-hearted mom whose little step son tried to kill her with a broken bottle in one of his rants. While his father was off at war, the doctor heavily medicated him and instructed that she lock him in his room during these explosive episodes. While she was telling me this, he was tucked under her arm, curled up sweetly against her body. This had been the influence of a demon.

In Mark 7 and 9, you find Jesus casting murdering demons out of a little girl and a young boy. Today they would have been sedated with potent cocktails of anti-psychotic and psychotropic drugs. The short and long term effects of these pharmaceutical treatments are devastating…and they do not resolve problems, only mask.
If I had taken Courtney to the doctor when she was ten, I would surely have walked out with a prescription for some kind of psychiatric mood modifier. She had a sudden bout with

anger and depression while on a trip with my brother Joey to visit family in Santa Fe, New Mexico. I was to join them a few days into the vacation. Before I got there, Joey called me, worried about Courtney's sudden change in behavior. She was uncharacteristically angry and mean; he couldn't understand her sudden personality change. I didn't understand it either and was anxious to get there. After my arrival, I was talking with her in the kitchen. She had a grimace on her face. Where was my little girl?

I asked, "Courtney, what is wrong with you? You have everything you want here. It is beautiful and fun and we get to do whatever we want. What's the matter honey?"
She narrowed her eyes and snapped, "I don't know!"
Immediately, like a rubber mallet on my head, I realized. This was a demon, not at all unusual in these parts. I said, "Come on Babe," and took her to the back room where we sat on the bed and I explained to her that she was being harassed by an evil spirit --and let's get rid of it. She agreed and I rebuked that rat thing. She was her little happy angel self again. Immediately.

Just be aware that although everything is not a demon's fault, they often inhabit people, places and even animals.

Tool #6 Temple Care

We need to reverse the increasing trend toward synthetic food and drugs. It is not as easy as it was 100 years ago to eat healthy and, although there have been amazing medical advances, we are creating medical emergencies at a faster rate than we are solving them. We would need far fewer cures if we had a clean food and water supply, and were free from toxins and over medication. We are sicker and more drug dependent than ever. I hope we get off this hamster wheel of malnutrition and pharmaceutically induced health decay.

Be wise as serpents in this world. Consider the source of all your information. This world's system is evil and we are warned against loving and following it. We should control the world; it should not control us. The evil forces in this dark system are to submit to us; we do not obey their dictates, no matter how angelic and wise they seem. Be careful where you entrust your family's health. This world does not love you. Earthly governments are not motivated by good will. Governments when unrestrained, always move to overpower and oppress. We saw from Nazi Germany that the first place governments go for control is national healthcare.

Be on guard from entities, whether governmental or medical, that assume any authority over your bodies, or the bodies of your children.

With all the wisdom and spiritual force that God has given you, protect your children and grand children from disease, accidents, over-medication and toxins. Our food source has become so polluted and the culprit for so much disease.

♥ *Nurse your babies as long as possible.*

The first couple weeks are the hardest to get used to; your body will toughen up. Any soreness will pass; use a little ointment. The rewards of your bond with baby are overwhelming, not to mention breast milk is easier, cheaper and profoundly, infinitely more healthy than formula --for baby first, but also for you.

Don't be discouraged by women who failed to nurse, or by nurses who push formula. Find supportive women who breast feed their babies. It is a myth and a lie that some women don't make enough milk. When babies cry and get frustrated because they aren't getting enough, it is because they aren't! They are growing and telling your body to produce more. It will!

This is no time to supplement with formula and mess up your production. Eat, drink and let the baby suck. Your milk will come in like a flood, a love potion of divine nutrients and essential elements that could only be composed by an all knowing, all powerful heavenly Father. If you had a baby, you can nurse a baby. Hush mother-in-laws.

♥ *Buy and Make More Healthy & Organic Food.*

Feed your family healthy and whole foods that are not genetically modified, full of sugar, high fructose corn syrup, partially hydrogenated oils, processed white or wheat flour, preservatives, colorings and chemicals. Grow vegetables if you can. Have yard chickens. We eat their eggs but not them since they greet us at the gate. Are we zoned for farm animals? (Don't ask, don't tell:)

Buy as much organic as you can, especially dairy and meat. Use extra virgin (not light) olive oil and organic coconut oil every day. I use coconut oil for everything --lotion, eye drops, eye make-up remover and in whatever food or smoothies I can add it. Shun fast food. Never microwave.

♥ *Pursue natural health solutions before synthetic drugs.*

Educate yourselves about essential oils and start using them as an alternative to running to the doctor or drug store for every little thing. All drugs have side effects. Frankincense and myrrh were not only used for incense and burial in ancient times. Myrrh was taken into battle by soldiers because of its rapid healing effect on open wounds. Hundreds of essential plant oils like these are loaded with antibacterial, antiviral, antifungal, antitumeral, anti-inflammatory, antiseptic, probiotic, cancer fighting and immune boosting properties. More information can be found on my website, BetsyB.tv. These oils have more than the value of gold to your body, whether sick or not. They are made in the bowels of plants by God. Like him, they are amazing.

God will heal you even if your primary food groups are soda, chips and candy, but you will keep getting sick if you continue to pollute your body so. That kind of eating is as sinful as doing drugs or smoking cigarettes. Is God mad when we do these things? No, it is sin because we destroy the beautiful bodies God gave us to use for dreams to come true.

Let's trust God for wellness. Let's wean off drug-dependence. Be cautious about falling in step with this cradle to grave drug culture.

Instead:

1) Marinate in scripture
2) Eat healthy
3) Play outside.

♥ *Guard Yourselves From Medical Abuse and Intimidation*

Carol, a school teacher and her husband Eric, a firefighter, would much rather have prevented their baby's juvenile arthritis than to have to believe for and struggle to see him walk or run like other boys. The medical procedures, drugs and suffering has been daunting. They have had to become wiser than, and even suspicious of some of their doctors. They had to overcame physician intimidation. Although the medical culture can do good, we as Christians need to be more keenly aware that it is still a part of this dark world's system.

The arthritis that attacked Liams' leg was the result of a vaccine. Juvenile arthritis is a vaccine side effect, along with hundreds of others --from serious to deadly. For the most part, parents are not aware of the potential for vaccine damage because, unlike any other medical procedure, neither doctors nor pharmaceutical companies are required to inform. No waiver is provided with lists of side effects. This lack of full disclosure n medicine is unique to vaccines, but why?

If parents were honestly informed of the damage and death that could follow their child's shots, most would opt out. Carol and Eric have said they would take measles or rubella any day in lieu of the damage that has been done to their son by a vaccine. Liam is on the road to recovery because of Eric and Carol's dedication to education and to faith. Baby boy number two is getting no shots.

Pediatricians and pharmaceutical companies depend on vaccines for multiple billions of dollars, for the shots themselves, but more so for the diseases and injuries that will result from vaccine damage. Congress has exempted both doctors and pharmaceutical companies from liability for vaccine injury and death. This makes it unnecessary to inform parents; it would ensure the loss of sales. If parents cannot sue, there is no need for the doctor to have a waiver signed.

Some people are not aware there is a vaccine controversy. As the vaccine schedule increases, we see more and more vaccine injured children. Child immunity is not being built; it is being destroyed. The number and toxicity of the vaccines have reached the tipping point for what their little bodies can tolerate.

Until now, we have been duped into thinking they have been inoculated from disease. The truth is they have been made more susceptible to disease.
Vaccine injury is easily avoidable. Thankfully, there is an awakening as people are doing their own research.

Vaccines are not safe.

They are legally classified as "unavoidably unsafe." A certain percentage of children will die or be disabled with each batch administered. Vaccines are far more dangerous than the diseases they purport to ward off. Vaccines, injected directly into the bloodstream, contain dozens of toxic chemicals such as formaldehyde, acetone, mercury, lead, aluminum, antifreeze, carbolic acid, DNA from animal tissues like dog and monkey kidney, pig blood, horse blood, rabbit brain, fetal bovine serum, neurotoxins, neomycin sulfate, phenol red indicator and aborted fetal tissues. These additives are far more toxic than the viral components.

In accordance with CDC guidelines, children are injected with 49 to 56 doses by age 5 in the vaccine schedule. More and more are being added to the schedule for every age after that.

Parents are often unaware of the ever increasing number of vaccines because of purposeful multi-dosing, several doses per shot, which requires more mercury for preservative, but gives the appearance of fewer doses.

As the number of required vaccines increases, so does the number of childhood disabilities and diseases like neurological damage, abnormal liver function, meningitis, prolonged high pitched screaming, respiratory arrest, eczema, gastrointestinal damage, rheumatic fever, brain tumors, autism, allergies, diabetes, anaphylaxis, heart disease, encephalopathy, bell's palsy, chronic illness, shock, chronic fatigue. arthritis, seizures, cancer, paralysis and SIDS, in spite of what some believe because of the amended reporting mechanism for crib death cases. Statistics are routinely manipulated to deceive the public about vaccines danger.

Vaccine safety is determined by the FDA based on testing that is done by the vaccine manufacturers. This is the fox guarding the hen house.

No testing has ever been done on the health of vaccinated verses unvaccinated children.

No testing has been done on the cumulative effect of vaccines.

Children are more drugged and vaccinated today than ever before in history. This begs the question. Why is this generation of kids the most sick in history? Why have diseases like autism, SIDS and cancer increased in direct proportion to the increases in government mandated shots? Why are perfectly healthy seeming little girls suddenly stricken and die with brain tumors?

Vaccines are ineffective in preventing disease.

Vaccinated diseases declined by as much as 95% before the advent of vaccines or antibiotics because of improved personal and public hygiene. People who are vaccinated get diseases they were vaccinated against.

Unvaccinated children have stronger immune systems to fight off those diseases and are generally much more healthy than the population of vaccinated children. Vaccines do not provide lifetime immunity.

Vaccines are NOT required for school/daycare admission.

Religious, medical and/or philosophical exemptions are still available in every state but one or two. Pray for the heroic parents that are fighting to maintain medical sovereignty over their own children.

I am alarmed at the number of people who submit to vaccines because they think if they do not, they cannot send their children to school. It is not as shocking to me that they are unaware that vaccines are *not* mandatory. This is the result of purposeful campaigning to hide the truth about exemptions. The really disturbing part to me, is that parents are willing to bow down to a dictatorial stance by a government that is usurping their God-given sovereignty over their children's bodies.

Know your rights, and fight for your rights. They are in jeopardy. I cannot tell you what to do. I just want you to be informed before you consent. Do not be bullied or intimidated into vaccinating. At a minimum, take your time --to study before you consent. In the meantime, your kids will be healthier than all their peers. Again, the ancient adage is true.

My people are destroyed for lack of knowledge. Hosea 4:6
If you have a vaccine injured child, or if you have a child with a condition you suspect is the result of a vaccine, it is not too late. You can get onto a path of hope by applying the principles of healing and filling their tummies with whole foods and essential oils.

To learn the truth about vaccines, stay away from the profiteers and beneficiaries: the government, the medical community and the pharmaceutical industry. I am all for huge profits and capitalism, but not at the expense of children's lives. Everything needs to be tempered with morality.

I recommend the book *Vaccine Epidemic,* and the vaccine links posted at BetsyB.tv

Do not trade the possibility of temporary, treatable illness for chronic, life-long disease or death.

BTW --Does God use doctors to heal?

Because I take a stand against the aggressive vaccine machine, some might think I am opposed to medicine and doctors. I am not. Pediatricians who peddle vaccines are often as ignorant about them as their patients. The entire premise of chemically induced herd immunity as taught in medical school is theoretical and unproven.

Most pediatricians are good, caring people who are too often mesmerized by a now tunnel-visioned, sold out, Western medicine. Vaccines are no more healing than abortion. Neither has a place in a community whose ethics are grounded in the Oath of Hippocrates that every doctor takes. The Hippocratic Oath holds the American Medical Association's Code of Medical Ethics and has remained in Western civilization as an expression of ideal conduct for the physician. Unfortunately, modified versions of the Hippocratic Oath are emerging to accommodate evolving ethics.

I vote to keep this portion of the original, "I will give no deadly medicine to any one if asked, nor suggest any such counsel; and in like manner I will not give a woman a pessary to produce abortion." This is routinely violated as a predictable, proven percentage of children and babies will die every year from their shots.

Doctors do best when they stick with facilitating healing. Yes, I appreciate doctors. I would probably have some dead loved ones now if it were not for doctors. But I also have loved ones who are dead because of doctors.

I do not believe God uses doctors to heal.
I believe that we use doctors to heal.

I believe that we should pray for them to be wise and successful in surgery. They are an amazing gift to us like dentists and lawyers and truck drivers and plumbers. Does God use plumbers to fix our pipes? Does he use grocers to feed us? Kind of I guess.

No matter the semantics, no matter how you formulate the argument, Jesus' atoning work on the cross, in fact, completed our healing. That is who God used to heal, his Son. No one can improve on or help that. There is nothing any man can do to add to the wounds that already healed us.

Jesus said over and over that according to our faith it would be unto us. We may need to be humble enough to realize that we may not yet be ready to fight some medical problems in the spirit alone. If a doctor helps us, then God in his great mercy provided a way for us to get help where we were unable to grasp the entirety of the benefits of the cross. According to our faith it is unto us. We are not always ready with our diabetes healing faith (or diet). It is not exhibiting unbelief to take my kid to the hospital. It would be foolish and immoral for me to withhold lifesaving medicine from my child because I was practicing my faith.

Don't be presumptuous. There have been several times I took Lucy to the doctor, okay a few times. My husband begrudgingly allowed me short amounts of time to believe after getting prescriptions in those cases. It was crunch time! As it turned out, I ended up not giving her the prescribed antibiotics because she got her healings --but I was careful not to endanger her in the process. I would not have put her life in jeopardy trusting God by withholding medicine.

Medicine is amazing. I just think its funny that we insinuate that God needs a doctor to heal sometimes. We are the ones who need it on this journey to becoming more like Jesus. Jesus never used gospel writer Dr. Luke's medical powers and savvy to heal.

Use medicine when you must, but beware. It is dangerously over-prescribed. Neurological drugs are handed out like candy. There is no scientific diagnosis for these mental disorders. Growing boys need to eat, play and sleep. Drugging them for behavior modification grossly inhibits their most important growth needs --their appetites and sleep patterns. There is not enough energy left for play. Children should be in 5th gear most of the day. Boys should be wild. Their drugs are intellectual steroids, the long term effects from which are only starting to be seen. Performance is enhanced, yes, just like the athletic performance improvements we see from steroid use in athletes, never mind the eventual damage.

Is academic success and behavior restraint worth it for kids who need to be swinging from trees and digging in the dirt for monster truck competitions? When they do not perform well stuck at a desk, packed and controlled in a stuffy room all day, should we force a performance with drugs?

They will only need more drugs to cope with the inevitable devastating side effects. I say no to drugs. Big Pharma has been successful in implementing their agenda --cradle to grave drugs.

Tool #7 Baptism in The Holy Spirit

The gift of your own prayer language builds you as a person -- spirit, soul and body, and by it you most effectively intercede for others. This tool is a key to everything. If you don't have it you need it. If you have it, now is the time to launch! It is your secret weapon. Much more on how this dynamic force for your physical, financial and relational success can be released in your life in *Part 4 Secret Weapon*.

Part Four
~~
Secret Weapon

Chapter 39

The Secret to Success

The first day of third grade is a stressful one for the little guy whose parents didn't get him any school supplies.

Usually, parents go to great lengths to make sure their kids have what they need to be successful and happy. They spend many years preparing them to take this life by the horns. Sometimes they have regrets. If only they had known, they may have done things differently. Ultimately, every child will learn that preparation is imperative for success.

It is never too late to find what you need to accomplish what you want. Finding it is one thing. Another is knowing what you are looking for. You may know something is missing...but what? Maybe you know what you want, but don't know there is something else you need in order to get it.

I can help you with all of this --so that you can be prepared for every lofty dream and every worthy fight. A big victory celebration comes after an intense battle. There is always victory in Jesus, but you need to be prepared. You need a secret weapon.

We have done a terrible job of convincing some Christians about a superpower called praying in tongues. Others, perhaps veteran tongue talkers, may need to re-evaluate its importance in their lives and re-establish it as a priority.

Why is the subject of tongues so critical for those who want to walk in the supernatural realm of the Holy Spirit? Why are tongues indispensable if we want to live as Jesus did? What is a prayer language and how does it link you to your destiny?

Jesus traversed the land as a miracle performing, kingdom preaching, people loving, wise provider for all who came to him. Clearly, the Bible teaches that emulating Jesus is our responsibility. God's expectations for us are not veiled in his word.

Whoever claims to live in him must walk as Jesus did. 1John 2:6

As he is so are we in this world. 1John 4:17

Jesus said, "As the Father has sent me, I am sending you." John 20:21

The disciples were suppose to be just like Jesus in this world. And so are we.

Anyone who has faith in me will do what I have been doing. John 14:12

This is a daunting task when we consider the things Jesus did; he healed the sick, drove out demons, raised the dead, loved his enemies. Alright, as he was in this world, so are we to be. We need access.

Tongues are the transmitter we need to access him. We need this connection with his Spirit so we can have the power to be like him, and do the supernatural works he did...and even greater works. The scriptures indisputably lay the burden of acting like Jesus on us. I cannot get this healing stuff to work, or anything else in the kingdom of God, without my personal arsenal of weapons that are obtained predominantly through my personal prayer language, or speaking in tongues.

As ground soldiers, we are building faith for war, for defending territory, for possessing new lands, for assailing the enemy of our souls, for loving others and for enjoying our lives. To accomplish these things we need supplies. Thankfully, Jesus supports his troops by sending this incredible weapon.

I am not talking about the sovereign impartation of a 'gift of tongues' as one would receive 'gifts' of healing, faith or words of knowledge for special ministerial purposes. I am talking about the everyday lifestyle of engaging the kingdom principles of healing, faith, knowledge, wisdom, miracles, discerning of spirits and yes, communing with God in tongues.

Not having a 'gift' of the Spirit, does not exempt us from having to exhibit these fruits.

"Ugh! Do I really have to be a participant in a lifestyle of divine health and miracles?!"

If so, you cannot afford to rush into battle ill-prepared. Tongues are basic training for operating in the Holy Spirit. Since we can do nothing without him, then the power we obtain through one on One, spirit to Spirit communication, also called speaking in tongues, must be our priority. Otherwise, living a righteous, successful, loving, signs and wonders filled Christian life is impossible.

Chapter 40

Charismatics Gone Wild

In practical terms, how can speaking in tongues affect us?

My little daughter Lucy has learned whenever she has an ailment, tummy ache, fever or pain, to request prayer. She is not satisfied with a tidy little, rote one. She will not even put up with my quoting a couple of healing verses over her. She, of course welcomes the praying of God's word.

"Thank you that you are the Lord, Lucy's healer. You keep her free from every disease. You send your word and heal her. You forgive all her sins and heal all her diseases." (Exodus 15:26, Deuteronomy 7:15, Psalm 107:20, Psalm 103:3)

But she will not let me get away until she is symptom free. So, I revert to my prayer language because I know my spirit is communing with God's Spirit in perfect agreement over his word, thereby affecting change in her body. I am powerless to bring such change in my own strength. I know that he is confirming the healing words that are spoken over her. Literally, her pain subsides when I place my hands on her and pray. English, not English, English, not English. If it takes me minutes or hours, I continue. God's word works if we work it and do not give up!

"Really, devil? You want to go 'round a few more times? You want to hear the word of Jesus Christ for several more hours? 'cause I am game baby!" At times, when she has fallen asleep and I have stopped praying, she has woken with a cry, only to go right back to sleep as soon as she hears the Holy Spirit's hushed medicating phrases in her mommy's mouth.

You know that I do not advise against medical attention. Being at the hospital does not preclude anyone from continuing to pray and believe God for a miracle. And you know I encourage prayerful research about the antibiotics and other drugs that are more and more often over-prescribed and unnecessarily administered. Research, research, research about vaccines. The more educated the population, the higher the rate of opting out on childhood vaccines. Follow the money. Study the ingredients. Study the history of epidemics. Do your homework.

If your child is sick, take baby steps toward learning how to believe God for healing. Lucy has never taken a prescription, but she and I have practiced our faith on health issues that were not critical, certainly not life threatening. In so doing, I have helped her build faith, not only for the serious medical problems of people she will encounter throughout her life and ministry, but so that she stays healthy and avoids sickness in her own life.

In all cases, speaking in tongues in conjunction with praying God's holy word is a powerful combination that will lead to measurable change in your family's health. You can be healed and then walk in divine health as you grow in faith. Sometimes the greatest challenge is to convince you of the need for speaking in tongues. Let's poke around a little and see if it hurts.

Are you stuck? Fresh out of ideas? You know you can't turn back, but you don't know how to move ahead. Your situation is not syncing up with the promises of God. Your circumstances are not in line with what you are sure he said. Your life is not what you know it should be. You are banging your head against a brick wall. You are going in circles. You are spinning your wheels. You are tired, weary and heavy laden. You want to give up, throw in the towel, jump ship, quit. Maybe you already have. You are depressed, discouraged, disillusioned, disheartened... powerless. If this is not you, then it probably has been at some time, and surely you know someone who is experiencing such frustration.

A pharmaceutical solution for these will solve little, make things worse or dull the pain at best. Your problem is nothing that speaking in tongues will not solve. Of course, there is no one, simple, ready-made solution for your complicated problems. Nevertheless, consider speaking in tongues.

I am not trying to trivialize your feelings or dilemmas --but when the omniscient, omnipotent, omnipresent God is given free reign to pray his perfect will out of your mouth, things happen. Things advance, things retreat, things look up.

The only problem is that speaking in tongues, the very phrase, conjures up all kinds of images from charismatics gone wild to The Exorcist. First of all, 'tongues' is the word for 'languages' and a bit archaic at that. Few in modern day vernacular use the word 'tongues.' I would prefer we use 'languages,' especially in the presence of people who are not savvy to Christian-speak. Say hang out instead of fellowship, bread and wine instead of sacraments, help instead of minister... prayer language instead of tongues. We would normally ask, "What language do you speak?" instead of, "In what tongue do you speak?" This terminology just adds unnecessarily to the reputed kookiness of tongues.

Perhaps this least understood gift is also the most powerful. It is no wonder that the devil would like to confine this alleged undignified display of spiritual excess to the ignorant and peculiar. For others, who recognize tongues as legitimate, their adversary need only detract them from activating their prayer language. So many Christians think tongues is fine for others. They do not believe they themselves need a prayer language, not a word of which they understand. I heartily disagree and I will persuade them otherwise!

I want to convince you that the benefits of a personal prayer language will shame the sneers of others. I promise that you will not be driven to freakish outbursts. Instead, your mouth will launch precision guided bombs when you speak -even in a whisper. Devil BEWARE.

This gift of tongues, or a new, freely imparted, God-given language is for all believers. It was not intended to be confined to Pentecostals and other holy-roller types.

When I was nineteen years old and had been a believer for a year, my grandfather kept telling me that I needed to be filled with the Holy Spirit. Outwardly I was agreeable, but inside, I quietly clung to the belief that it was not for me. I was not at all scandalized by other people's speaking in tongues, but I had the Holy Spirit resident within me as a Christian, and that should suffice. I could even be filled or baptized in the Holy Spirit but not speak in tongues, right? The Holy Spirit showed me otherwise when I went on a weekend retreat with the college kids from Seattle's Calvary Temple.

I was sitting after dark in the back row of a tiny chapel in the depths of the Pacific Northwest woods. Rich Wilkerson, a preacher in the great tradition of his cousin David Wilkerson, taught on the baptism of the Holy Spirit. I was not adverse, but it was not for me. As a relatively new Christian, I wanted to read my Bible and be with my Christian friends all the time. Jesus and I were good.

I did not understand the troubles that were heading in my direction: persecution, loneliness, sin, my ancestral past, sickness, the devil...things for which I would need to be a strong and mighty warrior not just a sweet little Christian girl.

I knew we were approaching the altar call. Rich did not say, "Raise your hand if you would like to be baptized in the Holy Spirit and speak in other tongues," to which I was ready with a reply.

"Maybe another time," I planned on telling myself, "Sounds good but some other time."

Instead he said, "Raise your hand if you have never been baptized in the Holy Spirit."

What a dirty trick! I couldn't lie. I mean, the Holy Spirit lived in me but I had not had the experience he was describing with the tongues and everything, so I raised my hand. How awkward.

My crush, sitting next to me, did not raise his hand. "*He* speaks in tongues?" I thought.

Then the preacher said to those of us raising our hands, "Stand up." I had to stand because everyone saw me raise my hand. Great! Now what spectacle would be made of me because I was not baptized in the Holy Spirit? "Get out of your seats and come to the front." I was being coerced! The guy I liked gave me an encouraging push. Gosh everyone was so pushy.

All of us non-tongue-talkers were huddled up front. Rich prayed for us to receive the baptism of the Holy Spirit and, since I was up there and everything, I wanted to be included. Within only one or two minutes, every single person was speaking in a language they did not learn from man...except for me.

"Praise the Lord! No more English!" Rich trumpeted.

Still nothing. See, I was right, not for me. "Someone has unforgiveness, God won't fill a dirty vessel," he informed the group. Yes, that was me. Immediately, my sister popped in my head and I forgave her. Later she would forgive me and we would become best friends. As soon as I did that, I started saying unfamiliar words that God put in my mouth.

I did not join a denomination or change my genre of Christianity. I did not feel different, become smarter or more spiritual. I received a gift that would help me as I committed to use it. I received the gift of being filled with the person of the Holy Spirit, Jesus. It would be years before I would realize the impact of my decision to welcome and exercise this gift.

Chapter 41

೧೪೨

Pink Slime or Filet Mignon?

It is the difference between having a race car and having a race car with nitrous oxide, a swing and a roller-coaster, pink slime (finely textured beef-based food additive) and filet mignon. It is the difference between God has a plan for your life and--

No eye has seen, no ear has heard, no mind has conceived what God has prepared for those who love him. 1 Corinthians 2:9

Experiencing the presence of the Holy Spirit starts at the new birth.

Jesus said, "I tell you the truth, no one can see the kingdom of God unless he is born again" John 3:3

When we are born again, we are born of the Spirit. We are transferred from the kingdom of darkness into the kingdom of light through the death, burial and resurrection of Jesus Christ. We get saved from hell. We get eternal life. Water baptism follows, reflecting this transformation. Water baptism is our statement of repentance; it is our burial with him in water and resurrection to new life as we come out of the water.

We are cleansed from sin through no effort of our own. The only condition of this eternal life is our decision to accept and walk in it. He is enough. But there is more of him! Isn't that the cry of the believer's heart? I want more of you Jesus!

The fire baptism that was spoken of by the last of the Old Testament Prophets, John the Baptist, is an experience subsequent to repentance. the new birth and water baptism. Again, as with the new birth, we have to partake of it by faith. It does not come by osmosis. John the Baptist describes the two baptisms.

Ironically, it was John the Water Baptist who was such an enthusiastic proponent of Jesus' Fire Baptism.

John answered, "I baptize you with water. But one more powerful than I will come, the thongs of whose sandals I am not worthy to untie. He will baptize you with the Holy Spirit and with fire." Luke 3:16

John's water baptism is one of repentance into Jesus, signifying the new birth. Jesus' fire baptism is full emersion in the Holy Spirit and is exercised at will just like any other of our acts of obedience in following Christ. Water baptism is the beginning of a life of following Jesus. Fire baptism is the beginning of an infusion that empowers us to reach our full potential in him.

Neither baptism is required to enter heaven once we are born again. The thief on the cross is indicative of that, so is the man that gets saved on his death bed or a woman who repents as her plane plunges to the ground from 10,000 feet. However, for those of us who are expected to survive and thrive in this world, both are necessary.

Peter and John prayed for some believers in Christ to receive the baptism of the Holy Spirit after they had become Christians. Similarly, Paul made sure the believers he found in Ephesus did the same.

Paul found some disciples and asked them, "Did you receive the Holy Spirit when you believed?"

They answered, "No, we have not even heard that there is a Holy Spirit."

So Paul asked, "Then what baptism did you receive?"

"John's baptism," they replied.

Paul said, "John's baptism was a baptism of repentance. He told the people to believe in the one coming after him, that is, in Jesus."

On hearing this, they were baptized into the name of the Lord Jesus. When Paul placed his hands on them, the Holy Spirit came on them, and they spoke in tongues and prophesied. Acts 19:1-6

So these people had already repented, believed in Jesus and been baptized in water. Some have claimed that these believers were not yet Christians. I believe the scripture clearly teaches that they were Christians because first of all, they were called disciples. Everywhere in the New Testament where 'disciples' are mentioned, they are Jesus' disciples. Any other disciples mentioned that are not Jesus' disciples are linked to their leader like 'John's disciples', 'the disciples of John' or 'the disciples of the Pharisees.' Just plain old 'disciple' --that's a Jesus disciple, everywhere.

Secondly, I believe they were Christians before Paul arrived because he asked them if they had received the Holy Spirit *"when they believed."* Already having received water baptism, an exclusively Christian baptism, Paul saw they were believers in Jesus. Why else would he have asked them if they had received the Holy Spirit *"when they believed?"* They said they received John's baptism when they believed, the water baptism of repentance in the name of Jesus, the only kind of baptism that John performed.

Paul, knowing that John pointed only to Jesus, affirmed this by saying to them, *"John's baptism was a baptism of repentance."* Since they had already been water baptized in Jesus' name, Paul was just assessing their needs at this point. It was clearly established that they did not need salvation. Instead, Paul placed his hands on them so they could receive the fire baptism, the baptism that Paul determined they lacked. He proceeded immediately to impart it to them by his hands. Paul was adamant about it.

The baptism in the Holy Spirit is an additional baptism to the water baptism. Water baptism is an outward washing away of your old life of sin. Fire baptism fills you up with abundance of new life. Without it you risk being fearful, fragile or perhaps unable to see your greatest dreams come true.

Chapter 42

Proving God

The Church is not armed to her potential with the weapons of war. It is scary to go to into battle ill-equipped, but still she stands there unprotected, unshielded and worse, unaware. Lack of knowledge about the baptism of the Holy Spirit has disabled much of the Church and made her vulnerable to enemy attack.

I take great joy in defrocking the friends of hell that subvert the mighty acts of God by concealing and delegitimizing the gift of the Holy Spirit. The outpouring of the Holy Spirit was the great priority of the Godhead; it was the event most anticipated by Jesus before and after his resurrection from the dead. He instructed the disciples to wait for it, even after his work on earth was done. It was the first gift to manifest in the body of Christ. The advent of the Holy Spirit heralded the Church Age.

Tongues ignited the Church with the fire she needed to power her mission on this earth.

Without the power of the Holy Spirit, we frustrate the plan of God in our lives by getting bogged down in so many areas unnecessarily. We do not avail ourselves of all the help we have been offered. Our congregations become frail. Our enemies grow strong.

While the devil has abandoned his attempts at destroying the Church's conviction about salvation through the blood of Christ, he has not relinquished his well-rewarded efforts of diffusing that same Church of explosive power. If he can just keep the Church bereft of the rocket fuel she needs to accomplish the supernatural works of Jesus, then he can disarm her. By convincing her of the insignificance of tongues, he can intimidate her with fear and bully her into submission.

Intimidation? Fear? Until the believers (yes, born-again believers) in the upper room were filled with the Holy Spirit, they were paralyzed by fear and intimidation. Boldness came with the infilling. It was after this that the disciples broke out confidently and fearlessly into the world. They were on their own for the first time without the earthly body of Jesus near them. Jesus had so eagerly anticipated this moment when his disciples would make him proud. They would courageously perform the miraculous signs and wonders that he had, and even greater ones. Jesus took the best seat in the house to watch his disciples prove him true.

Jesus had been a man attested (accredited) *"by miracles, signs and wonders."* Acts 2:22

Jesus proved himself to be God, but now *we* are to prove him to be God.

Jesus himself admitted that the force of his personality and his power of persuasion alone would not be enough to make people believe. Just before he healed the royal official's son, Jesus said,

Unless you people see signs and wonders, you will by no means believe, John 4:48

And he spent the rest of his ministry doing them.

He thought it was necessary to perform these supernatural feats to reach his goals, and he expects us to do the same. He does not command us to go into the world to preach the gospel without the accompanying force that confirms his word by miracles, signs and wonders.

If people believed Jesus only for the miracles' sake, we should obviously expect nothing different. We have to do them too. He begins with the baptism of in the Holy Spirit.

Jesus said, "Anyone who has faith in me will do what I have been doing. He will do even greater things than these, because I am going to the Father." John 14:12

Jesus went to the Father, sent the Holy Spirit and released his children to perpetuate the gospel. He watches as a proud father, considering the successes of his children to be more rewarding than his own, and more far-reaching in number and scope.

I would love to save a stadium full of people. I think there could be nothing better...until I imagine my son saving a stadium full of people or my daughter rescuing a sea of families. That would be greater. Those are the greater works, to see our offspring working in the anointing that we passed to them, reaching more people than we did. I imagine that is one of the things Jesus meant by greater works.

The gift of the Holy Spirit was the beginning; it set the disciples on fire. It was like rivers of living water rushing from their bellies, enabling them to obey his commands. Jesus left us with no less access to the force of heaven than he had.

This empowering gift is necessary for everyone and is thankfully available for everyone. So many Christians have excluded themselves from this outpouring, whether by pride, timidity or I believe in most cases, by lack of information. It is time for the Church of Jesus Christ, every single member, to go into weapons training and march fearlessly on the enemy.

Chapter 43

Are Tongues For Every Believer ?

On the last and greatest day of the Feast, Jesus stood and said in a loud voice, "If anyone is thirsty, let him come to me and drink. Whoever believes in me, as the scripture has said, streams of living water will flow from within him." By this he meant the Spirit, whom those who believed in him were later to receive. Up to that time the Spirit had not been given, since Jesus had not yet been glorified. John 7:37-39

When Jesus spoke of coming to him to drink, he was specifically talking about the Holy Spirit's visit that was yet to come, on the day of Pentecost. This was the event for which he directed the disciples to wait. This would mark the beginning of the Church Era. The message was universal; it was for everyone.

"If <u>anyone</u> is thirsty let him come," and then again, *"<u>whoever</u> believes will have streams of living water flow from within him."*

Streams of living water is not an ambiguous experience we have with the Lord. It is not a spiritual essence. This is not a mystery, open to interpretation. John immediately clarifies that by the streams of living water Jesus meant the Spirit who had not yet come. Jesus was speaking of the visitation of the Holy Spirit on the day of Pentecost when he spoke of streams of living water flowing from their bellies. And they spoke in unknown languages when they got it.

Would anyone argue that they have enough of the Spirit, that they don't need any more streams of living water or flowing whatever from God?

This is the day for which Jesus told them to wait. Before going back up into heaven, he instructed them,

Do not leave Jerusalem, but wait for the gift my Father promised, which you have heard me speak about. For John baptized with water, but in a few days you will be baptized with the Holy Spirit. Acts1:4-5

John foretold it as baptism by fire. But hadn't the Eleven (Judas not yet replaced) already received the Holy Spirit at this point? Yes. They had already received the Holy Spirit on the very first day Jesus was risen from the dead. He said that night,

"Peace be with you! As the Father has sent me, I am sending you." And with that he breathed on them and said, "Receive the Holy Spirit." John 20:21-22

Jesus had commissioned them, had given them authority and had given them the Holy Spirit. Still, they were not yet baptized in the Holy Spirit.

It was not until after this initial impartation of the Holy Spirit that Jesus said, "*Do not leave Jerusalem, but wait for the gift my Father promised, which you have heard me speak about.*"

They were ready to go, all except for this one thing. This impending incident was Jesus' focal point as he was preparing to ascend into heaven,

I am going to send you what my Father has promised; but stay in the city until you have been clothed with power from on high. Luke 24:49

This was the climactic event about which John the Baptist had prophesied and to which Jesus was so looking forward.

You will receive power when the Holy Spirit comes on you; and you will be my witnesses in Jerusalem, and in all Judea and Samaria, and to the ends of the earth. Acts 1:8

On the feast day of Pentecost, we know the disciples were in Jerusalem, obediently waiting because the scripture says,

When the day of Pentecost came, they were all together in one place. Suddenly a sound like the blowing of a violent wind came from heaven and filled the whole house where they were sitting. They saw what seemed to be tongues of fire that separated and came to rest on each of them. All of them were filled with the Holy Spirit and began to speak in other tongues as the Spirit enabled them. Acts 2:1-4

It was not until this event occurred that the Church was born. Three thousand people were saved and the tongues of fire that set the apostles ablaze began a worldwide conflagration that would come to be known as the Church of Jesus Christ. This was the historic incident that began a new era in the history of mankind.

Many Christians try to explain away the relevance of this first visitation. This was not an isolated incident for the original twelve apostles and their contemporaries in Jerusalem that day. This outpouring was to be for all people as Peter explained.

Let me explain this to you; listen carefully to what I say. These men are not drunk, as you suppose. It's only nine in the morning! No, this is what was spoken by the prophet Joel:

"In the last days, God says, I will pour out my Spirit on all people. Your sons and daughters will prophesy, your young men will see visions, your old men will dream dreams. Even on my servants, both men and women, I will pour out my Spirit in those days, and they will prophesy." Acts 2:14-18

Peter first refuted the accusations that they were drunk, even though they were obviously acting somewhat drunk. To those who dismiss this gift on the basis of the manner in which some Spirit-filled Christians behave, consider the apostles. They were not exactly carrying themselves in distinguished, priestly fashion that day. They were acting undignified, the way fans act at football games when their team scores a touchdown, undignified, the way a bride hikes up her dress and runs out the door of the chapel with her new husband, undignified, the way a grown man stumbles, sways and sobs over his son that was lost and has come home.

This gift cannot be likened to a demonic possession or visitation whereby a victim loses control of his members and psyche. A Christian can choose to be in a solemn posture when filled with the Holy Ghost --or not, as is illustrated here in the second chapter of Acts. The Holy Spirit makes no one lose control. The fruit of the Holy Spirit is self-control. It is the devil who wants to take control from people. That is his specialty.

God's wants to empower, not overpower.

I have to exercise everything he gives me by an act of my will, beginning with my very salvation. He gives me the car, fills up the tank and hands me the key, but I have to put in the key, turn on the engine and drive. He gives me freedom to obey him and freedom to act the way I want to act.

As with every aspect of truth there are legitimate excesses. But, we should be cautious about accusing believers of being in the flesh, emotional, in error, or of the devil, especially when a group of saintly apostles made such an odd spectacle of themselves under the influence of the first outpouring. Maybe it would be a good thing to be in such company.

We know this arrival of the Holy Spirit is the one Jesus so often spoke of and looked forward to. We know this because of what he instructed about this day and because of the account in Acts, but also because of Joel's prophesy. Peter quoted Joel's prophesy so it would be clear that this particular incident was the long awaited arrival of the Holy Spirit.

In his effort to explain, Peter quoted Joel, *"In the last days I will pour out my Spirit on all people."* Joel did not say, "Only on the first day of the last days I will pour out my Spirit." He said, *"in the last days."* We are in the big fat middle of the last days dispensation of time. The last days end at the return of Christ. They are now. Current events are last days events. The pouring out of the Spirit that Joel spoke of began its fulfillment with the baptism of fire that morning. Through Joel, God said he would likewise pour out his Spirit on all people including me. And he did. And he does.

Peter went on to explain to those whose hearts were cut and pleading for instruction,

Repent and be baptized, every one of you, in the name of Jesus Christ for the forgiveness of your sins. And you will receive the gift of the Holy Spirit. The promise is for you and your children and for all who are far off. Acts 2:39

This gift of the Holy Spirit to which Peter refers is contextually bound to be the gift that was witnessed by the assembly of locals and tourists in Jerusalem that morning. Peter clarified forever that the gift was for those present representing every nation under heaven, for their children, and just to be sure not to exclude anyone, for all who were far off. That's us. We were far off. Distance and time cannot separate us from the gift that was first shared on that Pentecost morning.

God will pour out his Spirit in the last days, of which today is one, on both men and women. The gibberish they were uttering was intelligible to those who were visiting Jerusalem from other parts of the world, who heard the uneducated Galileans speaking in their mother tongues. They heard lofty discourses, praises of the divine counsels and declarations of the wonders of God.

Amazed, perplexed, they heard such prophesying in their very own languages. Amazed, perplexed, thousands gave their lives to God on that day of silly behaviors. And it was only the beginning.

The scripture is clear that the gift of the Holy Spirit, evidenced by speaking in tongues, is intended for every believer. It is yours for the taking.

Chapter 44

Are Tongues Necessary?

Peter and John thought so.

Philip went into Samaria to preach the gospel. His ministry was so heavily validated by miraculous signs and wonders that even the followers of the amazing sorcerer Simon were astonished by the superior powers of Philip's God. As a result of these displays, they became believers in Jesus. But the fact that they had received the word of God, that they were water baptized in the name of the Lord Jesus unto repentance and were Christians --with the Holy Spirit in their hearts, did not exempt them from the need to be baptized in the Holy Spirit. Here is another scriptural example of followers of Christ who had an additional experience with the Holy Spirit, an experience that was accompanied by visible, audible evidence.

When the apostles in Jerusalem heard that Samaria had accepted the word of God, they sent Peter and John to them. When they arrived, they prayed for them that they might receive the Holy Spirit, because the Holy Spirit had not yet come upon any of them; they had simply been baptized into the name of the Lord Jesus. Then Peter and John placed their hands on them, and they received the Holy Spirit.

When Simon (the Sorcerer) saw that the Spirit was given at the laying on of the apostles' hands, he offered them money and said, "Give me also this ability so that everyone on whom I lay my hands may receive the Holy Spirit. Acts 8:14-19

The evidence of their receiving the Holy Spirit at the hands of Peter and John impressed Simon the Sorcerer enough that he coveted such power, to his demise. We can deduce from several other texts that what Simon initially witnessed was the divine gift of tongues dispersed on the believers. Simon the Sorcerer had already seen miraculous displays through Philip, perhaps more sensational than Peter and John's impartation of the Holy Spirit by the laying on of hands.

What was it about Peter and John's actions as opposed to Philip's spectacular miracles that appealed to Simon's lust for power? It was not the amazing supernatural manifestations he saw in Philip's ministry that wowed him the most. It was the fact that this power was being passed around by Peter and John and that it was being made available to all.

Simon the Sorcerer had become rich and famous with demonic power. Now he seized upon an opportunity to achieve more power and increase his stature as Simon the Great. Naturally, we abhor such abuse of God's power, but I caution those who are anxiously skeptical about ministries that welcome demonstrations of the Holy Spirit's power. Granted, there are plenty of Simon the Sorcerers today. This problem is not obsolete in the Body of Christ and has brought reproach upon the genuine gift of the Holy Spirit. But we should be careful not to be tainted by unscrupulous peddlers of the gospel who sensationalize the power of God for self promotion!

It is an easy cop out to site crooks and charlatans as an excuse to deny the legitimate power of the Holy Spirit. Jesus called them wolves in sheep's clothing. The author of Acts, Dr. Luke, calls one of them Simon the Sorcerer. We would be foolish to throw away God's gift for fear of a wolf or a warlock.

The benefits of this gift of the Holy Spirit are impossible to measure. It would be a tragic waste to refuse it for fear of misuse.

In spite of opposition, the leaders of the Early Church went out of their way, literally, to make sure that all believers had the experience of the baptism of the Holy Spirit because of its powerful implications in their lives. This is the power that fueled the evangelistic displays, which compelled crowds to come, but it is also the power that we need to live this otherwise impossible Christian life. Without the continuous infilling of God's Spirit we fall desperately short in loving, forgiving, persevering and battling sin, sickness, heartache, lack and poverty.

Praying in your own secret language accesses the force of God you need for being victorious in these areas. The question should really be -- Why wouldn't every believer want this?

Chapter 45

Satan's Plan For Sammy

This power that Simon coveted, I have. I want to use it for good. The purpose behind God's holy power is always the same, salvation that is provided through the blood sacrifice of Jesus Christ. The power of God is for salvation, in all of its ramifications -- healing, deliverance and protection.

Protection. This is a practical area any mother can appreciate. My boys, Joey and Sammy are professional inline rollerbladers, world class athletes in arguably the most dangerous sport in the world. Sliding and switching stances down high rails on wheels, flipping and spinning over towering cement walls, pounding the ground from roofs, taking falls that are unbearable to watch and banned from network television, all without helmets... these are some of the things that drive me into prayer. The boys are over eighteen so I have no control to change the no-helmet policy. All I can do is pray. These kind of people, and you may know some, need super-charged, supernatural, superman prayers. Thank God in his great mercy and wisdom that he allows us to pray in a language we do not understand.

Something happened to Sammy that, had I known what I was praying while I was praying, I would have been hysterical, frantic, panicked, hyper-ventilating and of no use whatsoever in intercession. I regularly pray the verses in Psalm 91 over my children, especially the boys because of their sport and because of the mean world that is constantly trying to stake a claim on them.

"Dear Lord, Command your angels concerning them to guard them in all their ways. Let no harm befall them, no disaster come near their tent," and then I pray for them in tongues.

Secret things, spoken in a prayer language, followed Sammy one dark night last summer.

As I slept, snuggled up to my little princess and husband, Sammy, a few miles away, walked with two friends into a violent fight. One man was left beaten and bloodied, another stabbed in the back. One friend was charged with attempted murder. All three boys were charged with crimes that carried many years in prison, and in one friend's case, up to life.

I know that my Spirit-lead prayers proceeding this event had a lifesaving impact on Sammy. . . spiritual warfare that I am grateful now I did not understand with my mind. For him to have walked away from that scene unhurt and not having permanently damaged anyone is a miracle. There is no doubt that God commanded his holy angels concerning Sammy to guard him in all his ways that night. They guarded us both.

Because of God's intervention following intercession, Sammy was protected not only from physical harm or death, but from years in prison. I was protected from unspeakable heartache.

I rely heavily on God's protection as a benefit to my salvation.

Christians do not avail themselves enough of God's protection, maybe because they feel disconnected. We, like Peter, John and Paul, should be ready to help others receive their baptisms of fire whereby they too can make tangible connections to God's power - a personal prayer language.

Chapter 46

Can You Be Filled Without The Tongues Part?

Is the baptism of the Holy Spirit necessarily evidenced by speaking in tongues?

There has to be an evidence. There has to be a fruit. There has to be something to receive.

Every gift of the Spirit manifests something that helps us. Every gift has an evidence that it was received by faith, from healing to prophesy. Every gift has substance, or it is not a gift. You can know you received the baptism of the Holy Spirit when you have your prayer language.

Tongues is the first gift, the easiest to receive, and it heralds the power that courses through them all. As with healing, there is no set formula by which we can ritualize the activities of God. And God knows we would. It seems God never does things the same way twice. Still, the results are the same. A variety of stories are told as to how people receive this baptism, but the result must be a prayer language.

The Biblical norm following the baptism in the Holy Spirit is speaking in tongues. Also, the prayer language is the necessary evidence of this fire baptism because it is the connection to the power. Practically speaking, how will you connect to the power source without lines? You need lines of communication to the source.

And what's the difference if you don't speak in tongues? Why bother? You had the Holy Spirit before. Right?

His words in your mouth are the difference. The Spirit-words he puts in your mouth make the difference. You are praying and speaking God's will. They are perfect prayers, perfect in wisdom and insight. You could never imagine big or smart enough -- to say those things on your own. They are excellent, pure and untainted praising, asking and receiving words. There is no other practical way to access God so effectively.

We see tongues follow the baptism in the Holy Spirit, even for believers that are not yet water baptized. Some Gentiles to whom Peter was preaching were baptized in the Holy Spirit and began to speak in tongues before they were water baptized. It is not the order in which these things are done that is important, it is that they are done. The hearing of the tongues made it plain to all that the Holy Spirit had been poured out. The differing order of things still yielded the same result, a fire and a water baptism.

While Peter was still preaching, The Holy Spirit came on all who heard the message. The circumcised believers who had come with Peter were astonished that the gift of the Holy Spirit had been poured out even on the Gentiles. For they heard them speaking in tongues and praising God. Then Peter said,

Can anyone keep these people from being baptized with water? They have received the Holy Spirit just as we have. So he ordered that they be baptized in the name of Jesus Christ. Acts 10:44-48

Speaking in tongues is the consequence of the baptism of the Holy Spirit. Many who receive prayer to receive this baptism, but do not speak in tongues believe that it is not a gift for them or that they received the baptism without the accompanying prayer language. Maybe there are other indications, they think.

I do not believe the Bible supports this theory because, first of all, there is such a preponderance of scripture whereby believers speak in tongues following prayer for the baptism of the Holy Spirit. This is our example starting from the first occurrence on Pentecost.

Second, Paul so strongly endorses the practice of speaking in tongues in his letters to the churches. People are missing an opportunity to press on, persevere and learn to receive a supernatural gift, an exciting task! Of all the gifts, speaking in tongues, which is arguably the most important gift, is the easiest to be entreated. You have to exercise faith to receive it. It is Learning to Receive 101. It is baby steps, faith in action. It is the poster child of faith with works. We should welcome such practice since faith without works is dead. Receiving by faith is the most foundational principle we must understand in order to move in the supernatural realm. If you can't receive your prayer language, it's gonna be real hard to receive a healing. Just sayin'.

We have to activate God's power by faith. Failure to understand the mechanics of his word is why we feel abandoned when we are not healed according to the overt and abundant healing promises. If there is a violation of Jehovah Rapha, Our Healer's covenant relationship with us, it is on our part, not his.

Instead of morphing the scriptures to line up with our inability to receive, we should push through and not give up until we get our language and get our cure. This gift of the Spirit does not fall on us like droplets after a rain dance. The benefits of the gospel do not whimsically appear when Jesus is feeling extra generous. God is not stopping your prayer language. Only you can stop it. The power is yours for the asking.

Whatever you ask for in prayer, believe that you have received it, and it will be yours. Mark 11:24

1) Ask
2) Believe
3) Receive

Do not give up on the believing part. Believing gets you from asking to receiving. If you believe that you have received-already, it will be yours.

If a trusted relative said he deposited a thousand dollars in your bank account, you would be excited, thankful and confident even though you had not seen the money yet. You know your relative's word is good and that he would not lie to you. He keeps his promises. Your trust would compel you to take action, a trip to the bank.

In the same way, have confidence in God's trusted word, before the gift materializes. Only when you believe without seeing will it be yours. If the gift has not manifested yet, keep building your faith. Changing the meaning of scripture or amending the word of God is not an option. Never give up. Never give in.

Ask for your prayer language and start talking. The great thing is that you can know when you made that faith connection when you get your prayer language. That feat alone gives you a deeper level of intimacy and confidence with God. Just do it. Pray. . . not in English!

If you feel silly then you are on the right track.

Chapter 47

Your All Access Pass

Your prayer language is a learning tool. It will teach you to commune intimately with God and to work intimately with him. The Holy Spirit will guide you in cooperation with him, in partnership. Other gifts will follow naturally. It is like the oil that gets everything started and keeps it going. Never let the machinery run dry. That is your job.

Peter illustrated man's perfect partnership with God in accomplishing a miraculous feat at the temple gate one day.

After making a lame man walk, he asked his accusers,

Why do you stare at us as if by our own power or godliness we made this man walk? It is Jesus' name and the faith that comes through him that has given this complete healing to him, as you can all see. Acts 3:12,19

Let there be no mistake, Peter and John did make the man walk as Peter testified, but it was not through their own power or godliness. It was through their faith that the power was tapped, faith in the name of Jesus. There is power in no other name.

This God and man cooperative is how the Red Sea parted. Moses did it. God did it. Moses could not do it without God. God would not do it without Moses. This is the foundational partnership that we so vigorously undermine by such pious phrases as 'Wait on the Lord' and 'God is in control.' Throwing your hands up in the face of obvious manifestations of the curse is not being reverent, respectful or patient. In fact it is the opposite. It is ignoring the catalog of tools that are carefully enumerated in our new covenant with God, tools for which Jesus paid the price of his own blood. He was tortured so we could have these gifts. Those Christian clichés become excuses and cop outs. Jesus' sacrifice was for a reason, to redeem us from the curse of the law by becoming a curse for us.

Christ redeemed us from the curse of the law by becoming a curse for us, for it is written: "Cursed is everyone who is hung on a tree." Galatians 3:13

So what are we going to do about it? Wait around? For what!? We need to practice our faith. We need to get going like the disciples did right there in Acts 1, the first chapter of the Church Age.

The disciples went out and preached everywhere, and the Lord worked with them and confirmed his word by the signs that accompanied it. Mark 16:20

The Lord worked with them. That means they were working, not waiting around anymore with their faces looking up into the clouds after he disappeared. They did not stay on the Mount of Olives waiting for him to come back and do something else for them.

Do we spend as much time getting about the Lord's business as we do quibbling over whether everyone can speak in tongues or not? Nowhere does the Bible it say that tongues are not for everyone, so we shouldn't say it either. We should not deprive anyone of a treasure that amplifies their ability to walk in faith and receive the impossible to imagine things that God has planned for them.

Your prayer language is the perfect gift because it completes you. Everything you dream can be achieved and experienced through your communication gift with God.

It is the all access pass to heaven.

Chapter 48

The Breakthrough Tool

We are so afraid of getting out of God's will, not knowing his will, or getting into a works mentality, that we don't do anything. We wait for God to do it all.

Things will never happen that way. Passive Christianity does not exist. Our problems will never just go away. It is just as bad to have faith with no works as it is to have works with no faith. Both are dead. James in Chapter 2 challenges believers to show him their faith without works. Impossible. It is a rhetorical statement because it cannot be done.

Show me your faith without works and I will show you my faith by what I do. James 2:18

Faith requires action or it does not exist.

James goes on to explain how faith without works is useless, dead. But you can start working your faith with your mouth, by speaking your prayer language. It is a great way of taking initiative. Be aggressive about God's promises. Don't take no for an answer.

All the promises in Christ are Yes. 2 Corinthians 1:20

Go get them. Remove old obstacles. Build new dreams. Solve your problem. When another comes, solve it too.

Walls will come down. Chains will break. Doors will open. Storm clouds will roll away. Light will break through.

I do not care how long you have been a Christian, how many letters are after your name, or to which denomination you are allegiant, if you get a grip of your prayer language and use it regularly, all the time, you will never be the same again. If you have let the gift fall dormant, revive! Pick up the pace! Double time! Move it, move it! Don't let that ol' Satan trick you into inertia. Wake up and strengthen the things that remain. It will benefit you and in turn, everyone around you. You will never be the same again!

Abandon all your pre-conceived ideas about tongues. Being filled with the Holy Spirit is not an exercise in feeling more spiritual. God is not interested in fluff. It is not a sense, aura or mind set. It is a practical gift for your benefit whether you feel anything or not. Your prayer language may not change anything about the way you feel. Well, maybe not right away. When you are speaking in an unknown tongue you may sense no changes. You may feel your spirit stand up inside. Sometimes you will know that things are happening and moving and changing, but you don't know what or how.

No matter how you feel or what you think, your Spirit words are swords clanking around in the atmosphere of your life.

Things will budge, move, come crashing down, heal, die, revive, break open, be saved, be rescued, be restored.

Chapter 49

The Gateway Gift

Your prayer language will lead you to flow in greater power gifts which will make you more productive, influential and effective in the earth.

My friend Tina, was with her pregnant daughter, Christi in Labor and Delivery. She asked for prayer because mother and baby were both suffering with some kind of disease. The doctors were saying it could be very dangerous to Christi and her unborn baby, potentially fatal. So, naturally, Tina was worried. The only way to stop its effects was to deliver the baby right away. She was far enough along that he would not be premature. Still, I was unnerved that the doctors were speaking words of disease and death in a situation that should be the most exciting celebration of health and life. When I asked Tina what disease it was, she could not remember the name. It didn't matter anyway, so she put me on speaker phone and we prayed so Christi could hear from her hospital bed.

Let's look at the mechanics of an effective prayer, not a formula. Under my breath I prayed in the Spirit, then in English, then in the Spirit quietly, then English. Was I interpreting as I went along? I don't know, but at a minimum the Holy Spirit guides us in our prayers when we pray like that. A verse came to my mind, which is always a good place to start.

I set before you today life and prosperity, death and destruction. Deuteronomy 30:15

I prayed, "Lord we speak over this situation, not words of death and destruction, but health, life and prosperity."

Unintelligible for a few seconds quietly so as not to freak out any nurse who may be listening and then English, "We speak health, life and prosperity......health, life, prosperity. H, L, P -- HELP. God will help this baby and he will be a helper. He will be the person that people will call when they are in trouble. This baby will be a helper."

I am not a big acronym person but that is what I got! The Lord would help him and this little guy would be a big help to others. That is what God spoke over that baby boy.

Funny God. The next day I went to the hospital. Christi and her newborn baby were perfectly fine. Christi's husband was handing the bundle to her when he mentioned how scared he was when he researched the disease Christi and the baby had been sharing, Help Syndrome. It was spelled like hell, HELLP, an acronym for the disease.

Before we knew this, God had shared with us a different acronym for the baby's condition, Health, Life and Prosperity. 'Help' it was interpreted at the time. God, not approving the medical label, re-labeled the baby.

Your prayer language is a mighty weapon that can cross into prophesy, healing, words of wisdom and knowledge-- whatever your people need! Be confrontational with it. The thief comes to steal your aggression toward him. Do not be passive and apathetic with this gift. If you do nothing, nothing will happen and you will have nothing.

If we pass nothing to our kids when they need a strong fortress in this corrupt generation, they will be exposed, overcome and defeated. Good grades and excellence in sports or music will be of no use against the aggressive evil that is surely crouching at their door.

This morning as my little girl lay in bed next to me, cherishing the last few minutes of snuggly covers before school, I cradled her head in my hands and prayed in a strange tongue. This foreign speech has become balm to her, refreshing, healing, strengthening, arming. I realize that protection, safety, healing and all of God's best is being prayed over her. The Holy Spirit ministers directly to hers without interruption. It's just Jesus and Lucy. Strengthening.

The ministries of Peter and John were dependent on the baptism of the Holy Spirit again and again as ours should also be. When the religious leaders were disturbed by their performing what they admitted to being an *"outstanding miracle,"* Peter and John were forbidden to speak in the name of Jesus.

As soon as the believers found out about these orders, they were again filled with the Holy Spirit. Why? Because it was no secret that non-compliance to such orders was at risk of death. They were filled again because they needed boldness to continue to speak, and power to continue to act in defiance to the law.

"Now, Lord, consider their threats and enable your servants to speak your word with great boldness. Stretch out your hand to heal and perform miraculous signs and wonders through the name of your holy servant Jesus." After they prayed, the place where they were meeting was shaken. And they were all filled with the Holy Spirit and spoke the word of God boldly Acts 4:29-31

They who cherished the Holy Spirit in their hearts already, were filled with him again. He was the direct answer to their prayer for boldness and for the miracles that God wanted to perform through them.

How many meals do you eat?

Will last week's dinner be enough?

You need to eat food everyday to be strong and healthy. How much more do you need to replenish your spirit on a regular basis by the Holy Spirit so you have the spiritual stamina to minister to others? Your prayer language is as practical a nutrient for your strengthening as food is.

A mystery of old, such a long time in coming, was now revealed. God in us would be the force needed to activate the miraculous and wonderful works of Jesus through our hands. Once baptized in fire, there should be no end to the need for infilling. If the Early Church fathers needed this baptism for ministry, then so do we.

Speaking in tongues was never intended by God to be elective for his followers. It is a requirement for a life full in the Spirit. It is imperative to accomplishing everything God desires for our lives and ministries.

The more you do it the better.

Chapter 50

Get Power Hungry

Energy: A vigorous exertion of power, usable power, capacity for intense activity

"Energy supplements have become one of the fastest growing categories of supplement. And that's because everybody, whether you're a man or woman young or old, wants more energy." –Andrew Shao, PhD from the Councl for Responsible Nutrition

Supernatural energy. Heavenly adrenalin. Divine power. You need more to do more --and don't let anyone talk you out of it.

Jesus said to them, "Go into all the world and preach the good news to all creation. Whoever believes and is baptized will be saved, but whoever does not believe will be condemned. And these signs will accompany those who believe: In my name they will drive out demons; they will speak in new tongues; they will pick up snakes with their hands; and when they drink deadly poison, it will not hurt them at all; they will place their hands on sick people and they will get well."

After the Lord Jesus had spoken to them, he was taken up into heaven and he sat at the right hand of God. Then the disciples went out and preached everywhere, and the Lord worked with them and confirmed his word by the signs that accompanied it. Mark 16:15-20

The infallible word of God states unapologetically that as a believer, supernatural signs will accompany my preaching should I choose to accept such a mission. I will drive out the same ancient demons that vexed people in Jesus' day and I will speak in a new language. Like Moses, I can pick up a snake for a sign to the world (Exodus 7). I have protection if I tread upon the cobra (Psalm 91). I will trample the serpent (Luke 10) and can shake a venomous snake into the fire without harm (Acts 28). The snakes will not hurt me. When I ingest something deadly, it will not poison me. Nothing will harm me. I will place my hands on sick people and they will get well.

How many times and in how many climactic ways does our God have to say it before we get it? All of these signs in the Great Commission are about healing, deliverance, protection, and the power to apply them to our lives via the Holy Spirit's supplications in our mouths.

The last commission of Jesus to the disciples at the end of Mark, at the end of Matthew and again at the end of Luke, was not really for them as much as for us. Except for the tongues which were soon to come, and greatly anticipated by Jesus, the disciples already knew about all that was said in the Great Commission passages.

They had already been casting out demons and healing people. The emphasis was instead on those who would believe through their ministries. The emphasis was on their teaching what they already knew. Jesus spoke of those who were yet to be saved and baptized, that the signs should also accompany them –all the believers through distance and ages to come.

Matthew recollects that Jesus told the disciples to preach, baptize and teach disciples of all nations everything that Jesus taught them to do. That is an enormous expectation when you consider the many miracles the disciples were performing at Jesus' direction. Yet, Jesus was clear that this commission would not begin until after they received the gift that was coming to them in Jerusalem, the tongues of fire. After that incident, and not a moment sooner, they would be emboldened and empowered for service.

The end of Mark has no new information that is not reinforced by other scriptures. Still, there are those who would try to dismiss this compelling passage (Mark 16:15-20) on the basis that it might not be 'reliable.' Some modern Bible translators take liberties to cast doubt on some passages that have always been included in the established and closed canon of scripture. Note that marginal text in some modern translations of the Bible questioning the authenticity of the end of Mark is not divinely inspired. These allegations are founded on nothing more than subjective conclusions by scholars who are influenced more by bias against the content than by any objective evidence that would validate the passage. It is an insidious way to inspire doubt about that cross-barrier speaking in tongues theology some of us espouse.

For example, the oldest and most reliable manuscripts around are not even the original ones that were divinely penned. Those are all gone. All we have is copies. The now oldest existing copies of the passage in question by modern scholars who are arrogant enough to challenge its authenticity, are still in existence precisely because they are errant. They were of no use to the transcribers because of their omissions and instances of tampering. Hence, they remain in tact from lack of use – nobody trusted them!

The original inspired manuscripts have long disintegrated from overuse by scribes who vigilantly copied them onto new paper, safe and sound. We have none of the original New Testament writings for this reason. The Mark 16 translation in your Bible is transcribed from manuscripts older than the oldest now-existing (errant) manuscripts that those dumb scholars like.

'Oldest manuscripts' is altogether different from 'oldest extant (existing) manuscripts.' It's the difference between an original document and a compromised copy. I would rather have a third generation exact copy of an original document than a first generation modified copy of the original document, even if the modified copy is older.

Simply put, the oldest manuscripts we have now are inferior.

Who do these 'scholars' think they are coming around changing the meaning of the established, unchanging word of God? Authenticity is not based on age. It is based on the accuracy of the scribes who themselves disposed of the authentic but greatly debilitated manuscripts, after having meticulously transcribed them. At least the King James Version has remained loyal to the sacred canon without casting doubt in the margins of the Bible.

Don't be intimidated by intellectual arguments against the fundamental and obvious tenants of your faith. Clearly, signs will follow those who believe, and in his name they will speak in new tongues. Never mind about those theologians that have an agenda. Anyway --

Where is the wise man? Where is the scholar? 1 Corinthians 1:25

Shoot. My motivation to debunk the academic arguments against tongues is to remove any impediment to your effective ministry tool. Your prayer language can open an opportunity for the Holy Spirit to work in you by bypassing your physical and natural limitations. You can freely move in the Spirit, not subjected to the confines of your own knowledge and wisdom.

God can move you into the complex realms of knowing unknown things, exerting other-worldly power and loving beyond your own capacity. The assignments of God are not things we can do in our own strength, neither can we pray for such monumental things with our own words. Since God intends for us to live in a supernatural atmosphere, tongues are expected.

Whether they realize it or not, everyone wants this connection to such an amazing power and energy source.

Chapter 51

Don't Trash Your Treasure

Biblical misinformation often results from scripture being taken out of context. Popular theology that restricts tongues comes from ignorance, lack of understanding or religious pride.

Some think, "If I can't do it, then obviously it is not for everyone" and although they would never admit it, "Tongues are for uneducated Christians." Most of the apostles met that qualification.

Christians are still getting in trouble with Paul's first letter to the Corinthians. They do not understand that Paul did not write the Chapter 14 portion of his letter to enumerate the pros and cons of speaking in tongues. He did not set out to write a treatise on the pitfalls of tongues, even though that is what it is often made out to be. Neither did he write to diminish the importance of tongues. It is not a chastisement for tongue-talkers as is popularly taught. Many lecture as if Paul said, "Follow the way of love instead of eagerly desiring spiritual gifts." No. He said,

Follow the way of love <u>and</u> eagerly desire spiritual gifts. 1 Corinthians14:1

It is not love *or* gifts; it is not love *instead* of gifts. It is love *and* gifts. Learning about tongues is assumed by Paul to have already occurred for the Corinthian Church. He is following up with corrections, teaching them to distinguish between tongues in corporate worship and tongues in private worship. Still, Christians miss this distinction and apply corporate standards of speaking in tongues to individual use of tongues.

Actually Paul is not even really concerned that much about tongues in this famous tongues chapter. He is concerned about motives and character. Almost the whole letter of 1 Corinthians is a rebuke. He admonishes their arrogance, divisions, idolatry, immorality and the resulting chaotic worship, including the misuse of the gift of tongues.

I have learned from my husband who can fix anything that I should not throw away the dryer just because a little rubber belt broke. Paul was telling them how to fix something, not to throw it away.

Just because their celebration of communion was a disaster does not mean they should stop communion. Just because there was impropriety in their worship services does not mean they should cease all worship. Just because the speaking in tongues was uncontrolled does not mean they were forbidden. He called for order,

Do not forbid speaking in tongues. But everything should be done in a fitting and orderly way. 1 Corinthians 14:39-40

His letter was sent to straighten them out, especially in their corporate gatherings.

Shall I come to you with a whip, or in love and with a gentle spirit? 1Corinthians 4:21

He was disturbed, not about their use of tongues, but the misuse, precisely because of its importance and power. It is the same reason we are so careful in the handling and use of nuclear weapons and bombs. It is because they are powerful and effective --when used responsibly.

The attitude in Paul's correction about speaking in tongues is similar to one you might hear from a parent regarding a teenager's cell phone. The parent is not against cell phones. In fact they promote them. Probably the parent even bought the kid a phone and maybe pays the bill. Yet the parent may scold, "Cell phones are not for driving. When you are driving and on the phone you are making plans well, communicating to friends and family, but you are driving dangerously! Talk and text all you want, but not while driving. Cell phones are for your personal use, not to be used in traffic with other drivers who are being endangered or cannot understand what you are doing on the road. I use a cell phone more than you do, but not in the car."

Do we conclude from this that cell phones are not valuable or helpful? The parent does not condemn cell phone usage but warns of improper use. The parent's reproof about the cell phone was not intended to teach about the benefits of a cell phone, those having been already understood by both parties. Instead it was to establish safe parameters of cell phone use.

Paul was not trying to discourage their use of gifts. He just wanted the Corinthians to use them responsibly. So much of the misunderstanding of tongues can be cleared up in 1 Corinthians 14 when we see there is a clear delineation between speaking in tongues in the corporate gathering of believers and in the believer's personal walk with the Lord.

The nine gifts of the Holy Spirit from 1 Corinthians 12 were given to the Church: the gifts of faith, healing, working of miracles, words of wisdom and knowledge, discerning of spirits, tongues, interpretation of tongues and prophesy. The operation of these gifts is intended for church gatherings, assemblies and other ministry events.

These ministry gifts to the Body of Christ corporately do not relinquish our individual responsibility to grow in areas of faith, healing, working of miracles, words of wisdom and knowledge, discerning of spirits, tongues, interpretation of tongues and prophesy. We should seek these gifts as ministry gifts to be dispersed in an assembly as God wills. I do not believe that precludes us from laboring in the spirit to exhibit all of these gifts in all areas of our individual lives.

Often people say they believe in healing but not for themselves because they don't have the 'gift of healing.' That is as ridiculous as saying I believe in faith but not for myself because I don't have the 'gift of faith.'

Everything is done more effectively when it is done decently and in order. The operation of the gifts where there may be unbelievers is no different. We should be gentle with unbelievers. We should be careful not to scare them away by reason of strange religious outbursts. Jesus is not weird. Would you go to the grocery store and start shouting in tongues? No. And if you would then you shouldn't. Whisper? Oh yeah I am up and down the grocery store aisles muttering about this and that –about I don't know what.

In this chapter of parental lecturing about behavior in group settings, we can glean valuable information about the value of implementing a personal prayer language, or speaking in tongues, while we are in private. The Message translation helps to clear up the confusion about the difference between speaking in tongues privately and corporately. Paul explained it well.

So, when you pray in your private prayer language, don't hoard the experience for yourself. Pray for the insight and ability to bring others into that intimacy. If I pray in tongues, my spirit prays but my mind lies fallow, and all that intelligence is wasted. So what's the solution? The answer is simple enough. Do both. I should be spiritually free and expressive as I pray, but I should also be thoughtful and mindful as I pray. I should sing with my spirit, and sing with my mind. If you give a blessing using your private prayer language, which no one else understands, how can some outsider who has just shown up and has no idea what's going on know when to say "Amen"? Your blessing might be beautiful, but you have very effectively cut that person out of it.

I'm grateful to God for the gift of praying in tongues that he gives us for praising him, which leads to wonderful intimacies we enjoy with him. I enter into this as much or more than any of you. But when I'm in a church assembled for worship, I'd rather say five words that everyone can understand and learn from than say ten thousand that sound to others like gibberish. 1 Corinthians 14:13-19

Hopefully I can prevent someone from discarding this powerful gift just because they never took a comprehensive look at the subject or because they witnessed a wacky religious tongue-talker.

It's not worth forsaking a fortune just because a weird guy has one too.

Chapter 52

A Baker's Dozen Benefits

Remember that Paul in no way discounts tongues. When he says for example, that prophesy is better than tongues, in a group setting that is true.

In a group setting everyone should understand. Tongues and interpretation in such an atmosphere has the same result as prophesy -- God speaking to the group.

In private, Paul coveted speaking in tongues. He boasted of doing it more than anyone else. When you're by yourself, you don't have to interpret. Take a break from coming up with the right words to say.

Our human language is far to restrictive to express the heights and depths to which our spirits can soar and be inspired. We need freedom from the confines of our infinitely limited vocabulary when we communicate with God.

The gift of tongues makes praying without ceasing a pleasure and possibility rather than a task. And we don't have to run our mouths the whole time to remain in a listening, conversational mode.

By this point, we have examined the miracle of speaking in a supernaturally endowed language. It is about power for the people. But what does that look like in practical terms? What are the benefits of a personal prayer language or speaking in tongues?

1) You speak straight to God. You have the direct spirit to Spirit connection that inevitably produces fruit in your life.

For anyone who speaks in a tongue does not speak to men but to God. 1 Corinthians 14:2

2) You speak hidden truths and secret things to God. You say things that evade your understanding, but these good things for which you pray, may suddenly appear in your life.

He utters mysteries with his spirit. 1 Corinthians 14:2

3) You edify yourself so you will be strong and bold. To 'edify' is to build oneself up from nothing or build from shambles as one restores a dilapidated house. When you are built up you are strong, confident, bold and fearless. . . not just your spirit, but your emotions, your mind *and* your body.

He who speaks in a tongue edifies himself. 1 Corinthians 14:4

4) You are in God's will. He would like you to do it. Parents know what is good for their kids. Even though it may take awhile, kids eventually realize the benefits too. Tongues helps you sync up with his desire and purpose for you.

I would like every one of you to speak in tongues. 1 Corinthians 14:5

5) You pray with your spirit, unhindered by the limitations of your mind. This two way spirit to Spirit transmission is your connection to all the attributes and character of God.

For if I pray in a tongue, my spirit prays, but my mind is unfruitful. So what shall I do? I will pray with my spirit, but I will also pray with my mind; I will sing with my spirit, but I will also sing with my mind. 1 Corinthians 14:14-15

6) You praise and thank God well and are edified. Enjoy these benefits in your private time with God

If you are praising God with your spirit, how can one who finds himself among those who do not understand say "Amen" to your thanksgiving, since he does not know what you are saying? You may be giving thanks well enough, but the other man is not edified. 1Corinthians 14: 17

7) You can improve your life by increasing the amount of time that you pray in tongues! Whether at home, in the car, pumping gas, in court, in the hospital or in a long line, a deliberate effort to do it more often will be productive enough to warrant saying....

I thank God that I speak in tongues more than all of you. 1Corinthians 14:18

8) You can be confident you are doing the right thing. The word of God backs you up. Those who forbid speaking in tongues do so in direct contradiction to God's word which clearly states we are not to forbid anyone to speak in tongues.

Therefore, my brothers, be eager to prophesy, and do not forbid speaking in tongues. 1 Corinthians 14:39

9) You can have revelation of God's plans and comprehension of his thoughts. Mysteries will be revealed.

No eye has seen, no ear has heard, no mind has conceived what God has prepared for those who love him – but God has revealed it to us by his Spirit. The Spirit searches all things, even the deep things of God. For who among men knows the thoughts of a man except the man's spirit within him? In the same way no one knows the thoughts of God except the Spirit of God. We have not received the spirit of the world but the Spirit who is from God, that we may understand what God has freely given us. 1 Corinthians 2:9-12

10) Your tutor will be the Holy Spirit.

This is what we speak, not in words taught us by human wisdom but in words taught by the Spirit, expressing spiritual truths in spiritual words. 1 Corinthians 2:13

11) You will have a Helper when you are weak and do not know what to say. The Holy Spirit rushes in to handle your situation when you are weak and do not even know where to begin. You will have relief from the vain repetitions that yield only frustration.

In the same way, the Spirit helps us in our weakness. We do not know what we ought to pray for, but the Spirit himself intercedes for us with groans that words cannot express. Romans 8:26

12) You will be praying God's perfect will in any given situation. This is earth shaking and world changing in its potential.

And he who searches our hearts knows the mind of the Spirit, because the Spirit intercedes for the saints in accordance with God's will. Romans 8:27

13) You will have God's power, the same power Jesus had while he was walking on earth.

You will receive power when the Holy Spirit comes on you; and you will be my witnesses in Jerusalem, and in all Judea and Samaria, and to the ends of the earth. Acts 1:8

Speaking in tongues is God Almighty's power harnessed by you. The ramifications of this are unfathomable.

My husband is a master handyman and a sea captain. He has a big tool box. A little job might just require one tool, but for most jobs it takes many. All the tools God gives us in the Bible work together. It's a great toolbox.

I pray you will begin to gather your tools and weapons, use them often and move into new realms of your spiritual adventure with Jesus Christ.

Chapter 53
The Night Before Last

I sit here at my kitchen table wondering how to end this book, how to sum it all up. Maybe I'll do it with the night before last.

I went with my three girls, Lucy, Courtney and her baby Hazel to my Sammy and Joey's little rental in downtown Orlando. Joey was going to take some promo pictures we needed and make us tacos.

In all the commotion of sisters, a toddler, costuming and a puppy, I heard that the boy's couch guy (a roommate who sleeps on the couch) Lucas, who is also a skater friend, was resting in Joey's room. We were not very quiet for him.

When Hazel was getting tired, it was time to leave. I walked through the hall and saw that the bathroom door was ajar and Lucas was sitting on the floor in the dark with his head down.

"Are you alright? I asked. "No you are not. What's wrong?"

He mumbled that he gets migraines and throws up, which usually makes them go away --but not this one.

I went to the living room to tell Joey, and ask him if I could offer to pray for Lucas. Joey shook his head and indicated that it wouldn't be a good idea. He went to the bathroom to check on Lucas, with me peeking over his shoulder. He asked if he was alright and if he wanted some peppermint oil, or to go lie down. It was too late for a homeopathic remedy but I was proud of Joey's naturopathic savvy. Lucas declined, explaining in low tones that normally after he throws up, the migraines start getting better, but this one felt like the whole left side of his head was on fire, and he couldn't even lie down. I followed Joey back into the living room using my best puppy dog eyes.

"Mom, no he won't...he'll be okay, just pray for him on your own."

I relented.

Oh but I couldn't stand it, and asked Joey one more time if I could pray for Lucas. I promised not to preach and to make it quick.

He relented --smiling at my obnoxious persistence. I just love Joey.

I tapped my nails gently on the bedroom door as I pushed it open. I could barely see Lucas sitting in the dark at the end of the bed with his head down. As I stepped in the room I asked, "Is it okay if I pray for your head Lucas? This is what I do for a job, teach people how to not be sick."

He said I could.

"Okay thanks because you know most people know Jesus died for their sins, but they don't know that he died for their sicknesses too. And you don't have to do anything to qualify for being healed except be his creation and you are. The Bible says that if we place our hands on sick people, they will get well, and that the prayer of faith will make the sick person well and the Lord will make him better....Is it okay if I touch your head?"

"Yes, do whatever you have to do," he quickly answered.

"You said on the left side right? Okay Lord, you have healed Lucas by your wounds and so we speak to this pain and tell it to leave in Jesus' name. ...spirit of infirmity you are bound from tormenting him anymore. Leave this room and this house right now. Holy Spirit fill this place. By the authority given to me in Jesus Christ I command you to be set free from this pain."

Although normally I decry symptom checking because healing is not according to our feelings or symptoms but according to truth, I asked him how he felt. Symptoms are little liars and need to be ignored most of the time. But, when praying for unbelievers, pagans or people whose spiritual situation is unknown, you might want to check. They need tangible results, not my seminar or book about how to effect a supernatural health lifestyle change. It also may help you to trouble shoot. Maybe it is a demon. Maybe you need to take another whack at it.

Even in the dark, I could tell he was assessing --he said it was a little better, but I wasn't sure if he just didn't want to hurt my feelings.

I told him it was leaving, it would not come back, he would continue to get better and that he would lie down in peace and sleep, that the Lord would make him to dwell in safety, his head included.

"I'll be praying," I told him as I snuck out. Courtney and I gathered up the chicks and left.

From time to time that night, I prayed for his health, his salvation and his happiness. The next morning, I called Joey and asked how Lucas was doing. He laughed a little and said he was going to call me.

"What? What happened?!" So exciting for me.

Joey answered, "Last night after you left, he came out of the room and said, "Dude, I think your mom healed me.'"

After I finished laughing, Joey added, "And then he asked me if you were a hugger because he said if you were, he wanted to give you a big hug."

Hearing that was the best hug ever.

Really, all I want to do is load this world up with healers and huggers.

Also available online at BetsyB.tv are books, dvds and other support materials ideal for individual, group and family study and edu-tainment.

Our Award Winning Word 4 Word Kids Programs teach Bible memory and application through adventure and music-video. Watch internet television BetsyB.tv for your spiritual spinach.

To share testimonies, ask questions or schedule a live event or speaking engagement with Betsy, visit BetsyB.tv and contact by email <u>me@betsyb.tv</u> or call (407)417-5351

Works Cited
1) Fox's Book of Martyrs Edited by William Byron Forbush
*1 page 8, *2 page 9, *3 page 8, *4 page 11, *5 page 16, *6 page 20, *7 pages 25, 26
2) History of the Christian Church: Apostolic Christianity, A.D. Philip Schaff, David Schley Schaff
*8 pages 381, 382

Made in the USA
Charleston, SC
23 January 2013